Course DRE 098
DURHAM TECH COMM COLLEGE
ENGLISH DEVELOP STUDIES

http://create.mheducation.com

ISBN-10: 1308179944   ISBN-13: 9781308179940

Contents

Credits

8

"Our behaviour toward each other is the strangest, most unpredictable, and most unaccountable of all the phenomena with which we are obliged to live. In all of nature, there is nothing so threatening to humanity as humanity itself."

Lewis Thomas, 1981

AGGRESSION

CHAPTER 8: AGGRESSION

What do we mean by the term 'aggression'? Broadly speaking, aggression defines behaviour that is destructive in some way, causing harm or injury. This can be towards other people, but may also include damage to inanimate objects (e.g. furniture or property), or animals. Of course, some examples of aggressive behaviour are very easily recognized when they accompany intentional violence towards others (e.g. in the time of war). However, not all aggression is so obvious. Aggression can take other more subtle forms such as the verbal aggression displayed in an argument, the occurrence of bullying in the school or workplace, or a scuffle in the street, and as such may be witnessed in our everyday lives. So aggression has many faces, and how social psychologists define it has implications for what they treat as evidence of it, how they measure it, explain it, and the solutions offered for reducing or preventing it. In this chapter we consider some empirical studies, theories and influences on aggression, and examine the diverse range of definitions and methodologies for studying this phenomenon.

In doing so we ask four more-specific questions:

1 Is aggression biologically predisposed, or do we learn it?

2 What circumstances prompt hostile outbursts?

3 Do the media influence aggression?

4 How might we reduce aggression?

First, however, we need to clarify the term 'aggression'.

WHAT IS AGGRESSION?

The lack of consistency in defining aggression in everyday language is reflected in social psychology. How aggression is defined often depends on the theoretical perspective and the methods used. If we define aggression in its most direct form, as physical acts, then we can only collect evidence of physical behaviour. However, if we define aggression in a more indirect form, perhaps as a subtle feature of language (e.g. spreading malicious gossip), then we would attend to what people say and perhaps how they say it. Some social psychologists/theorists have settled on a compromised definition of aggression as physical or verbal behaviour intended to cause harm, and this has been reflected in textbooks (e.g. Baron and Byrne, 2000; Carlson et al., 1989). However, this definition excludes unintentional harm such as collisions in the street, or the accidental spilling of a hot drink onto someone else; it also excludes actions that may involve pain as an unavoidable side effect of helping someone, such as dental treatments or – in the extreme – assisted suicide. It does include kicks and slaps, threats and insults, even gossip or snide 'digs'; and decisions, during experiments, about how much to hurt someone, such as how much of an electric shock to impose. It also includes destroying property, lying and other behaviour whose aim is to cause mental or physical hurt. However, even this compromise of 'intentional' aggression is not without its problems. Not all aggression is intentional. Some aggressive acts are caused accidentally, with no intention to cause harm. For example, over-exuberance at a music concert can result in harm to others if we accidentally hit or push them as we express our excitement. Unintentional aggression can also describe behaviour that harms others, but the individual causing that harm cannot be held responsible for that action. Children and adults with ADHD (Attention Deficit/Hyperactivity Disorder) may behave aggressively as a consequence of their disorder rather than intention to harm someone (Nigg, 2003).

Aggression can be indirect as well as direct. Consider Dan Olweus's work (1993) on bullying behaviour. Olweus defines bullying as negative behaviour that occurs to a victim 'repeatedly and over time' involving acts of direct physical aggression and indirect aggression. From his study of Norwegian schoolchildren he found that boys tended to conduct most of the bullying. As we shall see in this chapter, this finding is consistent with a lot of aggression research that suggests men are more aggressive than women. Biology, and the presence of hormones such as testosterone and cortisol, are a major contributing factor. But, as we shall also see in this chapter, it is possible to learn aggressive behaviour. So surely it is possible that women are as capable as men of aggression (Bjorkqvist, 1994). This raises issues surrounding the definition and methods used for capturing aggressive behaviour for the social psychologist. Larry Owens, Rosalyn Shute and Phillip Slee (2000a, 2000b) found from their interviews and focus groups with Australian teenage girls, that they use fairly subtle and indirect ways to bully other girls. This bullying can take the form of excluding girls from peer groups. Girls seem to value friendship groups more than boys, so excluding girls from their friends can be a very effective method of bullying. Teenage girls also report using other strategies such as verbal bullying (e.g. spreading malicious gossip), and non-verbal bullying (e.g. hostile staring), which can leave their marginalized victims feeling miserable. These indirect forms of aggression can be more difficult for the social psychologist to capture. Consequently how we define aggression may boil down to what we can see, capture and analyse.

SOME THEORIES OF AGGRESSION

In analysing the causes of aggression, social psychologists have focused on three main explanations: (1) aggression is the result of a biologically based aggressive drive; (2) aggression is a response to frustration; and (3) aggressive behaviour is learned. Here we shall focus on some key theories in social psychology, which have taken these explanations as their starting point for understanding aggression. Those theories outlined here are not exhaustive of social psychology's engagement with aggression (there are many others!), but they do offer some important insights for the discipline.

AGGRESSION AS A BIOLOGICAL PHENOMENON

Philosophers have debated whether our human nature is fundamentally that of a benign, contented, 'noble savage' or that of a brute. The first view, argued by the eighteenth-century French philosopher Jean-Jacques Rousseau (1712–78), blames society, not human nature, for social evils. His famous quote, 'Man is born free but everywhere he is in chains', summarizes his opinion that the natural state of man was good, but it was society that corrupted him. On the other hand, the second idea, associated with the English philosopher Thomas Hobbes (1588–1679), credits society for restraining the human brute. In the twentieth century, the 'brutish' view – that aggressive drive is inborn and thus inevitable – was argued by Sigmund Freud in Vienna and Konrad Lorenz in Germany.

CHAPTER 8: AGGRESSION

Instinct Theory and Evolutionary Psychology

Freud speculated that human aggression springs from a self-destructive impulse. It redirects towards others the energy of a primitive death urge (the 'death instinct', sometimes called Thanatos in post-Freudian theory). Lorenz, an animal behaviour expert, saw aggression as adaptive rather than self-destructive. The two agreed that aggressive energy is instinctual (unlearned and universal), that is, causes instinctive behaviour. If not discharged, it supposedly builds up until it explodes or until an appropriate stimulus 'releases' it, like a mouse releasing a mousetrap.

instinctive behaviour
an innate, unlearned behaviour pattern exhibited by all members of a species

The idea that aggression is an instinct collapsed as the list of supposed human instincts grew to include nearly every conceivable human behaviour. Nearly 6000 supposed instincts were enumerated in one 1924 survey of social science books (Barash, 1979). The social scientists had tried to *explain* social behaviour by *naming* it. It's tempting to play this rather circular explaining-by-naming game: 'Why do sheep stay together?' 'Because of their herd instinct.' 'How do you know they have a herd instinct?' 'Just look at them: they're always together!'

Instinct theory also fails to account for the variations in aggressiveness from person to person, culture to culture and across time and space. How would a shared human instinct for aggression explain the difference between the peaceful Iroquois before White invaders came and the hostile Iroquois after the invasion (Hornstein, 1976)? Although aggression may be biologically influenced, the human propensity to aggress does not qualify as instinctive behaviour.

Our distant ancestors nevertheless sometimes found aggression adaptive, according to evolutionary psychologists David Buss and Todd Shackelford (1997). Aggressive behaviour was a strategy for gaining resources, defending against attack, intimidating or eliminating male rivals for females, and deterring mates from sexual infidelity. In some preindustrial societies, being a good warrior made for higher status and reproductive opportunities (Roach, 1998). The adaptive value of aggression, Buss and Shackelford believe, helps explain the relatively high levels of male–male aggression across human history: 'This does not imply ... that men have an "aggression instinct" in the sense of some pent-up energy that must be released. Rather, men have learned from their successful ancestors psychological mechanisms' that improve their odds of contributing their genes to future generations.

Genetic Influences

Heredity influences the neural system's sensitivity to aggressive cues. For example, animals can be bred for aggressiveness. Sometimes this is done for practical purposes (the breeding of fighting cocks or dogs). Sometimes breeding is done for research. Finnish psychologist Kirsti Lagerspetz (1979) took normal albino mice and bred the most aggressive ones together; she did the same with the least aggressive ones. After repeating the procedure for 26 generations, she had one set of fierce mice and one set of placid mice. Chapter 14 discusses the impact of genes on our behaviour more holistically as well as in relation to gender differences.

Chapter 14 discusses the impact of genes on our behaviour more holistically as well as in relation to gender differences.

Aggressiveness varies among primates and humans (Asher, 1987; Olweus, 1979). Our temperaments – how intense and reactive we are – are partly brought with us into the world, influenced by our sympathetic nervous system's reactivity (Kagan, 1989). A person's temperament, observed in infancy, usually endures (Larsen &

Diener, 1987; Wilson & Matheny, 1986). A child who is non-aggressive at age 8 will very likely still be a non-aggressive person at age 48 (Huesmann et al., 2003). But it is not easy to say if this is due to genetic inheritance or social learning or socialization, or to tease these two things apart. Identical twins, when asked separately, are more likely than fraternal twins to agree on whether they have 'a violent temper' or have got into fights (Rowe et al., 1999; Rushton et al., 1986).

Do genes predispose the pit bull's aggressiveness?

SOURCE: © Jeff Share/Black Star

Long-term studies following several hundred New Zealand children reveal that a recipe for aggressive behaviour combines a gene, called monoamine oxidase-A (MAOA), that alters neurotransmitter balance with childhood maltreatment (Caspi et al., 2002; Moffitt et al., 2003). Avshalom Caspi and colleagues found that 12 per cent of males in their study had low levels of MAOA and had been subjected to abuse as children between the ages of 3 and 11 years old. Of this group, 85 per cent of them had engaged in antisocial behaviour, which in some cases led to convictions for violent conduct. Consequently, MAOA has been termed the 'warrior gene' (Gibbons, 2004) due to the effect it seems to have upon behaviour. The warrior gene has also been used successfully as a form of mitigating circumstances in murder convictions. In Italy, Abdelmalek Bayout, who confessed to murdering Walter Perez, had his sentence reduced on the grounds of having low levels of MAOA (Levitt, 2013). However, genes alone do not explain aggressive behaviour. Nature and nurture interact. Rose McDermott and her colleagues (2009) found that participants with low activity of MAOA would be aggressive to opponents in an experimental study, but only when they had been severely provoked. So it appears that biology interacts with the environment in producing aggressive responses.

Biochemical Influences
Blood chemistry also influences neural sensitivity to aggressive stimulation.

Alcohol
Both laboratory experiments and police data indicate that alcohol unleashes aggression when people are provoked (Bushman, 1993; Taylor & Chermack, 1993; Testa, 2002). Consider:

In experiments, when asked to think back on relationship conflicts, intoxicated people administer stronger shocks and feel angrier than do sober people.
    (MacDonald et al., 2000)

In Britain, a Home Office Study (Richardson & Budd, 2003) using survey and interview methods, conducted between 1998 and 2002 with young people aged 18–24 years, found that those who drank heavily at least once a week were five and a half more times likely to have committed a violent offence than those who got drunk less than once a month.

Alcohol and sexual assault. 'Ordinary men who drank too much' was the *New York Times*'s description of the mob that openly assaulted some 50 women attending a June 2000 NYC parade. 'Stoked with booze, they worked up from hooting at women, to grabbing them, to drenching them with water and pulling off their tops and pants' (Staples, 2000).
SOURCE: © Jose Mercado/Corbis Images

However, there is a question about the direction of causality here. In a study of young people aged 11–15

CHAPTER 8: AGGRESSION

susceptibility hypothesis *when features of someone's environment make him/her more susceptible to particular kinds of behaviour as a consequence*

years in the west of Scotland, Robert Young, Helen Sweeting and Patrick West (2007) found that antisocial behaviour can predict long-term alcohol (mis)use. The 'susceptibility hypothesis' suggests that people who are already engaging in antisocial behaviour, or who are likely to do so, are much more 'susceptible' to abuse alcohol in the short or long term. So here we have an example where the causal order is reversed (antisocial behaviour causing alcohol misuse). But, whatever the direction of the relationship between alcohol and aggression, what is clear is that alcohol enhances aggressiveness by lowering people's self-awareness and their thresholds for antisocial behaviour due to reduced control from social and cultural norms, by reducing their ability to consider consequences, and by people's mentally associating alcohol with aggression (Bartholow & Heinz, 2006; Ito et al., 1996; Steele & Southwick, 1985).

Testosterone

Hormonal influences appear to be much stronger in lower animals than in humans. But human aggressiveness does appear to correlate to some extent with the male sex hormone, testosterone. Consider:

Drugs that diminish testosterone levels in violent human males can subdue their aggressive tendencies.

Among the normal range of teen boys and adult men, those with high testosterone levels have been found to be prone to delinquency, hard drug use and aggressive responses to provocation (Archer, 1991; Dabbs & Morris, 1990; Olweus et al., 1988). After handling a gun, people's testosterone levels rise, and the more their testosterone rises the more aggression they will impose on another (Klinesmith et al., 2006). Shawn Geniole and his colleagues (2011) discovered that higher testosterone levels were associated with reactive aggression in men. Interestingly, Kimberly Cote and her research team (2013) found that sleep deprivation lowered testosterone levels and reactive aggression in men.

But we need to be careful here. Taken at face value this would lead us to the assumption that men must be more aggressive than women. As we shall see later in this chapter, this is not always the case. You may remember one of the lessons from Chapter 2: correlation does not mean causation. Winning a rugby match might cause a brief increase in testosterone levels among the players. Does this mean they will then behave aggressively? Most probably not.

Serotonin

Low levels of serotonin have been linked to heightened aggression (Birger et al., 2003; de Almeida et al., 2005).

Those studies which propose a link between aggression and serotonin include the dietary manipulation of tryptophan, which is an amino acid used in the production of serotonin. In one study by Gerard Moeller and his team (1996) participants were put on a low tryptophan diet for 24 hours to reduce the levels of serotonin produced. These participants were also asked to take part in a maths task that involved being provoked by a researcher. What the researchers discovered was that aggressive responses started to increase from 5 hours of being on the diet. Furthermore, when a low tryptophan diet is mixed with alcohol consumption serotonin levels drop even further, and aggressive behaviours are displayed in an experimental context (LeMarquand et al., 1998).

Studies such as these directly manipulate serotonin levels through diet. Yet these studies show us that our environment may interact with our biology. For example, those individuals who find themselves of low social status often have low levels of serotonin (Manuck et al., 2004). Deficiencies in this neurotransmitter are associated with risky and impulsive behaviour (Moeller et al., 1996). So is it the biology that determines the risky behaviour, or the social standing? Most probably, it's an interaction of both.

Neural Influences

Exerting self-control in a situation where we feel angry can be extremely difficult. And, as neuroimaging studies show, it can be more difficult for some people than others.

Reactive aggression defines a response to being provoked. We may want to respond to being threatened, frustrated or angry at someone's actions or a set of circumstances. Perhaps you've been insulted, tricked, embarrassed or put in a dangerous position. How do you react?

reactive aggression an aggressive response to being provoked

Denson and his colleagues (2012) outline 'I-Theory', which states that there are three processes behind aggression: instigation (being provoked), impellance (dispositional and situational factors which prepare you for an aggressive response) and inhibition (self-control). So your ability to avoid an aggressive reaction is based on the relative strength of your self-control (inhibition) over provocation (instigation) and impellance (preparedness to be aggressive). And it seems that processes within the brain have some influence over our ability to exercise self-control. Prefrontal cortex regions are involved in regulating our emotions and help us to maintain self-control. Damage to these regions is often linked to violent behaviour. But they can be temporarily impeded too by alcohol consumption (as we'll see later in this chapter) and depletion from feeling overwhelmed. The good news is that practice makes perfect, as we control our urge to react aggressively to provocation. Another tastier method of controlling our aggressive urges seems to be consuming sugar, which has been shown to improve those neural processes involved in self-control (Denson et al., 2010).

But not all aggression is reactive. Instrumental aggression defines behaviour that is aggressive in order to acquire a desired reward. For example, a son who murders his father for the inheritance would be an act of instrumental aggression. Instrumental aggression requires a lack of empathy with the victim. Research suggests that this lack of empathy is related to poor functioning of the amygdala. This is particularly evident in psychopathic populations, where personality is characterized by a lack of guilt for their actions. Dennis Reidy and his colleagues (2011) report examples of studies which have shown instrumental aggressive acts are much more likely to be conducted by psychopaths than non-psychopaths. It seems the amygdala, responsible for feelings of empathy and shame, plays a key role in instrumental aggression.

instrumental aggression a behaviour which requires aggression in order to obtain a desired (often material) reward

Biology and Behaviour Interact

It is important to remember that the traffic between hormonal influences, brain structure, alcohol, drugs and behaviour flows both ways. Testosterone, for example, may facilitate dominance and aggressiveness, but dominating or defeating behaviour also boosts testosterone levels (Mazur & Booth, 1998).

CHAPTER 8: AGGRESSION

After a World Cup football match or a big basketball game between arch-rivals, testosterone levels rise in the winning fans and fall in the losing fans (Bernhardt et al., 1998). That, plus celebration-related drinking, probably explains the finding of Cardiff University researchers that fans of *winning* rather than losing football and rugby teams commit more postgame assaults (Sivarajasingam et al., 2005). The more athletic competitions women enter, the more their levels of testosterone and cortisol rise (Edwards & Casto, 2013). As Thomas Denson and his colleagues discovered (2013), women with high levels of testosterone and cortisol reacted much more aggressively when insulted than women who had average or low levels of these hormones.

So, instinctive, genetic, neural and biochemical influences may predispose some people to react aggressively to conflict and provocation. But perhaps we need to be careful in interpreting these data, and not to assume that such features are solely responsible for aggressive behaviour.

Many of the tried and tested methods for treating and changing deviant behaviour do not involve biological intervention but concern adjustment of people's social environment and ways of thinking about themselves. Cognitive behavioural therapy (CBT) tackles the way in which people think about themselves, others and the world at large in order to alter their cognition and behaviour. So a complex array of factors is involved, and we need to think about 'what' we define as aggression and what we treat as evidence of it.

Some early social psychological theories of the causes of aggression focused on particular types: those aggressive acts which occurred as a result of frustration, and those that occurred as a consequence of relative deprivation. Let's consider each of these in turn.

AGGRESSION AS A RESPONSE TO FRUSTRATION

frustration-aggression theory *the theory that frustration triggers a readiness to aggress*

frustration *the blocking of goal-directed behaviour*

One of the first psychological theories of aggression, frustration-aggression theory, argues 'Frustration always leads to some form of aggression' (John Dollard and his colleagues, 1939). Frustration is anything that blocks our attaining a goal. Barker et al. (1941) found that young children who were shown a room full of attractive toys but prevented from playing with them displayed much more aggressive behaviour towards those toys, compared to other children who had been allowed to play with them immediately, when finally allowed to enter the room.

When Rupert Brown and his colleagues (2001) surveyed British ferry passengers heading to France, they found much higher than normal aggressive attitudes on a day when French fishing boats blockaded the port, preventing their travel. Blocked from obtaining their goal, the passengers became more likely (in responding to various vignettes) to agree with an insult towards a French person who had spilled coffee. In her study of queue-jumpers, Mary Harris (1974) found that when people were pushed in front of in a supermarket queue, the closer they were to the checkout when the incident occurred was related to the level of aggression they displayed. The nearer they were to the goal, the more intense the expression of aggression displayed became.

As Figure 8.1 suggests, the aggressive energy need not explode directly against its source. We learn to inhibit direct retaliation, especially when others might disapprove or punish; instead, we *displace* our hostilities to safer targets.

Displacement occurs in an old anecdote about a man who, humiliated by his boss, berates his wife, who yells at their son, who kicks the dog, which bites the mail-carrier (who goes home and berates his wife . . .). In experiments and in real life, displaced aggression is most likely when the target shares some similarity to the instigator and does some minor irritating act that unleashes the displaced aggression (Marcus-Newhall et al., 2000; Miller et al., 2003; Pedersen et al., 2000). When a person is harbouring anger from a prior provocation, even a trivial offence – one that would normally produce no response – may elicit an explosive overreaction (as you may realize if you have ever yelled at your room-mate after losing money in a malfunctioning vending machine).

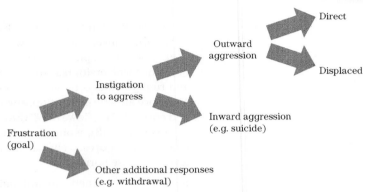

FIGURE 8.1 The classic frustration-aggression theory
Frustration creates a motive to aggress. Fear of punishment or disapproval for aggressing against the source of frustration may cause the aggressive drive to be displaced against some other target or even redirected against oneself.
SOURCE: Based on Dollard et al., 1939; Miller, 1941.

However, it is important to remember that frustration as well as aggression is culture dependent. In some cultures people do not have the same individual expectations as most people have in other cultures and they therefore do not feel frustrated for not reaching the individual goals. This also reduces the consequences of frustration and the prevalence of aggression.

A different approach to the aggression-frustration model is based in the work of Dolf Zillman (1979) and his excitation-transfer model. Zillman suggests that when we are physiologically aroused from a particular event or situation, this state of arousal does not simply disappear but can have effects on other situations we find ourselves in. Under such conditions a person may transfer feelings of frustration to a different situation and act aggressively.

Various commentators have observed that the intense American anger over 9/11 contributed to the eagerness to attack Iraq. Americans were looking for an outlet for their rage and found one in an evil tyrant, Saddam Hussein, who was once their ally. 'The "real reason" for this war', noted Thomas Friedman (2003b), 'was that after 9/11 America needed to hit someone in the Arab-Muslim world . . . We hit Saddam for one simple reason: because we could, and because he deserved it, and because he was right in the heart of that world.' One of the war's advocates, Vice-President Richard Cheney (2003), seemed to concur. When asked why most others in the world disagreed with America's launching war, he replied, 'They didn't experience 9/11.'

Frustration-Aggression Theory Revised

Laboratory tests of the frustration-aggression theory have produced mixed results: sometimes frustration increased aggressiveness but sometimes not. For example, if the frustration was understandable – if, as in one experiment, a confederate disrupted a group's problem solving because his hearing aid malfunctioned (rather than just because he wasn't paying attention) – then

displacement *the redirection of aggression to a target other than the source of the frustration. Generally, the new target is a safer or more socially acceptable target*

excitation-transfer model *when a state of physiological arousal is transferred from one situation to another, resulting in heightened expressive behaviour*

CHAPTER 8: AGGRESSION

Frustrated as the referee allows an own goal to stand, Patrice Eura of Manchester United begins to argue with him over his decision.
SOURCE: © Getty Images

FIGURE 8.2 A simplified synopsis of Leonard Berkowitz's revised frustration-aggression theory

frustration led to irritation, not aggression (Burnstein & Worchel, 1962).

Leonard Berkowitz (1978, 1989) realized that the original theory overstated the frustration-aggression connection, so he revised it. Berkowitz theorized that frustration produces *anger*, an emotional readiness to aggress. Anger arises when someone who frustrates us could have chosen to act otherwise (Averill, 1983; Weiner, 1981). A frustrated person is especially likely to lash out when aggressive cues pull the cork, releasing bottled-up anger (Figure 8.2). Sometimes the cork will blow without such cues. But, as we will see, cues associated with aggression amplify aggression (Carlson et al., 1990).

Frustration may be unrelated to deprivation. The most sexually frustrated people are probably not celibate. The most economically frustrated people are probably not the impoverished residents of African shanty towns. Likewise, Palestinian suicide bombers have not been the most deprived of Palestinians. Like Northern Ireland's IRA, Italy's Red Brigades and Germany's Bader-Meinhof gang, they are mostly middle class (Krueger & Maleckova, 2003; Pettigrew, 2003). So, too, were the 9/11 terrorists, who were professionally trained and world travelled.

Relative Deprivation

Frustration is often compounded when we compare ourselves with others. Workers' feelings of well-being depend on whether their compensation compares favourably with that of others in their line of work (Yuchtman, 1976). A raise in salary for a city's police officers, while temporarily lifting their morale, may deflate that of the firefighters.

relative deprivation the perception that one is less well off than others with whom one compares oneself

Such feelings are called relative deprivation. This goes some way to explaining why East Germans revolted against their communist regime: they had a higher standard of living than some Western European countries, but a frustratingly lower one than their West German neighbours (Baron et al., 1992).

One possible source of such frustration today is the affluence depicted in television programmes and commercials. In cultures where television is a universal appliance, it helps turn absolute deprivation (lacking what others have) into relative deprivation (feeling deprived). Karen Hennigan and her co-workers (1982) analysed crime rates in American cities around the time television was introduced. In 34 cities where television ownership became widespread in 1951, the 1951 larceny theft rate (for crimes such as shoplifting and bicycle stealing) took an observable jump. In 34 other cities, where a government freeze had delayed the introduction of television until 1955, a similar jump in the theft rate occurred – in 1955.

But of course, to claim that all aggression is simply the result of frustration and/ or relative deprivation is simply untrue. So social psychologists have examined other causes and explanations for aggressive behaviour.

AGGRESSION AS LEARNED SOCIAL BEHAVIOUR

Theories of aggression based on instinct and frustration assume that aggression arises from hostile urges which erupt from within the individual, which naturally 'push' aggression out into the social world from forces within. However, some social psychologists contend that the source of aggression may be located within the social world.

The Rewards of Aggression

By experience and by observing others, we learn that aggression often pays. People can learn the rewards of aggression. A child whose aggressive acts successfully intimidate other children is likely to become increasingly aggressive (Patterson et al., 1967). Aggressive hockey players – those sent most often to the penalty box for rough play – score more goals than non-aggressive players (McCarthy & Kelly, 1978a, 1978b). Canadian teenage hockey players whose fathers applaud physically aggressive play show the most aggressive attitudes and style of play (Ennis & Zanna, 1991). In these cases, aggression is instrumental in achieving certain rewards.

The same is true of terrorist acts, which enable powerless people to garner widespread attention. 'The primary targets of suicide-bombing attacks are not those who are injured but those who are made to witness it through media coverage,' note Paul Marsden and Sharon Attia (2005). Terrorism's purpose is, with the help of media amplification, to terrorize. Deprived of what Margaret Thatcher called 'the oxygen of publicity', terrorism would surely diminish, concluded Jeffrey Rubin (1986). It's like the 1970s incidents of naked spectators 'streaking' onto football fields for a few seconds of television exposure. Once the networks decided to ignore the incidents, the phenomenon ended.

Observational Learning

Albert Bandura (1997) proposed a social learning theory of aggression. He believes that we learn aggression not only by experiencing its rewards but also by observing others (also see Chapter 5). As with many social behaviours, we acquire aggression by watching others act and noting the consequences.

social learning theory
Bandura's theory that we learn social behaviour by observing and imitating others, and then by self-regulating our own behaviour accordingly

In one of Bandura's experiments (Bandura et al., 1961) a pre-school child is put to work on an interesting art activity. An adult is in another part of the room, where there are Tinker Toys, a mallet and a big, inflated, Bobo doll. After a minute of working with the Tinker Toys, the adult gets up and for almost 10 minutes attacks the inflated doll. She pounds it with the mallet, kicks it and throws it, while yelling, 'Sock him in the nose ... Knock him down ... Kick him'.

After observing this outburst, the child is taken to a different room with many very attractive toys. But after 2 minutes the experimenter interrupts, saying these are her best toys and she must 'save them for the other children'. The frustrated child now goes into yet another room with various toys designed for aggressive and non-aggressive play, two of which are a Bobo doll and a mallet.

Children who were not exposed to the aggressive adult model did not display any aggressive play or talk. Although frustrated, they nevertheless played calmly. However, those who had observed the aggressive adult were more likely to pick up the mallet and lash out at the doll. Watching the adult's aggressive behaviour lowered their inhibitions. Furthermore, the children often reproduced the model's specific acts and said her words. Observing aggressive behaviour had both lowered their inhibitions and taught them ways to aggress. Bandura argued that modelling this behaviour was enough for a child to acquire and perform aggressive behaviour.

In a later study Bandura tested whether the consequences of aggressive actions had any effect on children's modelling behaviour. He found that if children witnessed the adult being punished as a consequence of their negative actions towards the Bobo doll, the children did not mimic their actions. However, if they saw the adult rewarded, then their behaviour was re-enacted by the child towards the doll.

Since Bandura's studies there have been some questions raised over his claims. For example, Steve Hayes, Arnold Rincover and Diane Volosin (1980) replicated Bandura's study, and examined the levels of aggression children displayed to a free-moving Bobo doll as compared to one with limited movement. They found that when the Bobo doll was free-moving, providing the child with a lot of visual stimulation, this produced and maintained high levels of aggression. Athena Drewes (2008) reviews some further concerns that surround Bandura's studies, including the observation that Bobo dolls are 'meant to be hit', so it's unclear to what degree these are demonstrations of aggression. She also asks if behaviours that are allowed in a study are fair reflections of acts of aggression that occur in real life. That said, Drewes does not dispute that Bandura's work gives us some of the strongest evidence about how aggressive behaviour is acquired and performed.

Bandura (1979) believes that everyday life exposes us to three main aggressive models: the family, one's subculture and, as we will see, the mass media.

The Family

The role the family plays in the acquisition, maintenance and extinguishing of aggressive behaviour in children has been well documented within the research. While many children engage in physical aggression between the ages of 1 and 3 years, its subsequent decline is attributed to prosocial parenting and socialization

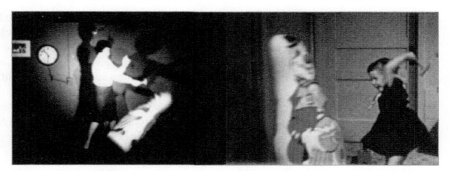

In Bandura's famous experiment, children exposed to an adult's aggression against a Bobo doll became likely to reproduce the observed aggression.
SOURCE: © Albert Bandura

by peers and teachers into non-violent ways of behaving. Jasmina Burdzovic Andreas and Malcolm Watson (2009) suggest that it is when children believe aggression is a justifiable and valuable tool in social interactions that they develop the habit of aggression. However, optimal family environments which exhibit low conflict and high levels of cohesion can reduce aggression in children. Anne Borge and colleagues (2004) found aggression was more common in children looked after at home in 'high-risk' families than those in daycare. She concluded that high physical aggression in children was associated with low maternal education, high number of siblings, low socio-economic status and very poor family functioning.

Sadly, not all family environments are havens of peace. Physically aggressive children often have had physically punitive parents, who disciplined them with screaming, slapping and beating (Patterson et al., 1982). These parents are likely to have parents who were themselves physically punitive (Bandura & Walters, 1959; Straus & Gelles, 1980). In Diane English and her colleagues' study (2009) with a non-clinical US sample, they found that children's outcomes were better when they came from homes that had never experienced domestic violence, neglect or maltreatment. But they also observed that much of the aggression reported was verbal rather than physical.

The presence of a violent parent or guardian within the family has received particular attention from psychologists. Timothy Ireland and Carolyn Smith (2009) reported a relationship between violent partner and homes during adolescence and adolescent conduct problems. The absence of a parent or guardian has also been studied for its role in aggression. A British study that followed more than 10 000 individuals for 33 years since their birth in 1958 found that a parental breakup during childhood had negative consequences for their mental health as adults (Chase-Lansdale et al., 1995). The point raised by these studies is not that children from single-parent homes are doomed to become delinquent, dysfunctional or violent, but rather, nurtured by a caring parent or guardian and extended family, most children thrive.

It is often thought that deprived neighbourhoods can be a harmful place for children and adolescents to grow up in. Yet, Candice Odgers and colleagues (2009) found quite the reverse. In deprived neighbourhoods with high social cohension and a willingness to intervene in family situations where it was thought to be for the greater good, these local communities with 'collective efficacy' were capable of reducing youth aggression and protecting children.

In fact it would seem that a complex array of factors inside and outside the family contribute to aggression in children. What this array of diverse research does alert us to is how difficult it is to produce simple cause-and-effect relationships to explain the role of the family in aggression. As Gayla Margolin and colleagues (2009) observed from their longitudinal study of children and adolescents, different forms of violence tend to co-occur within the lifetime of an individual. These can include marital aggression, parent–child abuse and community violence. To understand aggression and violence we need to look further than just the family, and to the broader social context in which it occurs.

The Culture

The social environment outside the home also provides models and societal norms. In communities where 'macho' images are admired, aggression is readily

CHAPTER 8: AGGRESSION

transmitted to new generations (Cartwright, 1975; Short, 1969). The violent subculture of teenage gangs, for instance, provides its junior members with aggressive models. Among Chicago adolescents who are otherwise equally at risk for violence, those who have observed gun violence are at doubled risk for violent behaviour (Bingenheimer et al., 2005).

Henri Tajfel (1974) pointed out that explanations of aggression must also consider the broader cultural context in which the individual is placed. For example, Conor McGuckin and Christopher Lewis (2003, 2008) have found that the prevalence of bullying in schools in Northern Ireland, where violent conflict between political and religious groups has been rife, is much higher than incidences found in Wales, England, Scotland and Ireland. In China and Japan, where the crime rates are low, children are thought not to be aggressive from an early age. Aggressiveness is looked upon as childish and a sign of being immature. In East Asian interdependent cultures the feeling of shame is also important in contributing to the low crime rates. To violate the law is to bring shame on oneself and the whole family, and to be caught means that the family is 'losing face'. These cultural norms reduce offending in East Asian shame cultures.

Richard Nisbett (1990, 1993) and Dov Cohen (1996, 1998) have explored the subculture effect within the USA. The sober, co-operative White folk who settled in New England and the Middle Atlantic region produced a different culture from that of the swashbuckling, honour-preserving White folk who settled much of the South. The former were farmer-artisans; the latter, more aggressive hunters and herders. To the present day, American cities and areas populated by southerners have much higher white homicide rates than those populated by northerners.

In their study of antigay aggression, Wilson Vincent and his colleagues (2011) note cultural influence in the development of heterosexual masculinity. Culture brings with it traditional expectations about how men 'ought' to behave, think and feel, and what the values and norms of men 'should' be. These cultural influences may underlie antigay aggression. Feeling insecure in one's own heterosexual masculine identity, or what Vincent and his colleagues call 'masculine gender-role stress', can express itself in antigay anger and aggression. It is the fear of being excluded from heterosexual groups and mainstream values that may motivate some reportedly straight men to be aggressive towards gay men, as an explicit reaffirmation of their heterosexual masculine identity.

Stanley Schachter's two-factor theory of emotion (1959) suggests that emotions, such as anger and frustration, are rooted in the physiology of the individual but also in how people interpret the situation and what is considered to be culturally appropriate behaviour. For example, Joe Vandello and Dov Cohen (2003) note how the cultural scripts in Brazil surrounding matters of 'honour' mean that under certain circumstances domestic violence is an acceptable way of punishing female infidelity and restoring a male's honour. Patricia Rodriguez Mosquera, Anthony Manstead and Agneta Fischer (2002) found differences in responses of Spanish and Dutch participants when confronted with threats and insults. Whereas Dutch participants became angered when the insults were directed towards their autonomy and individual achievements, Spanish participants displayed anger when their family honour was challenged. The researchers argue that these different patterns of responses mark the contrasting significance of

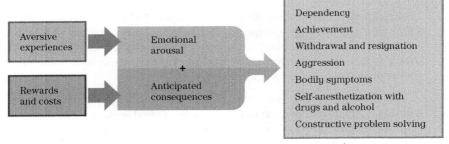

FIGURE 8.3 The social learning view of aggression
The emotional arousal stemming from an aversive experience motivates aggression. Whether aggression or some other response actually occurs depends on what consequences we have learned to expect.
SOURCE: Based on Bandura, 1979, 1997.

concepts of individualism (in the Netherlands) and honour (in Spain) provoking aggression when they are challenged or undermined. So, there are cultural scripts that influence what is regarded as an appropriate emotion to have under certain circumstances and what is an acceptable expression of it.

But when will aggressive responses actually occur? Bandura (1979) contended that aggressive acts are motivated by a variety of aversive experiences – frustration, pain, insults (Figure 8.3). Such experiences arouse us emotionally. But whether we act aggressively depends on the consequences we anticipate. Aggression is most likely when we are aroused, and it seems safe, appropriate and rewarding to aggress.

SOME INFLUENCES ON AGGRESSION

Under what conditions do we aggress? Here we examine some specific influences: aversive incidents, arousal, the media, hate and collective identity.

AVERSIVE INCIDENTS

Recipes for aggression often include some type of aversive experience: pain, uncomfortable heat, an attack or overcrowding.

Pain
Researcher Nathan Azrin (1967) was doing experiments with laboratory rats in a cage wired to deliver electric shocks to the animals' feet. Azrin wanted to know if switching off the shocks would reinforce two rats' positive interactions with each other. He planned to turn on the shock and then, once the rats approached each other, cut off the pain. To his great surprise, the experiment proved impossible. As soon as the rats felt pain, they attacked each other, before the experimenter could switch off the shock. The greater the shock (and pain) the more violent the attack. Of course today's ethical guidelines restrict researchers' use of painful stimuli.

Pain heightens aggressiveness in humans, too. Many of us can recall such a reaction after stubbing a toe or suffering a headache. Leonard Berkowitz and his associates demonstrated this by having students hold one hand in either lukewarm water

CHAPTER 8: AGGRESSION

or painfully cold water. Those whose hands were submerged in the cold water reported feeling more irritable and more annoyed, and they were more willing to blast another person with unpleasant noise. In view of such results, Berkowitz (1983, 1989, 1998) proposed that aversive stimulation rather than frustration is the basic trigger of hostile aggression. Frustration is certainly one important type of unpleasantness. But any aversive event, whether a dashed expectation, a personal insult or physical pain, can incite an emotional outburst. Even the torment of a depressed state increases the likelihood of hostile, aggressive behaviour.

Heat

People have theorized for centuries about the effect of climate on human action. Hippocrates (c. 460–377 BC) compared the civilized Greece of his day with the savagery in the region further north (what is now Germany and Switzerland) and decided that northern Europe's harsh climate was to blame. More than a millennium later, the English attributed their 'superior' culture to England's ideal climate. French thinkers proclaimed the same for France. Because climate remains relatively steady while cultural traits change over time, the climate theory of culture obviously has limited validity.

Pain attack. Frustrated after losing the first two rounds of his 1997 heavyweight championship fight with Evander Holyfield, and feeling pain from an accidental head butt, Mike Tyson reacts by biting off part of Holyfield's ear.

SOURCE: AP/Wide World Photos

Temporary climate variations can, however, affect behaviour. Offensive odours, cigarette smoke and air pollution have all been linked with aggressive behaviour (Rotton & Frey, 1985). But the most studied environmental irritant is heat. William Griffitt (1970; Griffitt & Veitch, 1971) found that compared with students who answered questionnaires in a room with a normal temperature, those who did so in an uncomfortably hot room (over 90°F) reported feeling more tired and aggressive, and expressed more hostility towards a stranger. Follow-up experiments revealed that heat also triggers retaliative actions (Bell, 1980; Rule et al., 1987).

Does uncomfortable heat increase aggression in the real world as well as in the laboratory? Consider:

In heat-stricken Phoenix, Arizona, drivers without air-conditioning have been more likely to display road rage (Kenrick & MacFarlane, 1986).

The riots that broke out in 79 US cities between 1967 and 1971 occurred on hotter rather than cool days; none of them happened in winter.

In 2007/08 violent crimes against the person fell considerably in London during the winter months.

'I pray thee, good Mercutio, let's retire; The day is hot, the Capulets abroad, And, if we meet, we shall not 'scape a brawl, For now, these hot days, is the mad blood stirring.'
Shakespeare, *Romeo and Juliet*

Do these real-world findings show that heat discomfort directly fuels aggressiveness? Although the conclusion appears plausible, these *correlations* between temperature and aggression don't prove it. People certainly could be more irritable in hot, sticky weather. And in the laboratory, hot temperatures do increase arousal and hostile thoughts and feelings (Anderson et al., 1999). There may be other contributing factors, though. Maybe hot summer evenings drive people into the streets. There, other group influence factors may well take over as group interactions increase. Then again (researchers are debating this), maybe there comes a point where stifling heat suppresses violence (Bell, 2005; Bushman et al., 2005b, 2005c; Cohn & Rotton, 2005).

Attacks

Being attacked or insulted by another is especially conducive to aggression. The reciprocity principle means we tend to react to a direct attack, which can of course lead to an escalation of violence. Several experiments, including one at Osaka University by Kennichi Ohbuchi and Toshihiro Kambara (1985), confirm that intentional attacks breed retaliatory attacks. In most of these experiments, one person competes with another in a reaction-time contest. After each test trial, the winner chooses how much shock to give the loser. Actually, each person is playing a programmed opponent, who steadily escalates the amount of shock. Do the real participants respond charitably? Hardly. Extracting 'an eye for an eye' is the more likely response.

Road rage has been found to be more likely in humid conditions.

SOURCE: © Carlofranco/iStock

reciprocity principle *asserts that we should treat like with like. So responses to a positive action should be positive, whereas those to a negative action should be negative*

INTERPRETING AROUSAL

So far we have seen that various aversive stimulations can arouse anger. Do other types of arousal, such as those that accompany exercise or sexual excitement, have a similar effect? Imagine that Lourdes, having just finished a stimulating short run, comes home to discover that her date for the evening has called and left word that he has made other plans. Will Lourdes more likely explode in fury after her run than if she discovered the same message after awakening from a nap? Or, since she has just exercised, will her aggressive tendencies be exorcised? To discover the answer, consider how we interpret and label our bodily states.

In a famous experiment, Stanley Schachter and Jerome Singer (1962) found we can experience an aroused bodily state in different ways. They aroused University of Minnesota men by injecting adrenaline. The drug produced body flushing, heart palpitation and more rapid breathing. When forewarned that the drug would produce those effects, the men felt little emotion, even when waiting with either a hostile or a euphoric person. Of course, they could readily attribute their bodily sensations to the drug. Schachter and Singer led another group of men to believe the drug produced no such side effects. Then they, too, were placed in the company of a hostile or a euphoric person. How did they feel and act? They were angered when with the hostile person, amused when with the person who was euphoric. The principle seemed to be: *a given state of bodily arousal feeds one emotion or another, depending on how the person interprets and labels the arousal.*

Other experiments indicate that arousal is not as emotionally undifferentiated as Schachter believed. Yet being physically stirred up does intensify just about any emotion (Reisenzein, 1983). For example, Paul Biner (1991) reports that people find radio static unpleasant, *especially* when they are aroused by bright lighting. And Dolf Zillmann (1988), Jennings Bryant and their collaborators found that

CHAPTER 8: AGGRESSION

research close-up

HARASSMENT ONLINE

Source: *Workman, M. (2010). A behaviourist perspective on corporate harassment online: Validation of a theoretical model of psychological motives.* Computers and Security, *29, 831–839.*

Introduction

Why do some people take to insulting and abusing others online? The phenomenon known as 'trolling' is receiving social psychological attention as its occurrence increases with the rise in our Internet use. So what motivates such cyber aggression? Perpetrators do not just abuse individuals, but also victimize companies. Cyber harassment can be dismissed as irritating, but at its worst can lead to considerable distress and in some cases suicide of their targeted victim. Corporate companies and their employees can be the targets of abuse, but also their employees can be the perpetrators. So what advice can be offered to businesses to prevent their employees from engaging in it?

This research draws on the findings of the Honeynet Project (2004; http://www.honeynet.org.uk), which identified six motives underlying individual attacks on computer systems. These included a need for entertainment, status-seeking, to promote a cause or ideology, a need for social acceptance, uncontrollable impulses and economic motives. Could motives such as these be behind cyber-attacks on individuals and corporations? The following six hypotheses were developed to predict who is likely to engage in trolling behaviour.

H1: People who are self-indulgent will be more likely to commit cyber harassment that people who are less self-indulgent.

H2: People who are more narcissistic will be more likely to commit cyber harassment than people who are less narcissistic.

H3: People who are more idealistic will be more likely to commit cyber harassment than people who are less idealistic.

H4: People who have a greater need for acceptance will be more likely to commit cyber harassment than people who have less need for acceptance.

H5: People who are less emotionally stable will be more likely to commit cyber harassment than people who are more emotionally stable.

H6: People who are more exploitative will be more likely to commit cyber harassment than people who are less exploitative.

Method

Of the 112 surveys given out to randomly sampled college students (mean age = 24 years), 54 were returned completed. The surveys consisted of a personality questionnaire to measure the characteristics of self-indulgence, narcissism, idealism, need for social acceptance, emotional stability and exploitation. This was a 7-point Likert scale that asked people how much they agreed with statements such as, 'My values are more important to me than offending people' (measure of idealism) and 'I seek to come out ahead no matter what' (a measure of exploitation). Participants were also asked whether they had ever written critical comments or something negative about people and companies on social media, which they knew was not true.

Results

A structured equation model was carried out. This provided correlations on the different personality measures (such as narcissism and self-indulgence) and having engaged in cyber harassment.

Statistical significance was found for all six hypotheses, and in the direction predicted by the research.

H1: People who are more self-indulgent are more likely to commit cyber harassment than people who are less self-indulgent ($\beta = -.55, p < .01$).

H2: People who are more narcissistic are more likely to commit cyber harassment than those who are less narcissistic ($\beta = -.33, p < .05$).

H3: People who are idealistic are more likely to commit cyber harassment than those who are less narcissistic ($\beta = -.25, p < .05$).

H4: People who have a greater need for acceptance are more likely to commit cyber harassment than those who have less need for acceptance ($\beta = -.46, p < .01$).

H5: People who are less emotionally stable are more likely to commit cyber harassment than those who are more emotionally stable ($\beta = -.27, p < .05$)

H6: People who are more exploitative are more likely to commit cyber harassment than people who are less exploitative ($\beta = .40, p < .01$).

Discussion

People who are more self-indulgent, narcissistic, idealistic, have high need for acceptance, emotionally unstable, and exploitative in their relationships with others are more likely to attack people and companies via social media, than those who are not strong on these personality characteristics.

So, what can companies do to discourage and prevent employees from getting involved in trolling, and protect themselves from becoming the victim of one? On a practical level companies can take out legal protection against incidences such as these happening. Software can be purchased that can trawl the Internet to detect any negative comments that have been posted up about a company. However, there are also things you can do to tackle perpetrators. These include ignoring the attacker in the hope that this will extinguish the behaviour. From a behaviourist perspective, this lack of reinforcement may be enough to stop the negative behaviour being continued. Alternatively, a company may wish to try and reason with an attacker to help him/her see the consequences of their behaviour. Finally, a company can punish the attacker either through corporate measures (such as dismissal) or via legal channels.

There are some limitations with this study. The truthfulness of participants' accounts may be compromised considering the sensitive and undesirable nature of the topic. The sample is also small in number (54) and young in age. This makes generalization to the wider population difficult. Moreover, these motives may not on their own explain trolling behaviour. There may be other attitudes involved, such as those about the legal system and fairness, which moderate trolling behaviour. We also have some potential discrepancy between individuals about what constitutes negative and critical comments. Furthermore, a study such as this does not consider any social factors involved in cyber-harassment including the context in which it is done. It assumes cyber-harassment is done by individuals.

Perhaps personality characteristics go some way to explaining cyber-harassment and targeted attacks on individuals and companies, but arguably other more social factors are involved.

CHAPTER 8: AGGRESSION

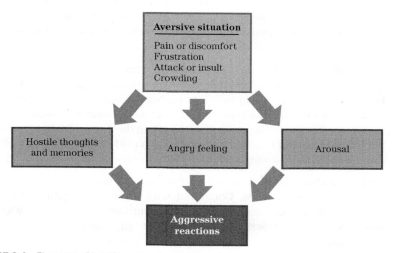

FIGURE 8.4 Elements of hostile aggression
An aversive situation can trigger aggression by provoking hostile cognitions, hostile feelings and arousal. These reactions make us more likely to perceive harmful intent and to react aggressively.
SOURCE: Simplified from Anderson et al., 1995.

people who have just pumped an exercise bike or watched a film of a Beatles rock concert find it easy to misattribute their arousal to a provocation. They then retaliate with heightened aggression.

Although common sense might lead us to assume that Lourdes's run would have drained her aggressive tensions, enabling her to accept bad news calmly, these studies show that *arousal feeds emotions*.

Sexual arousal and other forms of arousal, such as anger, can therefore amplify one another (Zillmann, 1989b). Love is never so passionate as after a fight or a fright. In the laboratory, erotic stimuli are more arousing to people who have just been frightened. Similarly, the arousal of a roller-coaster ride may spill over into romantic feeling for one's partner.

A frustrating, hot or insulting situation heightens arousal. When it does, the arousal, combined with hostile thoughts and feelings, may form a recipe for aggressive behaviour (Figure 8.4).

AGGRESSION CUES: THE INFLUENCE OF THE ENVIRONMENT

As we noted when considering the frustration-aggression hypothesis, violence is more likely when aggressive cues in the environment release pent-up anger. Leonard Berkowitz (1968, 1981, 1995) and others have found that the sight of a weapon is such a cue. In one experiment, children who had just played with toy guns became more willing to knock down another child's blocks. In another, angered University of Wisconsin men gave more electric shocks to their tormenter when a rifle and a revolver (supposedly left over from a previous experiment) were nearby than when badminton rackets had been left behind (Berkowitz & LePage, 1967). Guns prime hostile thoughts and punitive judgements (Anderson et al., 1998; Dienstbier et al., 1998). What's within sight is within mind. This is especially so when a weapon is perceived as an instrument of violence rather than a recreational item. So the labels and evaluative meanings we give people and objects influence our behaviour. For hunters, for example, seeing a hunting rifle does not prime aggressive thoughts, though it does for non-hunters (Bartholow et al., 2004).

Berkowitz notes how in the USA, a country with some 200 million privately owned guns, half of all murders are committed with handguns, or that handguns in homes are far more likely to kill household members than intruders. 'Guns not only permit violence,' he reported, 'they can stimulate it as well. The finger pulls the trigger, but the trigger may also be pulling the finger.' Perhaps this is echoed in the UK independent charity Crimestoppers report, that between 2007/08 and 2009, there was a rise in attempted murder with the use of knives.

Berkowitz also draws attention towards the fact that countries that ban handguns have lower murder rates. Compared with the USA, Britain has one-fourth as many people and one-sixteenth as many murders. The USA has 10 000 handgun homicides a year; Australia has about a dozen, Britain two dozen and Canada 100. When Washington, DC, adopted a law restricting handgun possession, the numbers of gun-related murders and suicides each abruptly dropped about 25 per cent. No changes occurred in other methods of murder and suicide, nor did adjacent areas outside the reach of this law experience any such declines (Loftin et al., 1991).

Researchers have also examined risks of violence in homes with and without guns. This is controversial research, because such homes may differ in many ways. One study sponsored by the Centers for Disease Control compared gun owners and non-owners of the same gender, race, age and neighbourhood. The ironic and tragic result was that those who kept a gun in the home (often for protection) were 2.7 times as likely to be murdered – nearly always by a family member or a close acquaintance (Kellermann et al., 1993; Kellermann, 1997). Another study found that the risk of suicide in homes with guns was five times as high as in homes without them (Taubes, 1992). A newer national study found a slightly weaker, but still significant, link between guns and homicide or suicide. Compared with others of the same gender, age and race, people with guns at home were 41 per cent as likely to be homicide victims and 3.4 times as likely to die of suicide (Wiebe, 2003).

However, once again we need to be careful about correlation not necessarily meaning causation. In his 2002 film documentary *Bowling for Columbine*, Michael Moore concluded that there is no direct cause between gun ownership and gun violence. Comparing the number of gun-related deaths and gun-ownership in Canada and the USA, he noted that of Canada's 7 million gun-owners there are very few gun-related deaths, compared to the USA. Moore suggests that what is responsible is a 'fear culture' created by the government, media and gun-making companies, which not only leads

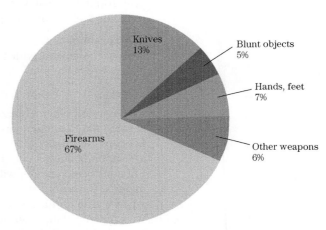

FIGURE 8.5 Weapons used to commit murder in the USA in 2002
SOURCE: FBI Uniform Crime Reports.

CHAPTER 8: AGGRESSION

Americans to arm themselves, but also makes them trigger-happy. So the cues in the environment may not simply be the presence of the gun but can extend to the social context in which we live.

Guns can not only serve as aggression cues but also put psychological distance between aggressor and victim. As Milgram's obedience studies taught us, remoteness from the victim facilitates cruelty. A knife can kill someone, but a knife attack requires a great deal more personal contact than pulling a trigger from a distance (Figure 8.5).

MEDIA INFLUENCES: PORNOGRAPHY AND SEXUAL VIOLENCE

As we've already seen, Bandura makes the claim that the mass media is an influential model for aggressive behaviour. Berkowitz's study, and the work of Schachter, illustrates how we may take cues from the environment in interpreting states of arousal, and express our behaviour in a way that seems appropriate.

Sadly, aggression in the form of violent crime seems to be on the rise. As the numbers of arrests for violent crime have increased across Europe and the USA since the 1960s, we may attribute some of this to better techniques of detection, but we might also wonder what has prompted such increases in aggressive behaviour. What social forces caused the mushrooming violence? Might the answer partially lie in the media's increasing modelling of unrestrained sexuality and violence, such that these acts become acceptable, and the individual becomes desensitized to their effects?

Increased rates of criminal violence, including sexual coercion, coincided with the increased availability of violent and sexual material in the media that started during the 'sexual revolution' of the 1960s. Is the historical correlation a coincidence? To find out, researchers have explored the social consequences of pornography (which *Webster's* defines as erotic depictions intended to excite sexual arousal) and the effects of modelling violence in movies and on television.

In many countries pornography has become a big business thanks to the billions a year spent on the industry's cable and satellite networks, on its theatres and pay-per-view movies, on in-room hotel movies, phone sex and sex magazines, and on for-profit websites (National Research Council, 2002; Rich, 2001; Schlosser, 2003). Gender differences in the reported use of Internet sex sites have been widely suggested. In a survey of 1845 Chinese college students, Yan Hong, Li Xiaoming, Mao Rong and Bonita Stanton (2007) found that 10 per cent of men claimed to have visited sex websites, while less than 1 per cent of women did so.

Social psychological research on pornography has focused mostly on depictions of sexual violence. A typical sexually violent episode finds a man forcing himself upon a woman. She at first resists and tries to fight off her attacker. Gradually she becomes sexually aroused, and her resistance melts. By the end she is in ecstasy, pleading for more. We have all viewed or read non-pornographic versions of this sequence: she resists, he persists. Dashing man grabs and forcibly kisses protesting woman. Within moments, the arms that were pushing him away are clutching him tight, her resistance overwhelmed by her unleashed passion. In *Gone with the Wind*, Scarlett O'Hara is carried to bed protesting and kicking, and wakes up singing.

Social psychologists report that viewing such fictional scenes of a man overpowering and arousing a woman can distort one's perceptions of how women actually respond to sexual coercion and increase men's aggression against women, at least in laboratory settings.

Distorted Perceptions of Sexual Reality

Does viewing sexual violence reinforce the 'rape myth' – that some women would welcome sexual assault – that 'no doesn't really mean no'? To find out, Neil Malamuth and James Check (1981) showed University of Manitoba men either two non-sexual movies or two movies depicting a man sexually overcoming a woman. A week later, when surveyed by a different experimenter, those who saw the films with mild sexual violence were more accepting of violence against women.

Other studies confirm that exposure to pornography increases acceptance of the rape myth (Oddone-Paolucci et al., 2000). For example, while spending three evenings watching sexually violent movies, male viewers in an experiment by Charles Mullin and Daniel Linz (1995) also became progressively less bothered by the raping and slashing. Compared with others not exposed to the films, three days later they expressed less sympathy for domestic violence victims, and they rated the victims' injuries as less severe. In fact, said researchers Edward Donnerstein, Daniel Linz and Steven Penrod (1987), what better way for an evil character to get people to react calmly to the torture and mutilation of women than to show a gradually escalating series of such films?

Did Ted Bundy's (1989) comments on the eve of his execution for a series of rape-murders acknowledge pornography's toll or make it a handy excuse? 'The most damaging kinds of pornography [involve] sexual violence. Like an addiction, you keep craving something that is harder, harder, something which, which gives you a greater sense of excitement. Until you reach a point where the pornography only goes so far, you reach that jumping off point where you begin to wonder if maybe actually doing it would give you that which is beyond just reading it or looking at it.'

SOURCE: © Bettman/Corbis Images

Note that the sexual message (that many women enjoy being 'taken') was subtle and unlikely to elicit counter-arguing. Given frequent media images of women's resistance melting in the arms of a forceful man, we shouldn't be surprised that even women often believe that some *other* women might enjoy being sexually overpowered – though virtually none think it of themselves (Malamuth et al., 1980).

'Pornography that portrays sexual aggression as pleasurable for the victim increases the acceptance of the use of coercion in sexual relations.'

> Social science consensus at Surgeon General's Workshop on Pornography and Public Health (Koop, 1987)

You may recall our discussion from Chapter 2 about the ecological validity such experiments have. What do they tell us about the real world? The extent to which these can be translated into explanations of how and why sexual violence occurs remains a topic of debate within social psychology.

Aggression against Women

Although limited to the sorts of short-term behaviours that can be studied in the laboratory, controlled experiments reveal what correlational studies cannot: cause and effect. A consensus statement by 21 leading social scientists summed up the results: 'Exposure to violent pornography increases punitive behaviour toward women' (Koop, 1987). One of those social scientists, Edward Donnerstein (1980), had shown 120 University of Wisconsin men a neutral, an erotic or an aggressive-erotic (rape) film. Then the men, supposedly as part of another experiment, 'taught' a male or female confederate some nonsense syllables by choosing how much shock to administer for incorrect answers. The men who had

CHAPTER 8: AGGRESSION

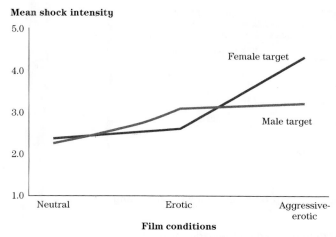

FIGURE 8.6   After viewing an aggressive-erotic film, college men delivered stronger shocks than before, especially to a woman.
SOURCE: Data from Donnerstein, 1980.

watched the rape film administered markedly stronger shocks (Figure 8.6), especially when angered and with a female victim.

The ethical implications of such experiments are very serious considering the controversial and powerful experience they are giving participants. Only after giving their knowing consent do people participate, and they are free to withdraw from such studies at any time. Moreover, after the experiment, researchers effectively debunk any myths the films communicated (Check & Malamuth, 1984). Justification for this experimentation is not only scientific but also addresses real-world concerns:

☐   According to the Worldwide Sexual Assault Statistics, one in three women worldwide has experienced rape or sexual assault (2001; http://www.nsvrc.org/publications/fact.sheets/worldwide-sexual-assault-statistics).

☐   From a sample of 198 850 women in North America, 40 per cent reported having been raped (2003).

☐   In a random study of 1200 young girls in Geneva, Switzerland, 20 per cent revealed they had been the victim of some form of sexual assault (2002).

☐   Between 10 and 12 per cent of women in Peru, Samoa and Tanzania have suffered sexual violence by someone who is not their partner, by the time they reach 15 years of age.

☐   In Canada, 12 per cent of women, and in New Zealand and Australia up to 20 per cent of women, report some form of sexual assault from non-partners during their lifetime (World Health Organization, 2005).

☐   Surveys in industrialized countries offer similar results (Table 8.1). Three in four stranger rapes and nearly all acquaintance rapes went unreported to police. Thus, the official rape rate greatly underestimates the actual rape rate.

Repeated exposure to erotic films featuring quick, uncommitted sex also tends to:

☐   decrease attraction for one's partner

☐   increase acceptance of extramarital sex and of women's sexual submission to men

☐   increase men's perceiving women in sexual terms (see D. G. Myers, 2000).

MEDIA INFLUENCES: TELEVISION

We have seen that watching an aggressive model attack a Bobo doll can unleash children's aggressive urges and teach them new ways to aggress. And we have seen that, after viewing movies depicting sexual violence, many angry men will

TABLE 8.1 Percentage of women in five countries reporting rape experiences

Country	Sample of women	Completed and attempted rape
Canada	Student sample at 95 colleges and universities	23% rape or sexual assault
Germany	Berlin late adolescents	17% criminal sexual violence
New Zealand	Sample of psychology students	25%
United Kingdom	Student sample at 22 universities	19%
United States	Representative sample at 32 colleges and universities	28%
Seoul, Korea	Adult women	22%

SOURCE: Studies reported by Koss et al. (1994) and Krahé (1998).

act more violently towards women. Does everyday television viewing have any similar effects?

Although very recent data are scarce (funding for media monitoring waned after the early 1990s), these facts about television watching remain: today, in much of the industrialized world, nearly all households (99.2 per cent in Australia, for example) have a television set, more than have telephones (Trewin, 2001). Most homes have more than one set, which helps explain why parents' reports of what their children watch correlate minimally with children's reports of what they watch (Donnerstein, 1998). With MTV in 140 countries and CNN spanning the globe, television is creating a global culture (Gundersen, 2001).

Women watch more television than men, pre-schoolers and retired people more than those in school or working, and the less educated more than the highly educated (Comstock & Scharrer, 1999). For the most part, these facts characterize the viewing habits of Americans, Europeans, Australians and Japanese (Murray & Kippax, 1979).

During all those hours, what social behaviours are modelled? From 1994 to 1997, bleary-eyed employees of the National Television Violence Study (1997) analysed some 10 000 programmes from the major networks and cable channels. They found 6 in 10 programmes contained violence ('physically compelling action that threatens to hurt or kill, or actual hurting or killing'). During fistfights, people who went down usually shook it off and came back stronger – unlike most real fistfights that last one punch (often resulting in a broken jaw or hand). In 73 per cent of violent scenes, the aggressors went unpunished. In 58 per cent, the victim was not shown to experience pain. In children's programmes, only 5 per cent of violence was shown to have any long-term consequences; two-thirds depicted violence as funny. By the end of elementary school, the average child has witnessed some 8000 television murders and 100 000 other violent acts (Huston et al., 1992). Reflecting on his 22 years of cruelty-counting, media researcher George Gerbner (1994) lamented: 'Humankind has had more bloodthirsty eras but none as filled with *images* of violence as the present. We are awash in a tide of violent representations the world has never seen ... drenching every home with graphic scenes of expertly choreographed brutality.' Sally Black and Alice Hausman's (2008) study of gun-carrying behaviour among adolescents from high-violence communities, points to the role the media plays in displays of 'flossing'. Flossing

CHAPTER 8: AGGRESSION

describes copying gunplay as seen in the media which can involve shooting the gun into the air. The authors note how this often results in self-inflicted injuries. They suggest that this behaviour isn't just showing off, but also serves as a release of aggressive excitement.

Does prime-time crime stimulate the behaviour it depicts? Or, as viewers vicariously participate in aggressive acts, do the shows drain off aggressive energy? The latter idea, a variation on the catharsis hypothesis, maintains that watching violent drama enables people to release their pent-up hostilities. For example, Seymour Feshbach and Robert Singer (1971) in their study of 9- to 15-year-old boys from underprivileged backgrounds and boarding schools, found that those who observed a diet of aggressive television displayed fewer acts of hostility (e.g. arguments and fights) than those who had watched non-aggressive programmes such as comedy shows. Defenders of the media cite this theory frequently and remind us that violence pre-dates television.

catharsis emotional cleansing. In psychodynamic theory this is the process of expressing repressed emotions, so these no longer cause neurotic problems

'One of television's great contributions is that it brought murder back into the home where it belongs. Seeing a murder on television can be good therapy. It can help work off one's antagonisms.'
   Alfred Hitchcock

Television's Effects on Behaviour
Correlating Television Viewing and Behaviour

Researchers often use correlational and experimental studies to examine the effects of viewing violence. One technique, commonly used with schoolchildren, correlates their television watching with their aggressiveness. The frequent result: the more violent the content of the child's television viewing, the more aggressive the child (Eron, 1987; Turner et al., 1986). The relationship is modest but consistently found in North America, Europe and Australia. The finding also extends to 'indirect aggression', which has recently attracted psychological attention. This includes behaviour such as gossiping, manipulating others, spreading malicious gossip, and social exclusion. Sarah Coyne and John Archer (2004) found that in a content-analytic study of over 200 hours of television programmes watched by British adolescents, 92 per cent of these programmes contained indirect aggression. Moreover, the indirect aggressor was most likely to be an attractive female who was rewarded in some way for her actions. They discovered that, of 347 British female teenagers studied, those who engaged in indirect aggression were more likely to watch television that contained indirect aggressive acts than their non-aggressive counterparts.

However, because these are often correlational studies, the cause–effect relation could also work in the opposite direction. Maybe aggressive children prefer aggressive programmes. Or maybe some underlying third factor, such as lower intelligence, predisposes some children to prefer both aggressive programmes and aggressive behaviour.

Researchers have developed two ways to test these alternative explanations. They test the 'hidden third factor' explanation by statistically pulling out the influence of some of these possible factors. For example, William Belson (1978; Muson, 1978) studied 1565 London boys. Compared with those who watched little violence, those who watched a great deal (especially realistic rather than cartoon violence) admitted to 50 per cent more violent acts during the preceding six months (for example, vandalizing a public telephone). Belson also examined 22 likely third factors, such as family size. The 'heavy violence' and 'light violence' viewers still differed after the researchers equated them with respect to potential third factors. So Belson surmised that the heavy viewers were indeed more violent *because* of their television exposure.

Similarly, Leonard Eron and Rowell Huesmann (1980, 1985) found that violence viewing among 875 children aged 8 correlated with aggressiveness even after statistically pulling out several obvious possible third factors. Moreover, when they re-studied those individuals as 19 year olds, they discovered that viewing violence at age 8 modestly predicted aggressiveness at age 19, but that aggressiveness at age 8 did *not* predict viewing violence at age 19. Aggression followed viewing, not the reverse. Moreover, by age 30, those who had watched the most violence in childhood were more likely than others to have been convicted of a crime (Figure 8.7).

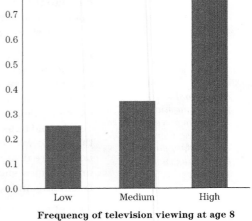

FIGURE 8.7 Children's television viewing and later criminal activity

Violence viewing at age 8 was a predictor of a serious criminal offence by age 30.

SOURCE: Data from Eron & Huesmann, 1984.

Follow-up studies have confirmed these findings in various ways, including:

☐ correlating 8 year olds' violence viewing with their later likelihood of adult spouse abuse (Huesmann et al., 1984, 2003)

☐ correlating adolescents' violence viewing with their later likelihood of assault, robbery and threats of injury (Johnson et al., 2002)

☐ correlating elementary schoolchildren's violent media exposure with how often they got into fights when re-studied two to six months later (Gentile et al., 2004).

In all these studies, the investigators were careful to adjust for likely 'third factors' such as pre-existing lower intelligence or hostility.

Also it seems to be the case that where television goes, increased violence follows. Even murder rates increase when and where television comes. In Canada and the USA, the homicide rate doubled between 1957 and 1974 as violent television spread. In census regions where television came later, the homicide rate jumped later, too. And in a closely studied rural Canadian town where television came late, playground aggression doubled soon after (Williams, 1986).

Notice that these studies illustrate how researchers are now using correlational findings to *suggest* cause and effect. Yet an infinite number of possible third factors could be creating a merely coincidental relation between viewing violence and aggression.

Television Viewing Experiments

The Bobo doll experiments by Albert Bandura and Richard Walters (1963) sometimes had young children view the adult pounding the inflated doll on film

instead of observing it live – with much the same effect. Then Leonard Berkowitz and Russell Geen (1966) found that angered college students who viewed a violent film acted more aggressively than did similarly angered students who viewed non-aggressive films. These laboratory experiments, coupled with growing public concern, seemed to confirm that viewing violence amplifies aggression (C. A. Anderson et al., 2003).

For example, research teams led by Ross Parke (1977) in the USA and Jacques Leyens (1975) in Belgium showed institutionalized American and Belgian delinquent boys a series of either aggressive or non-aggressive commercial films. Their consistent finding: 'Exposure to movie violence ... led to an increase in viewer aggression.' Compared with the week preceding the film series, physical attacks increased sharply in cottages where boys were viewing violent films. Dolf Zillmann and James Weaver (1999) similarly exposed men and women, on four consecutive days, to violent or non-violent feature films. When participating in a different project on the fifth day, those exposed to the violent films were more hostile to the research assistant. Likewise, Jennifer Linder and Douglas Gentile (2009) found that teachers reported higher levels of aggression in students who had watched televised physical and verbal aggression than those who had not. Furthermore, they found that the television industry's age-based rating system for the coding of material was not a valid reflection of its aggressive content.

The aggression provoked in these experiments is not assault and battery; it's more on the scale of a shove in the lunch queue, a cruel comment, a threatening gesture. Nevertheless, the convergence of evidence is striking. 'The irrefutable conclusion,' said a 1993 American Psychological Association youth violence commission, is 'that viewing violence increases violence'. This is especially so among people with aggressive tendencies, and when an attractive person commits justified, realistic violence that goes unpunished and that shows no pain or harm (Bushman, 1995; Donnerstein, 1998).

All in all, conclude researchers Brad Bushman and Craig Anderson (2001), violence viewing's effect on aggression surpasses the effect of passive smoking on lung cancer, calcium intake on bone mass, and homework on academic achievement. As with smoking and cancer, not everyone shows the effect – other factors matter as well. Media executives have discounted the evidence. But the evidence is now 'overwhelming', say Bushman and Anderson: 'Exposure to media violence causes significant increases in aggression.' The research base is large, the methods diverse and the overall findings consistent, echoes a National Institute of Mental Health task force of leading media violence researchers (C. A. Anderson et al., 2003): 'Our in-depth review ... reveals unequivocal evidence that exposure to media violence can increase the likelihood of aggressive and violent behaviour in both immediate and long-term contexts.'

Why Does Television Viewing Affect Behaviour?

Given the convergence of correlational and experimental evidence, researchers have explored *why* viewing violence has this effect. Consider three possibilities (Geen & Thomas, 1986). One is that it is not the violent content that causes social violence but the *arousal* it produces (Mueller et al., 1983; Zillmann, 1989a). As we noted earlier, arousal tends to spill over: one type of arousal energizes other behaviours.

Other research shows that viewing violence *disinhibits*. In Bandura's experiment, the adult's punching of the Bobo doll seemed to make those outbursts legitimate and to lower the children's inhibitions. Viewing violence primes the viewer for aggressive behaviour by activating violence-related thoughts (Berkowitz, 1984; Bushman & Geen, 1990; Josephson, 1987). Listening to music with sexually violent lyrics seems to have a similar effect (Barongan & Hall, 1995; Johnson et al., 1995; Pritchard, 1998).

Media portrayals also evoke *imitation*. The children in Bandura's experiments re-enacted the specific behaviours they had witnessed. The commercial television industry is hard-pressed to dispute that television leads viewers to imitate what they have seen: its advertisers model consumption. Are media executives right, however, to argue that television merely holds a mirror to a violent society? Actually, on television programmes, acts of assault have outnumbered affectionate acts four to one. In other ways as well, television models an unreal world.

But there is good news here, too. If the ways of relating and problem solving modelled on television do trigger imitation, especially among young viewers, then television modelling of prosocial behaviour should be socially beneficial.

prosocial behaviour
positive, constructive, helpful social behaviour; the opposite of antisocial behaviour

Television's Effects on Thinking

We have focused on television's effect on behaviour, but researchers have also examined the cognitive effects of viewing violence: does prolonged viewing desensitize us to cruelty? Does it give us mental scripts for how to act? Does it distort our perceptions of reality? Does it prime aggressive thoughts?

Desensitization

Repeat an emotion-arousing stimulus, such as an obscene word, over and over and the emotional response will 'extinguish'. After witnessing thousands of acts of cruelty, there is good reason to expect a similar emotional numbing. Victor Cline and his colleagues (1973) observed when they measured the physiological arousal of 121 Utah boys who watched a brutal boxing match. Compared with boys who watched little television, the responses of those who watched habitually were more a shrug than a concern.

Of course, these boys might differ in ways other than television viewing. But in experiments on the effects of viewing sexual violence, similar desensitization – a sort of psychic numbness – occurs among young men who view 'slasher' films. Moreover, experiments by Ronald Drabman and Margaret Thomas (1974, 1975, 1976) confirmed that such viewing breeds a more blasé reaction when later viewing a brawl or observing two children fighting. In one survey of 5456 middle-school students, exposure to movies with brutality was widespread (Sargent et al., 2002). Two-thirds had seen *Scream*. Such viewing patterns help explain why, despite the portrayals of extreme violence (or, should we say, *because* of it), Gallup youth surveys show that the percentage of 13 to 17 year olds feeling there was too much movie violence has declined, from 42 per cent in 1977 to 27 per cent in 2003.

Today's teens 'appear to have become considerably more desensitized to graphic depictions of violence and sex than their parents were at their age', concludes Gallup researcher Josephine Mazzuca (2002).

CHAPTER 8: AGGRESSION

Social Scripts and Social Representations

social scripts *culturally provided mental instructions for how to act in various situations*

When we find ourselves in new situations, uncertain how to act, we rely on social scripts ('schemas'), or what Serge Moscovici termed 'social representations' (see Chapter 4) – which are culturally provided mental instructions for how to act. These are acquired through experience of the social world and in interactions with others. In the case of television viewing of so many action films, youngsters may acquire a script that is played when they face real-life conflicts. Challenged, they may 'act like a man' by intimidating or eliminating the threat. Likewise, after viewing multiple sexual innuendoes and acts in most prime-time television hours – mostly involving impulsive or short-term relationships – youths may acquire sexual scripts they later enact in real-life relationships (Kunkel et al., 2001; Sapolsky & Tabarlet, 1991). Thus, the more sexual content that adolescents view (even when controlling for other predictors of early sexual activity), the more likely they are to perceive their peers as sexually active, to develop sexually permissive attitudes, and to experience early intercourse (Escobar-Chaves et al., 2005; Martino et al., 2005).

Altered Perceptions

Does television's fictional world also mould our conceptions of the real world? George Gerbner and his associates (1979; Gerbner, 1994) suspected that this is television's most potent effect. Their surveys of both adolescents and adults showed that heavy viewers (four hours a day or more) are more likely than light viewers (two hours or fewer) to exaggerate the frequency of violence in the world around them and to fear being personally assaulted. Similar feelings of vulnerability have been expressed by South African women after viewing violence against women (Reid & Finchilescu, 1995). For those who watch much television, the world becomes a scary place.

Cognitive Priming

Some evidence also reveals that watching violent videos primes networks of aggressive-related ideas (Bushman, 1998). After viewing violence, people offer more hostile explanations for others' behaviour (was the shove intentional?). They interpret spoken homonyms with the more aggressive meaning (interpreting 'punch' as a hit rather than a drink). And they recognize aggressive words more quickly.

Perhaps television's biggest effect relates not to its quality but to its quantity. Compared with more active recreation, television watching sucks people's energy and dampens their mood (Kubey & Csikszentmihalyi, 2002). Moreover, television annually replaces in people's lives a thousand or more hours of other activities. If, like most others, you have spent a thousand-plus hours per year watching television, think how you might have used that time if there were no television. What difference would that have made in who you are today? In seeking to explain the post-1960 decline in civic activities and organizational memberships, Robert Putnam (2000) reported that every added hour a day spent watching television competes with civic participation. Television steals time from club meetings, volunteering, congregational activities and political engagement.

MEDIA INFLUENCES: VIDEO GAMES

Researchers have shifted their attention to video games, which have exploded in popularity and are exploding with increasing brutality. In 2007 the video-game industry celebrated its thirty-fifth birthday. Since the first video game in 1972, we have moved from electronic ping-pong to splatter games (Anderson, 2004; Gentile & Anderson, 2003). Today's mass-murder simulators are not obscure games.

As Lillian Bensley and Juliet van Eenwyk (2001) have observed, society's attitudes on the impact video games have on individuals is mixed. It perhaps shouldn't surprise us then that social psychology's view of their potential harm or educational benefits is also mixed. While many argue the kind of aggression displayed in playing video games is fundamentally different to that shown in real life (as no one gets hurt in gamespace), others argue they can foster violent thoughts, feelings and actions (e.g. Sherry, 2001).

However, educational research shows that there are many benefits from video games. Gentile and Anderson (2003) argue that 'video games are excellent teaching tools', but 'If health video games can successfully teach health behaviours, and flight simulator video games can teach people how to fly, then what should we expect violent murder-simulating games to teach?'

The Games Children Play

In one survey of fourth-graders in the USA, 59 per cent of girls and 73 per cent of boys reported their favourite games as violent ones (Anderson, 2003, 2004). Games rated '18' are supposedly intended for sale only to those 18 and older but often are marketed to those younger.

'We had an internal rule that we wouldn't allow violence against people.'
    Nolan Bushnell, Atari founder

In the popular *Grand Theft Auto: San Andreas*, youth are invited to play a psychopath, notes Gentile (2004). 'You can run down pedestrians with the car, you can do car-jackings, you can do drive-by shootings, you can run down to the red-light district, pick up a prostitute, have sex with her in your car, and then kill her to get your money back.' In effective three-dimensional graphics, you can knock people over, stomp on them until they cough up blood, and watch them die. And as research by Susan Persky and James Blascovich (2005) demonstrates, virtual-reality games promise even more realism, engagement and impact.

Effects of the Games Children Play

'There is absolutely no evidence, none, that playing a violent game leads to aggressive behaviour', contended Doug Lowenstein (2000), president of the Interactive Digital Software Association. Gentile and Anderson (2003) nevertheless offer some reasons why violent game playing *might* have a more toxic effect than watching violent television. With game playing, players:

☐ identify with, and play the role of, a violent character

☐ actively rehearse violence, not just passively watch it

☐ engage in the whole sequence of enacting violence – selecting victims, acquiring weapons and ammunition, stalking the victim, aiming the weapon, pulling the trigger

☐ are engaged with continual violence and threats of attack

☐ repeat violent behaviours over and over

☐ are rewarded for effective aggression.

CHAPTER 8: AGGRESSION

For such reasons, military organizations often prepare soldiers to fire in combat (which many in the Second World War reportedly were hesitant to do) by engaging them with attack-simulation games. Craig Anderson (2003, 2004; Anderson et al., 2004) offers statistical digests of three dozen available studies that reveal five consistent effects. Playing violent video games, more than playing non-violent games:

1 *increases arousal.* Heart rate and blood pressure rise.

2 *increases aggressive thinking.* For example, Brad Bushman and Anderson (2002) found that after playing games such as *Duke Nukem* and *Mortal Kombat*, university students became more likely to guess that a man whose car was just rear-ended would respond aggressively, by using abusive language, kicking out a window or starting a fight.

3 *increases aggressive feelings.* Frustration levels rise, as does expressed hostility.

4 *increases aggressive behaviours.* After violent game play, children and youth play more aggressively with their peers, get into more arguments with their teachers, and participate in more fights. The effect occurs inside and outside the laboratory, across self-reports, teacher reports and parent reports, and for reasons illustrated in Figure 8.8. Is this merely because naturally hostile kids are drawn to such games? No, even when controlling for personality and temperament, exposure to video-game violence desensitizes people to cruelty and increases aggressive behaviour (Fraser et al., 2012). Moreover, observed Douglas Gentile and his co-researchers (2004) from a study of young adolescents, even among those who scored low in hostility, the percentage of heavy violent gamers who got into fights was ten times the 4 per cent involved in fights among their non-gaming counterparts. And after they start playing the violent games, previously non-hostile kids become more likely to have

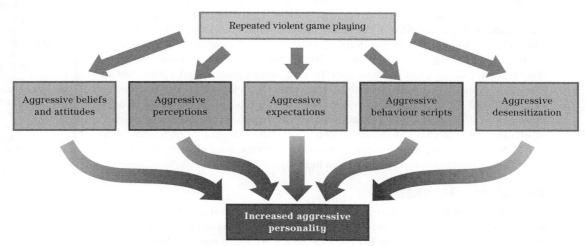

FIGURE 8.8   Violent video-game influences on aggressive tendencies

SOURCE: Adapted from Bushman & Anderson, 2001.

fights. Playing violent video-games has a negative impact on our ability to empathize with others, and this lack of empathy may be responsible for behaviours such as cyber-bullying (Ang and Goh, 2010) and vandalism (Carrasco et al., 2006).

5 *decreases prosocial behaviours.* After violent video-game playing, people become slower to help a person whimpering in the hallway outside and slower to offer help to peers. On a later monetary decision-making task, they become more likely to exploit rather than to trust and co-operate with a partner (Sheese & Graziano, 2005). They also, as revealed by decreased brain activity associated with emotion, become desensitized to violence (Bartholow et al., 2006).

Does playing violent video games lead to aggressive behaviour?

SOURCE: © R-J-Seymour/iStock

Moreover, the more violent the games played, the bigger the effects. Video games *have* become more violent, which helps explain why newer studies find the biggest effects. Although much remains to be learned, these studies indicate that, contrary to the catharsis hypothesis, practising violence breeds rather than releases violence.

Anderson (2003, 2004) therefore encourages parents to discover what their kids are ingesting and to ensure that their media diet, at least in their own home, is healthy. Parents may not be able to control what their child watches, plays and eats in someone else's home. Nor can they control the media's effect on their children's peer culture. But parents can oversee consumption in their own home and provide increased time for alternative activities. Networking with other parents can build a child-friendly neighbourhood. And schools can help by providing media awareness education.

However, we may need to question whether what's being observed reflects real aggression or 'play' aggression. In their study of aggressive play and aggressive behaviour Joel Cooper and Diane Mackie (1986), concluded that violent video games affect the former and not the latter. Mark Griffiths (1997) found that while partaking in violent video games increases aggression in young children, it had no effect on teenagers. The discrepancy in these figures may reflect either that video games do not have the same effect on older children as they do on younger children, or that what is being defined as evidence of aggressive behaviour is present only in the younger sample. Interestingly, recent research suggests that violent video games do have an effect on older children and adults, but on lowering prosocial behaviour rather than directly heightening aggression. In their study of 780 young adults (mean age 19.60 years), Ashley Fraser and his colleagues (2012) found that playing violent video games lowers empathy levels which results in decreased prosocial behaviour towards strangers. So although displays of aggression may be absent from studies with older children and adults, what is more apparent are reductions in helping behaviour.

> Observation of aggression can heighten aggression; the same can be said for helping with prosocial models promoting altruism. See Chapter 10 for further discussion of prosocial behaviour, specifically helping.

GENDER AND AGGRESSION

The research on bullying alerts us to something of a stereotype within common sense and social psychological understandings of aggression: that men are more aggressive than women. On the face of it, this might seem to be a sensible assumption as official crime statistics repeatedly show that men are much more

likely to appear as perpetrators of aggressive crimes. Academic work notes gender differences across cultures and situations. For example, Eleanor Maccoby and Carol Jacklin (1974) report a gender difference in the display of aggression from 2 years of age.

Within social psychology, it's often assumed that women are not as aggressive as men for socio-biological reasons. First, there is the argument that claims men are more aggressive than women due to the presence of higher testosterone levels. We noted earlier in this chapter the link between hormones and violent behaviour in human beings, and men in particular. The second argument is evolutionary, documenting that women nurture their young. Conversely it is the role of men to protect women and their children from threats, which may mean using aggression to do so. Reinforcing these socio-biological arguments are processes of socialization into specific gender roles, such that while young boys might be rewarded for behaving aggressively, young girls may be punished.

However, there have been some studies that have examined the onset of physical aggression in girls. In a 15-year longitudinal study of 6- to 12-year-old girls, Nathalie Fontaine and colleagues (2008) found that those with high levels of hyperactivity and high physical aggression were also more likely to report nicotine addiction, low educational attainment, physical aggression in intimate relationships, and early pregnancy. Fontaine concludes that targeted intensive prevention programmes would be useful in tackling these problems.

Jacquelyn White and Robin Kowalski (1994) make the point that aggressive women tend to be seen as social deviants and even mentally ill. Media attention on 'ladettes' has pointed to this stigmatization of women who do not present normative gender-role behaviour. Reidy et al. (2009) found that hyper-masculine men were more likely to be aggressive towards women who violated feminine gender-role behaviour.

White and Kowalski consider crime statistics that report a difference in men and women as perpetrators of aggressive crimes. They note a number of factors that might account for this, including the following.

- Willingness of a victim to report a crime. Men who are subject to domestic violence from their female partners may be less willing to report the crime for fear of being stigmatized.

- The act must be regarded as being 'serious' for it to be reported. This may be less likely where women are the perpetrators.

- Women may be treated much more leniently by the criminal justice system than men, and as such may not show up in the official crime statistics.

In a culture where the norm, or the stereotype, is of the 'unaggressive woman', recognizing aggressive behaviour may prove tricky. As men are predominantly used in social psychology studies of aggression, White and Kowalski argue that the definition and understanding of 'what' aggression is, comes from a male perspective. They suggest that if researchers examine female aggression in situations that are congruent with their gender role, such as family settings, and extend the definition of aggression to include non-physical acts as well as just physical ones, then the evidence points to women being as, if not more, aggressive than men under such circumstances.

As well as the difficulties in defining aggression, we also have the problem of collecting evidence. If we rely on a method of collecting self-reports, which many of these studies do, then what we might be seeing are differences between men and women in terms of what *they* define as aggression rather than accurate reflections of its occurrence. In Penny Tinkler and Carolyn Jackson's (2007) study of 'ladettes' in the media, they consider how aggression is defined in particular ways to stigmatize young women. This is interesting when you consider Steven Muncer and his colleagues' (2001) report that, for the young women themselves, there is no correlation between holding laddish attitudes and engaging in aggressive behaviour.

The point? There is no simple explanation or definition of aggression. Nor is there any simple way of collecting evidence of it. As we've seen throughout this chapter, there is a tendency to study examples of aggression which can be easily identified and measured in some way. This can mean an over-reliance on evidence of physical violence to represent aggression. We noted at the start of this chapter that aggression comes in many guises, but this complexity is arguably not reflected in social psychological studies of the topic. Indeed, it might be the attempt to simplify the behaviour that is partly responsible for the generalization that women are not as aggressive as men. Is this true? In Chapter 14 we discuss the relationship between gender and behaviour in terms of biological influences and cultural socialization.

Collective Identity

Behaviour is seldom random and is often organized around a shared sense of social identity which provides the group with norms about what is, and what is not, appropriate behaviour. Youths sharing antisocial tendencies and lacking close family bonds and expectations of academic success may find social identity in a gang (Staub, 1996). Members give themselves over to the group, often feeling a satisfying oneness with the others.

Social identity theory argues that crowds will be violent to the extent that violent actions are consistent with the group's identity. Where this does turn into acts of aggression they do not occur randomly but are aimed at very specific targets who represent a meaningful outgroup.

Hate crimes can occur when someone is attacked on the basis of being a member of a group. We have already seen in this chapter that individuals identified as members of a minority group, such as homosexuals, may be the victims of verbal and physical aggression. Often this is because these people represent deviance away from cultural norms and values. Prejudice towards the group they represent underlies these attacks. Rebecca Stotzer and Emily Hossellman (2012) consider how the increased presence of US students from ethnic and racial minority groups in higher education can lead to greater harmony between them, or aggravate tensions between them leading to heightened prevalence of hate crime on university campuses. On the one hand, increased contact between students of different racial and ethnic groups can lead to racial tolerance. We shall consider Gordon Allport's 'contact hypothesis' in Chapter 13, which suggests that when certain optimal conditions are in place (most notably equal status of

Membership of a gang can give individuals a sense of social identity which shapes its activities.
SOURCE: © monkeybusinessimages/iStock

CHAPTER 8: AGGRESSION

all groups), increasing contact between groups can lead to reduced prejudice. On the other, increased contact can intensify racial and ethnic tensions leading to the occurrence of hate crimes. Stotzer and Hossellman note that which way things go partly depends on the communication of values from the academic institution to its students, but also the values of the students themselves and how the white majority perceive the legitimacy of ethnic diversity in higher education.

In Chapters 4 and 13 we consider how behavioural expectations shape perception. There we have examples from the extensive research on football hooligans that has shown how the presence and perception of the police, opposing fans, and their actions, influences the levels of aggression displayed by the supporters (Drury et al., 2003; Reicher et al., 2004; Stott et al., 2001). Where opposing team supporters are perceived to be engaging in illegitimate acts of violence towards the ingroup, that group will respond by asserting its own identity in 'legitimate' violent ways towards the outgroup. We will discuss these ideas in more detail in Chapter 13 when we consider intergroup relations.

The twentieth-century massacres that claimed over 150 million lives were 'not the sums of individual actions', notes Robert Zajonc (2000). '*Genocide is not the plural of homicide.*' Massacres are *social* phenomena fed by 'moral imperatives' – a collective mentality (including images, rhetoric and ideology) that mobilizes a group or a culture for extraordinary actions. The massacres of Rwanda's Tutsis, of Europe's Jews and of America's native population were collective phenomena requiring widespread support, organization and participation. Before launching the genocidal initiative, Rwanda's Hutu government and business leaders bought and distributed 2 million machetes.

Experiments in Israel by Yoram Jaffe and Yoel Yinon (1983) confirm that groups can amplify aggressive tendencies. In one, university men angered by a supposed fellow participant retaliated with decisions to give much stronger shocks when in groups than when alone. In another experiment (Jaffe et al., 1981), people decided, either alone or in groups, how much punishing shock to give someone for incorrect answers on a task. As Figure 8.9 shows, individuals gave progressively more of the assumed shock as the experiment proceeded, and group decision making magnified this individual tendency. When circumstances provoke an individual's aggressive reaction, the addition of group interaction will often amplify it (see Research Close-Up: When Provoked, Are Groups More Aggressive than Individuals?).

Aggression studies provide an apt opportunity to ask how well social psychology's laboratory findings generalize to everyday life. Do the circumstances that trigger someone to deliver electric shock or allocate hot sauce really tell us anything about the circumstances that trigger verbal abuse or a punch in the face? Craig Anderson and Brad Bushman (1997; Bushman & Anderson, 1998) note that social psychologists

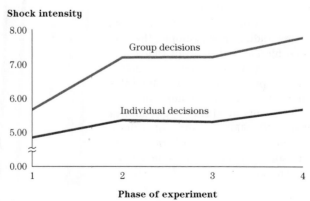

FIGURE 8.9 Group-enhanced aggression
When individuals chose how much shock to administer as punishment for wrong answers, they escalated the shock level as the experiment proceeded. Group decision making further polarized this tendency.

SOURCE: Data from Jaffe et al., 1981.

have studied aggression in both the laboratory and everyday worlds, and the findings are strikingly consistent. In *both* contexts, increased aggression is predicted by the following:

- ☐ male actors
- ☐ aggressive or Type A personalities
- ☐ alcohol use
- ☐ violence viewing
- ☐ anonymity
- ☐ provocation
- ☐ the presence of weapons
- ☐ group interaction.

The laboratory allows us to test and revise theories under controlled conditions. Real-world events inspire ideas and provide the venue for applying our theories. Aggression research illustrates how the interplay between studies in the controlled laboratory and the complex real world advances psychology's contribution to human welfare. Hunches gained from everyday experience inspire theories, which stimulate laboratory research, which then deepens our understanding and our ability to apply psychology to real problems.

CAN AGGRESSION BE REDUCED?

We have examined instinct, frustration-aggression and social learning theories of aggression, and we have scrutinized biological and social influences on aggression. How, then, can we reduce aggression?

Theory and research suggest that aggression can be tackled at the level of the individual, the group and society. For example, we can try to implement measures to control alcohol abuse, improve relationships within families, educate people about the effects of war and genocide, and enable groups in society to learn about one another, thus promoting shared understanding. For example, the role of society in educating young people has been highlighted in Sally Black and Alice Hausman's study of gun-carrying behaviour among adolescents (2008). They suggest that, 'Primary prevention starts by producing meaningful roles and economic opportunities for youth in inner cities and providing culturally competent prevention education. Generally, adolescents need safe opportunities for independence and the resources to build identity' (p. 606). However all of these measures are complex to implement due to the multifaceted nature of aggression, but that is not to say we shouldn't try. There are some key factors that have been outlined in this chapter that are worth bearing in mind.

CATHARSIS?

'Youngsters should be taught to vent their anger.' So advised Ann Landers (1969). If a person 'bottles up his rage, we have to find an outlet. We have to give him an opportunity of letting off steam'. So asserted the once prominent psychiatrist Fritz Perls (1973). 'Some expression of prejudice ... lets off steam ... it can siphon

CHAPTER 8: AGGRESSION

research close-up

WHEN PROVOKED, ARE GROUPS MORE AGGRESSIVE THAN INDIVIDUALS?

Source: Meier, B. P., and Hinsz, V. B. (2004). A comparison of human aggression committed by groups and individuals: An interindividual-intergroup discontinuity. Journal of Experimental Social Psychology, *40, 551–559.*

Introduction

At the time of writing their study Brian Meier and Verlin Hinsz point out that despite some classic examples, such as Sherif and Sherif's Robber's Cave Study (see Chapter 13), there is very little social psychological study into aggression that is carried out by groups. In our social world we are faced with lots of incidences of groups aggressing against others, yet we seem to have little study on why this occurs. The social psychological literature tells us that groups tend to be more competitive towards one another than individuals. A famous example is the Prisoners' Dilemma where if both parties are groups, they choose competition to obtain rewards rather than co-operation. Why? Chester Insko and his colleagues (2001) suggest that group situations provide people with anonymity and a diffusion of responsibility (see Chapters 11 and 13), which may explain their behaviour. This is known as the interindividual-intergroup discontinuity effect. So if a sense of competition is heightened in a group context, can we anticipate that people will behave more aggressively towards one another in these circumstances than they would do if they were in an individual context?

Aggression researchers are noted for their creative methods for measuring aggression, which in various experiments has involved such tactics as administering shock, blasting sound and hurting people's feelings. Holly McGregor and her colleagues (1998) took their cue from a cook's arrest for assault after lacing two police officers' food with tabasco sauce, and from child abuse cases in which parents have force-fed hot sauce to their children. This inspired the idea of measuring aggression by having people decide how much hot sauce someone else must consume.

That is what Gettysburg College psychologist Bruce Meier and North Dakota State University psychologist Verlin Hinsz (2004) did when comparing aggressive behaviour by groups and individuals.

Method

The researchers told participants, either as individuals or in groups of three, that they were studying the relationship between personality and food preferences, and that they would be tasting and rating hot sauce. The experimenter explained that he needed the participants to choose the size of the portion given to the rest of the participants (either individuals or groups of three). After having the participants sample the intense hot sauce using a wooden stick, the experimenter left to collect the amount of hot sauce that the individuals or groups had selected. In reality he actually ignored the amount they had decided to give the other participants, and handed everyone a cup filled with 48 grams of the sauce, which each participant expected later to consume. Now was the chance for revenge! Once the second set of participants had been given the hot sauce, chosen for them by the first set of participants, to consume, they could now return the favour! This second set of participants were now to spoon as much or as little hot sauce as they wished into a cup for the supposed other people to consume. (In reality, no participant was forced to consume anything.)

TABLE 8.2 Mean amount of hot sauce dished out (GRAMS)

Source	Target	
	Individual	**Group**
Individual	58.2	71.0
Group	71.1	92.9

SOURCE: Meier & Hinsz, 2004.

Results

The striking result, seen in Table 8.2, was that groups retaliated by dishing out 24 per cent more hot sauce than individuals did. So groups were more aggressive than individuals in dishing out the hot stuff! Furthermore, they were dishing it out to other groups! In fact groups received 24 per cent more hot sauce than individuals. Thus, given toxic circumstances, interaction with a group (as a source or target) amplifies individual aggressive tendencies. This finding was particularly evident in the intergroup condition. Group members, after each receiving a nasty 48 grams of hot sauce, retaliated by dishing out 93 grams of hot sauce for each member of the group that had given them hot sauce. Apparently, surmised Meier and Hinsz, groups not only respond more aggressively to provocation but also perceive more hostility from other groups than they do from individuals.

Discussion

What Meier and Hinsz's study had shown was that more hot sauce (the measure of aggression) was allocated in intergroup contexts than interindividual interactions. Groups allocate hot sauce to other groups. However, groups are also more likely to receive hot sauce from individuals, than other individuals are. So groups influence aggressive behaviour either when they are the cause of the aggression or on the receiving end.

Why? The researchers suggest that what may be going on is group polarization (see Chapter 11). Individuals' attitudes strengthen within a group context. If a dominant response of individuals within a group is towards aggression anyway this becomes intensified in a group situation. Chester Insko wonders if trust may also be an issue here. Groups are considered less trustworthy than individuals. So increased competition and feelings of aggression may become heightened in the context of people we distrust.

As entertaining as this study might appear, it has limitations as well as strengths. While it tells us something about the context in which aggression is more likely to occur, we may want to question the measure of aggression. Hot sauce. Is this the same as physical or verbal aggression which can have long-lasting consequences for all concerned? How generalizable are studies such as this to the real-world? Does it have ecological validity?

off conflict through words, rather than actions.' So argued Andrew Sullivan in a *New York Times Magazine* article on hate crimes (1999).

The concept of catharsis is usually credited to Western thinking, especially to Aristotle. Although Aristotle actually said nothing about aggression, he did argue that we can purge emotions by experiencing them, and that viewing the classic tragedies therefore enabled a catharsis (purging) of pity and fear. To have an emotion excited, he believed, is to have that emotion released (Butcher, 1951). The catharsis hypothesis has been extended to include the emotional release supposedly obtained not only by observing drama but also through our recalling and reliving past events, through our expressing emotions, and through our actions.

Assuming that aggressive action or fantasy drains pent-up aggression, some therapists and group leaders have encouraged people to ventilate suppressed aggression by acting it out – by whopping one another with foam bats or beating a bed with a tennis racket while screaming. If led to believe that catharsis effectively vents emotions, people will react more aggressively to an insult as a way to improve their mood (Bushman et al., 2001). Some psychologists, believing

that catharsis is therapeutic, advise parents to encourage children's release of emotional tension through aggressive play.

Many laypeople have also bought the catharsis idea, as reflected in their nearly two-to-one agreement with the statement 'Sexual materials provide an outlet for bottled-up impulses' (Niemi et al., 1989). But then, other national surveys reveal that most Americans also agree, 'Sexual materials lead people to commit rape'. So is the catharsis approach valid or not?

Actually, notes researcher Brad Bushman (2002), 'Venting to reduce anger is like using gasoline to put out a fire'. Consider: if viewing erotica provides an outlet for sexual impulses, places with high consumption of sex magazines should have low rape rates. After viewing erotica people should experience diminished sexual desire and men should be less likely to view and treat women as sexual objects. But studies show the opposites are true (Kelley et al., 1989; McKenzie-Mohr & Zanna, 1990).

The near consensus among social psychologists is that – contrary to what Freud, Lorenz and their followers supposed – viewing or participating in violence fails to produce catharsis (Geen & Quanty, 1977). For example, Robert Arms and his associates report that Canadian and American spectators of football, wrestling and hockey games exhibit *more* hostility after viewing the event than before (Arms et al., 1979; Goldstein & Arms, 1971; Russell, 1983). Not even war seems to purge aggressive feelings. After a war, a nation's murder rate has tended to jump (Archer & Gartner, 1976).

In laboratory tests of catharsis, Brad Bushman (2002) invited angered participants to hit a punching bag while either ruminating about the person who angered them or thinking about becoming physically fit. A third group did not hit the punching bag. Then, when given a chance to administer loud blasts of noise to the person who angered them, people in the punching bag plus rumination condition felt angrier and were most aggressive. Moreover, doing nothing at all more effectively reduced aggression than did 'letting off steam' by hitting the bag.

In some real-life experiments, too, aggressing has led to heightened aggression. Ebbe Ebbesen and his co-researchers (1975) interviewed 100 engineers and technicians shortly after they were angered by layoff notices. Some were asked questions that gave them an opportunity to express hostility against their employer or supervisors – for example, 'What instances can you think of where the company has not been fair with you?' Afterwards, they answered a questionnaire assessing attitudes towards the company and the supervisors. Did the previous opportunity to 'vent' or 'drain off ' their hostility reduce it? On the contrary, their hostility increased. Expressing hostility bred more hostility.

'He who gives way to violent gestures will increase his rage.'
    Charles Darwin, *The Expression of Emotion in Man and Animals*, 1872

Recall as we noted in analysing Stanley Milgram's obedience experiments (see Chapter 7), little aggressive acts can breed their own justification. People derogate their victims, rationalizing further aggression.

Retaliation may, in the short run, reduce tension and even provide pleasure (Ramirez et al., 2005). But in the long run it fuels more negative feelings. Should we therefore bottle up anger and aggressive urges? Silent sulking is hardly more effective, because it allows us to continue reciting our grievances as we conduct conversations in our head. Brad Bushman and his colleagues (2005a) experimented with the toxic effect of such rumination. After being provoked by an obnoxious experimenter with insults such as 'Can't you follow directions? Speak louder!' half were given a distraction (by being asked to write an essay about their campus landscape) and half were induced to ruminate (by writing an essay about their experiences as a research participant). Next, they were mildly insulted by a supposed fellow participant (actually a confederate), to whom they responded by prescribing a hot sauce dose this person would have to consume. The distracted participants, their anger now abated, prescribed only a mild dose, but the still-seething ruminators displaced their aggressive urge and prescribed twice as much.

Fortunately, there are non-aggressive ways to express our feelings and to inform others how their behaviour affects us. Across cultures, those who reframe accusatory 'you' messages as 'I' messages – 'I feel angry about what you said' or 'I get irritated when you leave dirty dishes' – communicate their feelings in a way that better enables the other person to make a positive response (Kubany et al., 1995). We can be assertive without being aggressive.

A SOCIAL LEARNING APPROACH

If aggressive behaviour is learned, then there is hope for its control. Aversive experiences such as frustrated expectations and personal attacks predispose hostile aggression. So it is wise to refrain from planting false, unreachable expectations in people's minds. Anticipated rewards and costs influence instrumental aggression. This suggests that we should reward co-operative, non-aggressive behaviour.

In experiments, children become less aggressive when caregivers ignore their aggressive behaviour and reinforce their non-aggressive behaviour (Hamblin et al., 1969). Punishing the aggressor is less consistently effective. Threatened punishment deters aggression only under ideal conditions when the punishment is strong, prompt and sure; when it is combined with reward for the desired behaviour; and when the recipient is not angry (Baron, 1977).

Moreover, there are limits to punishment's effectiveness. Most homicide is impulsive, hot aggression – the result of an argument, an insult or an attack. If mortal aggression were cool and instrumental, we could hope that waiting until it happens and severely punishing the criminal afterwards would deter such acts. In that world, states that impose the death penalty might have a lower murder rate than states without the death penalty. But in our world of hot homicide, that is not so (Costanzo, 1998). Thus, we must *prevent* aggression before it happens. We must teach non-aggressive conflict-resolution strategies.

Physical punishment can also have negative side effects. Punishment is aversive stimulation; it models the behaviour it seeks to prevent. And it is coercive (recall that we seldom internalize actions coerced with strong external justifications). These are reasons why violent teenagers and child-abusing parents so often come from homes where discipline took the form of harsh physical punishment.

To foster a gentler world, we could model and reward sensitivity and co-operation from an early age, perhaps by training parents how to discipline without violence. Training programmes encourage parents to reinforce desirable behaviours and to frame statements positively ('When you finish cleaning your room, you can go play', rather than, 'If you don't clean your room, you're grounded'). One 'aggression-replacement programme' has reduced re-arrest rates of juvenile offenders and gang members by teaching the youths and their parents communication skills, training them to control anger, and raising their level of moral reasoning (Goldstein et al., 1998).

If observing aggressive models lowers inhibitions and elicits imitation, then we might also reduce brutal, dehumanizing portrayals in films and on television – steps comparable to those already taken to reduce racist and sexist portrayals. We can also inoculate children against the effects of media violence. Wondering if the television networks would ever 'face the facts and change their programming', Eron and Huesmann (1984) taught 170 Oak Park, Illinois, children that television portrays the world unrealistically, that aggression is less common and less effective than television suggests, and that aggressive behaviour is undesirable. (Drawing upon attitude research, Eron and Huesmann encouraged children to draw these inferences themselves and to attribute their expressed criticisms of television to their own convictions.) When re-studied two years later these children were less influenced by television violence than were untrained children. In a more recent study, Stanford University used 18 classroom lessons to persuade children to simply reduce their television watching and video-game playing (Robinson et al., 2001). They reduced their television viewing by a third – and the children's aggressive behaviour at school dropped 25 per cent compared with children in a control school.

Aggressive stimuli also trigger aggression. This suggests reducing the availability of weapons such as handguns. In 1974 Jamaica implemented a sweeping anti-crime programme that included strict gun control and censorship of gun scenes from television and movies (Diener & Crandall, 1979).

Suggestions such as these can help us minimize aggression, but we should be aware that this isn't as simple as flicking a magic wand. Given the complexity of aggression's causes and the difficulty of controlling them, who can feel the optimism expressed by Andrew Carnegie's forecast that in the twentieth century, 'To kill a man will be considered as disgusting as we in this day consider it disgusting to eat one.' Since Carnegie uttered those words in 1900, some 200 million human beings have been killed. It is a sad irony that although today we understand human aggression better than ever before, humanity's inhumanity endures. Nevertheless, cultures can change.

focus on

TEACHING THEM A LESSON: MOTIVATIONS FOR DRIVER AGGRESSION

Road rage is increasing in those countries where we rely heavily on vehicles to take us from A to B. Many of us have been subject at some point to actions such as someone honking their horn at us, sharply swerving in front of the car you're in, making obscene hand gestures, or driving far too close to the rear of the car. Statistics show that the majority of drivers in the UK, US and Australia have been on the receiving end of these behaviours. We're a little less willing to admit that we've been the person doing these behaviours to other motorists, however. But why does road rage happen? Are we stressed out? Are other drivers so bad that they deserve these actions? Do we enjoy the danger? Do we think we're invincible once we're behind the wheel of a car? Is it mostly young men who get road rage? All of these factors, and more besides, have been found to play a role in explaining road rage (Lennon & Watson, 2011). However, what is less clear is, do people who commit road rage intend on harming the recipient of their aggressive behaviour?

In their qualitative study of motorists, Alexia Lennon and Barry Watson found they explained their mildly aggressive acts (such as horn-honking and light-flashing) as points of information to let another driver know s/he was driving badly. The potential negative impact upon the other driver was denied or mitigated. So whilst these motorists recognized their behaviour as mildly aggressive, there was no intention to actually harm the other motorist. However, if the motorist perceived other drivers as intending on harming them then they regarded their subsequent actions towards them as 'justified retaliation'. Such people needed to be 'taught a lesson'. What Lennon and Watson found was that despite aggression being a socially undesirable behaviour, motorists were fairly open about admitting to it when they felt their actions had been deserved. However, many drivers downplayed the potential consequences of their actions leading to harm to the other driver. So whilst the aggression may be seen as justified, the intention to cause harm is denied.

So the distinction between intentional and unintentional aggression may not be quite so clear-cut. As we can see from this example, aggressors may admit their behaviour but deny the intent. Does this make the act any more palatable? Is it still aggression?

QUESTIONS

1 Who should define what counts as aggressive behaviour? The social psychologist? The person who commits the act?

2 Should we treat unintentional aggression with the same seriousness as intentional aggression?

3 If you were to design a study into aggression, what behaviours would you focus on? How would you collect evidence of them and analyse them?

SUMMING UP: AGGRESSION

WHAT IS AGGRESSION?

☐ Aggression has been defined in various ways by social psychologists. Broadly speaking its definition can include direct and/or indirect physical and verbal acts. It can refer to intentional and/or unintentional behaviour.

☐ How we define aggression has implications for what we treat as evidence of it and the conclusions we reach about its presence in human society.

SOME THEORIES OF AGGRESSION

We have considered three broad theories of aggression.

☐ The *instinct* view, most commonly associated with Sigmund Freud and Konrad Lorenz, contended that aggressive energy will accumulate from within, like water accumulating behind a dam. Although the available evidence offers little support for that view, aggression is biologically influenced by heredity, blood chemistry and the brain.

☐ According to the second view, *frustration* causes anger and hostility. Given aggressive cues in the environment may provoke aggression. Frustration stems not from deprivation itself but from the gap between expectations and achievements.

☐ The *social learning* view presents aggression as learned behaviour. By experience and by observing others' success, we sometimes learn that aggression pays. Social learning enables family, cultural and subcultural influences on aggression, as well as media influences (which we will discuss in the next section). In some cultures children are taught not to be aggressive since it is an immature reaction.

SOME INFLUENCES ON AGGRESSION

☐ Many factors exert influence on aggression. One factor is aversive experiences, which include not only frustrations but also discomfort, pain and personal attacks, both physical and verbal.

☐ Arousal from almost any source, even physical exercise or sexual stimulation, can be transformed into anger.

☐ Aggression cues in the environment, such as the presence of a gun, increase the likelihood of aggressive behaviour.

☐ Viewing violence (1) breeds a modest increase in *aggressive behaviour*, especially in people who are provoked, and (2) *desensitizes* viewers to aggression and alters their *perceptions* of reality. These two findings parallel the results of research on the effects of viewing violent pornography, which can increase men's aggression against women and distort their perceptions of women's responses to sexual coercion.

☐ Television permeates the daily life of millions of people and portrays considerable violence. Correlational and experimental studies converge on the conclusion that heavy exposure to televised violence correlates with aggressive behaviour.

☐ Repeatedly playing violent video games may increase aggressive thinking, feelings and behaviour even more than television or movies do, as the experience involves much more active participation than those other media.

☐ A special kind of aggression is committed by groups. Circumstances that provoke individuals may also provoke groups. By diffusing responsibility and polarizing actions, group situations amplify aggressive reactions.

CAN AGGRESSION BE REDUCED?

☐ How can we minimize aggression? Contrary to the catharsis hypothesis, expressing aggression by catharsis tends to breed further aggression, not reduce it.

☐ The social learning approach suggests controlling aggression by counteracting the factors that provoke it: by reducing aversive stimulation, by rewarding and modelling non-aggression, and by eliciting reactions incompatible with aggression.

CRITICAL QUESTIONS

1 How have social psychologists defined aggression?

2 What implications does the definition of aggression have for research on its occurrence?

3 What are some of the causes social psychologists have identified for aggression?

4 Why does aggression occur?

5 What can we do to reduce aggression?

RECOMMENDED READINGS

Below are some recommended classic and contemporary readings within social psychology on aggression.

Classic Books and Papers

Dollard, J., Doob, L., Miller, N., Mowrer, O. & Sears, R. (1939). *Frustration and Aggression.* New Haven, CT: Yale University Press.

This book outlines John Dollard and his colleagues' frustration-aggression hypothesis.

Berkowitz, L. (1989). Frustration-aggression hypothesis: Examination and reformulation. *Psychological Bulletin,* **106**(1), 59–73.

A revision of John Dollard's frustration-aggression hypothesis that includes the conditions under which frustration leads to aggression.

Bandura, A., Ross, D., & Ross, S.A. (1961). Transmission of aggression through imitation of aggressive models. *Journal of Abnormal and Social Psychology,* **63**, 575–582.

Classic social learning demonstration which shows how children learn aggressive behaviour through observation.

Zillmann, D., & Bryant, J. (1974). Effect of residual excitation on the emotional response to provocation and delayed aggressive behavior. *Journal of Personality and Social Psychology,* **30**(6), 782–791.

Offers a good explanation and demonstration of Dolf Zillman's excitation-transfer model.

Contemporary Papers

Hayes, S.C., Rincover, A., & Volosin, D. (1980). Variables influencing the acquisition and maintenance of aggressive behavior: Modelling versus sensory reinforcement. *Journal of Abnormal Psychology,* **89**(2), 254–262.

Discusses Bandura's social learning experiments (Bobo doll studies), and argues that there may be other facilitatory sensory factors involved in aggressive behaviour, which have been previously ignored.

Workman, M. (2010). A behaviourist perspective on corporate harassment online: Validation of a theoretical model of psychological motives. *Computers & Security,* **29**, 831–839.

A qualitative study that investigates how cultural norms shape aggressive and prejudiced behaviour, such as antigay violence.

BH 411

Business Horizons (2010) **53**, 571—579

Available online at www.sciencedirect.com

ScienceDirect

KELLEY SCHOOL OF BUSINESS
INDIANA UNIVERSITY
www.elsevier.com/locate/bushor

'Where everybody knows your name': Lessons from small business about preventing workplace violence

Anthony C. Klotz, M. Ronald Buckley *

Price College of Business, University of Oklahoma, Norman, OK 73019, U.S.A

KEYWORDS
Workplace violence;
Small business
practices;
Work groups

Abstract   Recently, we have seen a number of high profile examples of workplace violence. Large organizations are armed with many of the programs that have been developed to minimize the occurrence of workplace violence. In contrast, smaller organizations—which constitute the majority of businesses in the United States—possess neither the resources nor the manpower to implement the aforementioned programs. Additionally, due to a number of individual, social, and situational factors, small businesses appear to be more vulnerable to workplace violence than large businesses. Despite these disadvantages, however, it seems that small businesses do not experience higher levels of workplace violence than their more sizeable counterparts. In this article, we uncover a number of small business practices that may counteract the threat of workplace violence, and proffer these as lessons for all managers who wish to work toward that goal.
© 2010 Kelley School of Business, Indiana University. All rights reserved.

It seems to me that there were repeated signals being sent off by Major Hasan that he was potentially a danger.

~ *U.S. Senator Joseph Lieberman*

The system is not doing what it's supposed to do.
~ *Dr. Val Finnell, who studied with Hasan at the military's Uniformed Services University of the Health Sciences*

* Corresponding author.
  E-mail addresses: klotz@ou.edu (A.C. Klotz),
mbuckley@ou.edu (M.R. Buckley).

1. No safe haven: Violence in the workplace

What motive could possibly foment such a heinous act as that perpetrated by Major Nidal Hasan upon Fort Hood on November 5, 2009? Why would someone want to harm co-workers? In spite of what appear to be easily confronted questions, it is not difficult to find myriad examples of employees who engage in workplace violence, and wound and kill their colleagues.

- On January 7, 2010, at an ABB manufacturing facility in St. Louis, Missouri, a 51-year-old employee in the midst of a pension dispute walked

0007-6813/$ — see front matter © 2010 Kelley School of Business, Indiana University. All rights reserved.
doi:10.1016/j.bushor.2010.06.004

into his workplace with an assault rifle, a handgun, and a shotgun, and proceeded to kill three co-workers and injure five more before turning the gun on himself. Although the company employed a security firm to stem these and other horrifying acts of workplace violence, the attack could not be prevented.

- On January 26, 2005, at a Chrysler plant in Toledo, Ohio, a 54-year-old employee arrived late for his scheduled shift armed with a shotgun and a list of co-workers to kill. The man murdered a supervisor and wounded two other co-workers before killing himself. One of the wounded employees, the assailant's team leader, still carries 68 pieces of metal shot in his body from that day. The shooter had received a negative performance appraisal the day before, and it sent him over the edge. Although the plant employed security guards, they could not thwart this tragedy.

- On February 12, 2010, while attending a routine department meeting, Amy Bishop, a professor of biology at the University of Alabama at Huntsville, abruptly stood up, pulled out a 9 mm handgun, and used it to kill three of her colleagues and wound three others. The shooter had recently been denied tenure—which, per university policy, meant that she would not be retained at the end of the following semester. In the wake of the especially violent Columbine and Virginia Tech slayings, schools across the country have tightened security and standardized procedures in response to acts of violence. This professor, however, was seemingly unimpeded in her quest to cause violence to her co-workers.

The aforementioned are high profile examples of workplace violence. To be considered workplace violence, an act must meet three criteria (Baron & Richardson, 1994; Buss, 1961):

1. It must be a physical act of aggression. Although unpleasant, a screaming match between two employees is not considered violence. As soon as one of those employees shoves the other, though, the push qualifies it as an act of violence.

2. The incident must be active, not passive. To illustrate, seeing that a box is going to fall off the top shelf of a rack and hit a co-worker on the head, and yet failing to warn the co-worker would not be considered an act of workplace violence. However, grabbing that box and throwing it at the co-worker's head would be an active act of violence.

3. Finally, workplace violence must be direct, and not indirect. For example, cutting the brake lines on a co-worker's forklift—although very harmful—would be an indirect act, and thus not constitute an act of workplace violence. Ramming into another employee with a forklift would be direct, and thereby be considered an act of workplace violence.

Incidents of workplace violence capture media attention and chillingly remind us of the fragility of human life. These events may cause some of us to fret over whether a similar incident could happen at our work, while others may view them as a reminder of the importance of kissing a spouse goodbye in the morning and saying "I love you." For managers, however, a different set of feelings may emerge. The latest workplace rampage may force a manager to think about how incensed an employee became at a recent disciplinary meeting, or how quiet and brooding a new employee has been since being hired. Another thought is likely to quickly follow: "What should I do, or could I do, to prevent this from happening on my watch?" If these managers are part of large organizations like the ones in the aforementioned examples, they likely have at their disposal a number of tools, such as violence prevention and recognition training, security guards, and employee assistance programs (EAPs). Many companies, though—primarily those of small and medium size—do not provide these tools to managers (Bureau of Labor Statistics, 2005). Furthermore, as previously illustrated, these measures are often ineffective at circumventing workplace violence.

The juxtaposition of two observations—(1) smaller organizations lack the resources to develop sophisticated responses to the threat of workplace violence; and (2) even though managers in large organizations do possess resources, they are often ineffective against determined would-be assailants—focused our analysis toward what was happening in small businesses. An informal review of co-worker driven workplace violence resulting in death over the past two decades suggests that, although over half of the nation's workers are employed by small businesses (i.e., companies with fewer than 500 employees), only a handful of these extreme acts of co-worker on co-worker violence occurred in small businesses. In addition, because larger organizations dedicate more resources to violence prevention (Bureau of Labor Statistics, 2005), one might expect that the rate of incidents of co-worker violence would decrease as organizational size increases. Data from a recent Bureau of Labor Statistics (2005) survey suggest this is not the case, however, and that rates of co-worker

rybody Knows Your Name': Lessons from Small Business about preventing Workplace Violence by M. Ronald Buckley and Anthony C. Klotz

49

'Where everybody knows your name': Lessons from small business about preventing workplace violence 573

Figure 1.   Antecedents of workplace violence

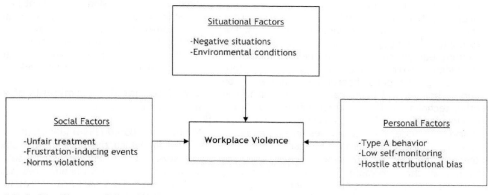

*Adapted from Neuman and Baron (1998)

violence are fairly constant regardless of company size.

This paradox led us to consider the factors in small businesses that may contribute to their increased vulnerability to workplace violence. More importantly, we consider how the more intimate and personal feel of the small business setting—where 'everybody knows your name'—counteracts this increased susceptibility to workplace violence. We explain how managers in these settings, while lacking the resources of large firms, use individualized tactics to make employees feel valued ('and they're always glad you came') and one with the rest of the organization ('our troubles are all the same'), thereby curbing the possibility of a violent outburst. Based on these observations, we proffer a set of practical recommendations that managers in all types and sizes of organizations can proactively use to minimize the threat of workplace violence.

2. The vulnerability of small business to workplace violence

A number of causes of workplace violence have been suggested (see Stone, 1995). We intend to look at these causes through a small business lens to understand whether smaller organizations are at an advantage or disadvantage in thwarting workplace violence. In a review of workplace violence, Neuman and Baron (1998) divide the antecedents of workplace violence into three categories: social factors, situational factors, and personal determinants. In many incidents of workplace violence, it is determined all too late how these antecedents have combined to cause individuals to combust in a fit of violence. In the

aforementioned example regarding the University of Alabama at Huntsville, accounts suggest that elements of the tenure situation, the perception of social injustice, and Amy Bishop's personal instability may have all played a proximal role in the gruesome outcome. In this way, these three antecedents (shown in Figure 1) lead to internal states in would-be aggressors that are conducive to acts of workplace violence.

2.1. Social determinants of violence in small businesses

Social determinants of workplace violence include unfair treatment, frustration-inducing events, increased workforce diversity, and norm violations. Unfair treatment is a major cause of workplace violence. Perceptions of injustice have been clearly linked to a number of hostile workplace behaviors, including theft and other forms of retaliation. In the examples cited earlier, there is evidence that all three acts of violence were set off by perceptions of unfairness concerning pension disbursements, performance appraisals, or tenure evaluations; clearly, Amy Bishop felt that she was being treated unfairly when she was denied tenure by the University of Alabama at Huntsville. In large organizations, standard procedures, and the watchful eye of human resources departments, are institutionalized in order to reduce the probability of injustice and to deal with these perceptions in a controlled manner when necessary. Small businesses lack these formal institutions, however, and instead give much more leverage to the manager or owner in determining outcomes for employees. This absence of procedures to ensure fair treatment likely makes small businesses more vulnerable to perceptions of injustice by employees, and, therefore, acts of workplace violence.

Frustration-inducing events, characterized as impediments to goal-directed behavior, may also stoke the fire of workplace violence in employees. For example, if a body shop has only one piece of welding equipment and all of the technicians at the facility need the welder on occasion to complete their assigned repairs, hoarding of the welder by one technician will likely cause frustration in the other technicians. This frustration may lead to acts of violence if the selfish technician does not begin sharing. Because small businesses often operate in an environment characterized by scarce resources, there are more opportunities for frustration-inducing events in this environment. Indeed, frustrating episodes such as running out of toner for the copy machine or being denied credit for a needed part from a new vendor are more likely to occur in the resource-strapped and less standardized world of small business. For this reason, we would expect more violent activity to take place in this setting.

Interpersonal attraction between workers in organizational settings has been linked to the similarity that two individuals perceive to exist between one another. Therefore, when individuals are similar, the positive interpersonal feelings from similarity lower the likelihood that acts of violence will occur. Thus, diverse workforces are more fertile breeding grounds for acts of violence than are homogeneous ones. Although diversity is often thought of in terms of race or gender, differences in age, socioeconomic status, religious views, political stance, and so on, also increase workplace diversity and can, therefore, be sources of workplace violence. While small businesses are likely no more or less diverse than large organizations, they may be less equipped to deal with the challenges associated with diversity if it exists. In a study of human resource professionals, Rynes and Rosen (1995) found that diversity training is positively related to large organization size. Thus, small businesses may be less capable of blunting the negative effects of diversity in organizations, which may make them more susceptible to workplace violence.

The final social determinant of violence pertains to workplace norm violations. Norms refer to informal rules of expected behavior to regulate and regularize the behavior of a close-knit group or community. Because of the competitive environment in which many entrepreneurial firms must operate, there may be a higher likelihood that an aggressive climate and set of normative behavior emerges within the organization. When this type of climate emerges in a group within a large organization, there are mechanisms in place—such

as interactions with other groups in the company, oversight by higher levels in the hierarchy, and even board supervision—to prevent the norms from growing (although high profile examples such as Goldman Sachs and AIG show that this is not foolproof). Small businesses lack these controls, which may increase the chance that an aggressive set of norms emerges and breeds workplace violence.

2.2. Situational determinants of violence in small businesses

Neuman and Baron (1998) identified two broad factors under which the odds of workplace violence increase. The first encompasses a set of negative situations, such as layoffs and breaches of psychological contracts, which are becoming more common in the modern workplace. The second category, physical environmental conditions, captures working conditions that make employees especially susceptible to lashing out at co-workers. We discuss both of these factors as they relate to violence in small organizations.

Clearly, high-stress situations such as layoffs, downsizings, and contract negotiations can have a negative impact on employees. As detailed in the introductory cases, these stimuli can lead employees to commit egregious acts of workplace violence. The University of Alabama at Huntsville is no different from other universities in that gaining tenure is a stressful event of paramount importance in the life of a professor. This high stakes situation likely contributed to the negative feelings inside Amy Bishop that culminated in her violent act. In addition to the victims of these high-stress situations, employees left working for the company may deal with depression in losing their co-workers, guilt at having been 'spared,' and increased workloads that result from a reduction in staffing.

As illustrated in the recent Academy Award-nominated movie *Up in the Air*, large organizations have the practice of laying off employees down to a science. It is not uncommon for an employee to receive a severance package, including a monetary allowance, emotional counseling, and professional job hunting services to help make the transition to a new career. Further, retained employees are typically able to use counseling services via the company's EAP to help them through their own transition. Likewise, during stressful times—such as plant labor negotiations, acquisitions, or divestitures—large organizations supplement their human resources coverage in the areas most impacted by the changes. Due to resource constraints in small businesses, however, it is much less likely that severance packages will be provided

'Where everybody knows your name': Lessons from small business about preventing workplace violence   575

for employees that are laid off, or that extra counseling can be provided for those employees most impacted by large changes in the organization. Therefore, it would seem probable that these smaller companies would be more exposed to the threat of violence during these events.

Conditions in the physical environment may also lead to higher levels of violence in individuals (Bushman, Wang, & Anderson, 2005). Conventional wisdom would also indicate that comfortable working conditions would be associated with lower levels of violence, while working in environments with extreme levels of heat, cold, noise, humidity, crowding, darkness, and so forth would shorten tempers and increase the odds of violent behavior. While poor working conditions may exist in large or small organizations, it is more likely that large businesses have used some resources to reduce the impact of these physical discomforts. For example, in most large manufacturing plants, ear plugs are provided by the company. In large construction companies, water to prevent dehydration is provided at every job site. In smaller versions of these firms, the availability of these items is more likely to be left to the employee's discretion and cost. Consequently, in small businesses, there are likely to be more situations where unpleasant physical conditions lead to workplace violence.

2.3. Personal determinants of violence in small businesses

Along with social and situational causes of violence in organizations, several individual antecedents make employees more prone to behave violently in the workplace. Type A behavior, low self-monitoring, and the hostile attributional bias all contribute to the likelihood of workplace violence in employees. Next, we discuss the implications of these personal characteristics on workplace violence in small business settings.

Individuals with Type A behavior patterns can be described—among other things—as controlling, competitive, and aggressive. These individuals are impatient with delays, display hostility quickly, and are concerned with their social status. As officials later discovered, Amy Bishop had killed her own brother 24 years earlier during an argument, and was a suspect in an attempted bombing at Harvard when she was a student there. Clearly, she possessed some aggressive and hostile tendencies. As Neuman and Baron (1998) argue, with these characteristics, it is not a stretch to see why these individuals are likely candidates for sources of violence in the workplace. Indeed, Baron, Neuman, and Geddes (1999) demonstrated a positive

relationship between three types of aggression and Type A behavior patterns. Naturally, this type of behavior is likely to increase the chances of workplace violence in large and small organizations. However, small businesses may be especially at risk due to the fact that Type A behavior has consistently been found to associate with the personality characteristics of entrepreneurs (Crant, 1996). If entrepreneurs—the leaders of small businesses— act in a Type A manner, it is more likely that a norm of that behavior will become institutionalized, setting the stage for later acts of workplace violence.

High self-monitors have been described as social chameleons because of their ability to read the social landscape and, in response, frequently and accurately adjust their impressions to suit the specific target or situation (Turnley & Bolino, 2001). On the other end of the spectrum, low self-monitors behave in a manner consistent with their own personal values and beliefs without care regarding the reactions or perceptions of others. Therefore, when the situational or social factors previously discussed set the stage for violence in the workplace, high self-monitors are likely to react by trying to diffuse the situation with apologies, excuses, or other impression management tactics. Low self-monitors will make no attempt to diffuse the situation, thereby allowing the likelihood of a violent incident to increase. Although one could make the case that entrepreneurs are less tolerant of politics and are more 'straight-shooting' than managers in traditional organizations, there is no evidence to support this. Thus, it is unlikely that a difference in the level of self-monitoring contributes to workplace violence in small businesses.

Finally—and not surprisingly—individuals with a hostile attribution bias are more likely to perpetrate an act of workplace violence than are those with more benevolent attributions. When individuals possess this bias, they are more likely to interpret the act of others as hostile, and therefore reciprocate with additional hostility. This can quickly spiral into larger acts of hostility, eventually culminating in violence. We have all worked with this type of individual, who views an innocent act such as drinking the last cup of coffee as a personal attack on his or her right to a hot caffeinated beverage.

While the hostile attribution bias likely exists in equal parts in large and small businesses, it brings up an interesting point regarding the management of these 'problem' employees in small businesses. In large businesses, there is a formal procedure for managing bad employees out of the organization and replacing them with new hires. In small businesses, it is less likely that these processes exist. While it may be simpler to terminate a bad employee in a small business, it is likely more cumbersome to hire and

Table 1. The difference in how large and small businesses deal with social, situational, and personal sources of workplace violence

Source of violence	Large business solution	Small business solution	Lesson
Employees have personal problems	Refer employees with personal problems to HR or EAPs	Dedicate time to help employees through difficult personal times	1. Get personal with employees
Workloads are perceived as unfair among employees	Give employees the tools they need and leave them alone	Ensure every employee pulls their weight	2. Focus more on accountability than autonomy
Stressful work situations arise (cyclically and sporadically) in organizations	Adjust resources and "human capital" as necessary to adjust for changes in business cycle	Personally monitor employees during scheduled and unexpected times of stress	3. Get in rhythm with stressful work cycles
Aggressive personalities lead to increased frustration in work groups	Work is work. "Play" happens outside of work.	Find small and simple activities in which employees can interact informally on a regular basis	4. Provide an outlet for aggression
Work scheduling leads to perceptions of unfair treatment and individual needs are not met	Headquarters-dedicated work scheduling policies	Be consistently sensitive and flexible, to the unique scheduling needs of every employee	5. Practice consistent flexibility with work schedules

train a new member as a replacement without the support of a human resources department. This lack of flexibility leads small business managers to put up with toxic behavior, such as those that result from the hostile attribution bias. Because of this retention, small businesses may be more likely than large employers to retain sources of workplace violence.

3. How small businesses compensate for workplace violence vulnerability

Most large organizations institute a number of policies and practices to deal with the threat of workplace violence. These include, but are not limited to: employment pre-screening; written procedures for dealing with violent behavior; uniform guidelines for employee termination; use of full- or part-time security services; psychiatric resources or outplacement counseling; and managerial training. These are all worthwhile endeavors, and ones which small businesses should emulate to the extent that it is possible. However, most small businesses lack the time and resources to implement such extensive measures, especially considering the fairly low likelihood that a co-worker act of violence will occur in the organization.

Given the fact that most small businesses do not use these established measures of workplace violence prevention (Bureau of Labor Statistics, 2005), we offer a set of five lessons from small business for managers of all types of organizations to reduce

acts of aggression in the workplace, thereby lowering the probability of workplace violence in their organization. First, get personal with employees. Second, focus on accountability, not autonomy. Third, get in rhythm with stressful work cycles. Fourth, provide an outlet for aggression. Fifth, and finally, practice consistent flexibility with work schedules. We feel that by incorporating these lessons (when possible) into work groups, managers will reduce the potential for workplace violence, and perhaps even improve the group's effectiveness. Each of these lessons is explicitly considered next, and illustrated in Table 1.

3.1. Lesson #1: Get personal

Throughout the course of the movie *Office Space*, Milton, a quiet and mumbling office worker at the fictional Initech Corporation, is dehumanized through a number of cost cutting steps including wrestling away his prized red Swingline stapler, moving his cubicle to the storage area in the basement, and ceasing his flow of paychecks. Each action is taken without concern for Milton's personal well-being, and with each insult, Milton's anger grows until one day he resorts to workplace violence to exact his revenge on the company by burning down the building.

Though exaggerated, the depersonalized nature of these actions is common in many large organizations. Managers are pushed to supervise greater numbers of employees, and rely on technology such

rybody Knows Your Name': Lessons from Small Business about preventing Workplace Violence by M. Ronald Buckley and Anthony C. Klotz

53

'Where everybody knows your name': Lessons from small business about preventing workplace violence 577

as electronic surveillance to assist them. To quote musician Bob Seger (1978), in these settings, employees begin to "feel like a number. . . .The boss can't even recall my name. . . .I feel like just another spoke in a great big wheel. . . .I'm not a number, dammit. . . .I'm a man. . . .I said I'm a man." This unhealthy working atmosphere becomes a breeding ground for violent events. In small businesses, however, it is much more common that 'everybody knows your name,' and employees are unable to hide and let minor issues grow into outbursts of violence; on the contrary, the familial feel of many small businesses affirms the idea that each employee matters, which reduces violent tendencies in the workplace. Managers in large organizations would be wise to foster this inclusive atmosphere within their work groups.

Further, in large organizations, it is a common stigma for managers to take a deep interest in the personal lives of their direct reports. Indeed, in a Fortune 500 company, it is an HR director's nightmare to have hundreds of managers engage in delicate discussions concerning marital problems, drug abuse issues, or weight loss fad diets with their thousands of employees. That is why EAPs work so well: managers are ever-equipped with a stack of cards featuring a toll-free 800 number, which can be handed to employees in these sticky situations. While EAP programs can be extremely helpful, small business owners and managers are left to deal with these issues on their own. Indeed, because of their acute awareness that without their employees they are sunk, these leaders often spend relatively small, but quite meaningful, amounts of time and energy listening to and coping with on a personal level the issues that employees encounter. We spoke with some companies whose owners even work long and hard to rattle their social network to find jobs for employees that must be let go because of financial hardship or fit issues. In return for this investment, these managers receive increased loyalty, cultivate employees who know that they are personally cared for, and create individuals that are more emotionally capable of extinguishing the embers which can ignite the powder keg of workplace violence.

3.2. Lesson #2: Focus more on accountability than autonomy

The term 'autonomy' has been a buzzword in management for some time now. From individual autonomy to autonomous work teams, the belief that giving employees the tools they need to do the job and then letting them do the rest is embedded within the collective management psyche. The purpose of this lesson is not to discuss whether the use of autonomy is an effective tactic for managers; it is in many situations and is not in many others. The point is to highlight our observation that, out of necessity, small businesses place much greater emphasis on accountability than on autonomy. That is, small business managers are much more concerned with whether each employee is pulling their weight and contributing their fair share to the organizational pie.

This focus on accountability impedes the growth of workplace violence in two ways. First, by ensuring that no team member is shirking the duties expected by the organization and its members, one of the primary sources of perceptions of injustice in the workplace is eliminated. As we have discussed, perceptions of unfair treatment are antecedents to violent behavior. Second, when a manager personally holds each employee accountable, no one falls through the cracks. This increases the likelihood that each employee understands their specific role as a valuable member of the group, thereby lowering the chance that negativity will fester and grow into violent eruptions. Thus, in addition to the ethical benefits associated with adopting an 'accountability lens' (Hall, Bowen, Ferris, Royle, & Fitzgibbons, 2007), managers can also increase the workplace safety of their employees by embracing this view.

3.3. Lesson #3: Get in rhythm with stressful work cycles

Each organization, each work location, each manager, and each employee ebbs and flows through periods of high and low stress. For some—such as accountants as tax time nears, national park rangers in the summertime, and farmers at harvest—these periods are easily discernable and predictable. For others, however, periods of high stress—and, therefore, higher chances of workplace violence—are more subtle and unpredictable. For example, an unexpected hailstorm may batter an unlikely part of the country, causing insurance adjustors to work for weeks on end without a break. A highly publicized recall on a competitor's product may instantly send demand soaring, pushing workers to the brink. In small businesses, leaders are involved in every aspect of the operation. Therefore, they are in a position to detect these spikes in stress and are able to personally get involved in making it more bearable, by doing things like working alongside employees and buying meals for the workplace to show appreciation. This not only increases the spirit of camaraderie during a taxing time, but also allows these managers to watch for employees that may be reaching the breaking point, and to react before the stress leads to an act of workplace aggression or violence.

3.4. Lesson #4: Provide an outlet for aggression

As we have argued, small business may be especially vulnerable to the increased likelihood of workplace violence associated with Type A behavior patterns, adverse working conditions, and diversity in the workforce. Therefore, many small businesses develop rituals that simultaneously provide an outlet for pent-up aggression and encourage camaraderie. We are not referring to the ubiquitous annual company picnic, which typically becomes a 'must-attend' event and not the team building exercise that is intended. Rather, we are referring to small but meaningful rituals that are not burdensome to employees and allow socialization with their managers in non-work atmospheres. Many of the new technology firms have retained these rituals and incorporated them into their now-large organizations. For example, Google has a volleyball court at its company headquarters, and PayPal has basketball courts.

While most small businesses do not have the resources to make these grand gestures, many use creativity and input from their employees to create inexpensive, yet meaningful rituals. We spoke with one collision center owner who built a horseshoe pit, and every Friday after work the employees stay for varying lengths of time to play horseshoes. According to the owner, this not only provides an outlet to let off some steam from the previous week's work, but also allows internal 'rivals'—in this case, the estimators and the parts department—to compete alongside one another in a healthy environment. Perhaps most importantly, these rituals allow the manager to observe the interpersonal dynamics of the group in a casual setting, and provide early warning signals regarding employees that carry grudges from work over into other settings. These employees can then be dealt with promptly, decreasing the likelihood of aggression escalating to a violent level in the organization.

3.5. Lesson #5: Practice consistent flexibility with work schedules

In large organizations, it is often easiest—and may even be required—for managers to set strict rules concerning work schedules. We appreciate the efficacy of this approach, as it dovetails well with our comments concerning the importance of fairness and justice. However, in small businesses, managers often do not have strict scheduling policies, and this can provide them with opportunities to decrease the accumulation of hostility in the workplace. Free from formal flextime or attendance policies, small business managers often treat each individual's schedule on a case-by-case basis.

An extreme example can be found in the outdoor apparel company Patagonia, which began small and has retained its most important organizational practices even as it has grown into a large company. Patagonia's Let My People Surf policy allows employees to take advantage of a nice day, a good tide, a stiff breeze, or whatever suits their personal interest, without notice—provided they have their work done. Clearly, this would be difficult for most companies to emulate; yet, it does demonstrate the significance of a small business owner recognizing that each employee has different priorities outside of work, and designing a system which allows them to pursue their personal interests. Of course, this must be done in a fashion that is fair and consistent. The point is that work schedules can be a critical source of feelings on unfair treatment or frustration-inducing events in organizations. By mitigating some of the strain and anxiety associated with it, managers can reduce a source of potential violence in their workplace.

4. Concluding thoughts

The causes of workplace violence are not going to disappear; indeed, it is likely that they will become even more prevalent as the pace of life and work continues to quicken. Thus, it is up to managers to proactively diagnose and treat the causes of workplace violence. We feel it is critical that managers not only rely on traditional HR-driven remedies to workplace violence, but also supplement them with creative and custom solutions for their work group so that each employee feels they spend the majority of their waking hours in a place where everybody knows their name. Could an Amy Bishop situation have happened in a small business? Of course. But, there are a number of factors in small businesses which may have intervened and defused those triggers which elicited the violent behavior. It is our hope that the set of lessons we have developed, based on our observations and informal research regarding small business practices, provides managers with some tools to develop and implement those solutions. By learning from one another, managers in large and small businesses can reduce workplace violence, and to that we sing "Cheers!" (Portnoy, 2003) and invite you all to sing along;

rybody Knows Your Name': Lessons from Small Business about preventing Workplace Violence by M. Ronald Buckley and Anthony C. Klotz

55

'Where everybody knows your name': Lessons from small business about preventing workplace violence 579

Sometimes you want to go
Where everybody knows your name
And they're always glad you came;
You want to be where you can see
Our troubles are all the same;
You want to be where everybody knows
your name.

References

Baron, R. A., Neuman, J. H., & Geddes, D. (1999). Social and personal determinants of workplace aggression: Evidence for the impact of perceived injustice and the Type A behavior pattern. *Aggressive Behavior, 25*(4), 281–296.

Baron, R. A., & Richardson, D. R. (1994). *Human aggression* (2nd ed.), New York: Plenum Press.

Bureau of Labor Statistics. (2005). *Survey of workplace violence prevention, 2005* (USDL 06-1860). Washington, DC: Government Printing Office.

Bushman, B. J., Wang, M. C., & Anderson, C. A. (2005). Is the curve relating temperature to aggression linear or curvilinear? Assaults and temperature in Minneapolis reexamined. *Journal of Personality and Social Psychology, 89*(1), 62–66.

Buss, A. H. (1961). *The psychology of aggression.* Hoboken, NJ: John Wiley & Sons.

Crant, J. M. (1996). The proactive personality scale as a predictor of entrepreneurial intentions. *Journal of Small Business Management, 34*(3), 42–49.

Hall, A. T., Bowen, M. G., Ferris, G. R., Royle, M. T., & Fitzgibbons, D. E. (2007). The accountability lens: A new way to view management issues. *Business Horizons, 50*(5), 405–413.

Neuman, J. H., & Baron, R. A. (1998). Workplace violence and workplace aggression: Evidence concerning specific forms, potential causes, and preferred targets. *Journal of Management, 24*(3), 391–419.

Portnoy, G. (2003). Where everybody knows your name [CD]. On *Keeper.* Los Angeles: Argentum Records.

Rynes, S., & Rosen, B. (1995). A field survey of factors affecting the adoption and perceived success of diversity training. *Personnel Psychology, 48*(2), 247–270.

Seger, B. (1978). Feel like a number. On *Stranger in Town* [record]. Los Angeles: Capitol Records.

Stone, R. A. (1995). Workplace homicide: A time for action. *Business Horizons, 38*(2), 3–10.

Turnley, W. H., & Bolino, M. C. (2001). Achieving desired images while avoiding undesired images: Exploring the role of self-monitoring in impression management. *Journal of Applied Psychology, 86*(2), 351–360.

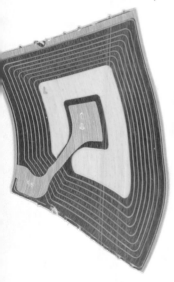

IVEY BUSINESS JOURNAL

IMPROVING THE PRACTICE OF MANAGEMENT

Workplace bullying: Escalated incivility

By Gary Namie

Reprint # 9B03TF09

IVEY MANAGEMENT SERVICES • November/December 2003
COPYRIGHT © 2003

Workplace bullying: Escalated incivility

The time has come to treat workplace bullying the same as sexual harassment or racial discrimination, to identify the perpetrators, establish rules of conduct and penalties, and even pass laws prohibiting and penalizing bullying. This author, an expert on the subject, draws a compelling picture of workplace bullying and suggests a blueprint that can help employers reduce or even eliminate it.

By Gary Namie

Gary Namie is co-founder of The Workplace Bullying & Trauma Institute, an education, research and advocacy organization (bullyinginstitute.org) and co-author of *The Bully At Work* (Sourcebooks, 2003). He is a social psychologist and consultant, and former professor of management at the University of Southern California.

> *"Violence in the workplace begins long before fists fly or lethal weapons extinguish lives. Where resentment and aggression routinely displace cooperation and communication, violence has occurred."*
> Bernice Fields, Arbitrator

The bullying phenomenon

Bullying in the workplace is far too widespread today, but before we can come to understand it, we must understand that bullying is different from harmless incivility, rudeness, boorishness, teasing and other well-known forms of interpersonal torment. Bullying is a form of violence, but only rarely involves fighting, battery or homicide. It is mostly sub-lethal, non-physical violence. And as our research data show, bullying crosses boundaries of gender, race and organizational rank.

Consider that workplace incivility, bullying and physical violence lie on a 10-point continuum of organizational disruption. Incivilities range from 1 to 3, while bullying covers mild to severe interference with the accomplishment of legitimate business interests, reflecting scores of 4 to 9. The highest score is reserved for battery and homicide which grind work completely to a halt. A parallel dimension views the consequences from the perspective of the mistreated individual. Incivilities cause little to no harm, bullying can cause mild to severe harm, and physical violence can result in death.

A short history of workplace bullying

The founder of the international anti-bullying movement, Heinz Leymann, cared most about bullying's impact on the health of individuals. Leymann was a German psychiatrist who established the world's first Work Trauma clinic in Sweden in the 1980's. He documented the traumatization that can result from sustained "psychological terrorization" in the workplace He used the term "mobbing." The term "workplace bullying" was coined by the pioneering British journalist Andrea Adams in 1992, who applied bullying to adulthood misery.

Dr. Ruth Namie and I introduced the term "workplace bullying" to the U.S. in the popular press in 1998. Our associate, David Yamada, professor of law at Suffolk University in Boston, wrote the seminal article for the legal community in March, 2000 (*Georgetown Law Journal*, 2000, vol.88, issue 3, "The Phenomenon of Workplace Bullying and the Need for Status-Blind Hostile Work Environment Protection," Pp. 475-536.)

We define workplace bullying as "status-blind" interpersonal hostility that is deliberate, repeated and sufficiently severe as to harm the targeted person's health or economic status. Further, it is driven by perpetrators' need to control another individual, often undermining legitimate business interests in the process.

The best estimate of bullying's prevalence in the U.S. comes from a year 2000 survey that randomly sampled Michigan residents. The researchers found that 16.7 percent of respondents reported a severe disruption of their lives from workplace aggression. Thus, we can extrapolate and say that about one in six workers is bullied. (Loraleigh Keashly and Karen Jagatic, Wayne State University, 2000.)

Characteristics of bullying

How can a problem so prevalent not trigger societal outrage? Silence by targeted persons is understandable because shame stems from being controlled and humiliated. Co-workers' silence makes sense in a fear-

Regardless of how bullying is manifested -- either verbal assaults or strategic moves to render the target unproductive and unsuccessful -- it is the aggressor's desire to control the target that motivates the action

plagued environment when people are unsure if they might next be targeted.

More puzzling is the typical employer response in light of internal anti-harassment and anti-violence policies. In a survey conducted by the Workplace Bullying & Trauma Institute, respondents described the nature of support, or lack of it, provided by others at work. Targets who had reported the abusive misconduct to the perpetrator's (bully's) manager and had asked for relief, elicited positive, helpful responses in only 18 percent of cases. In 42 percent of instances the bully's boss actually compounded the problem. And in 40 percent of cases, the boss did nothing, which is not a neutral response after help was explicitly requested. Human Resources and anti-discrimination officers were similarly unhelpful: 17 percent took positive steps to stop the bullying, 32 percent reacted negatively, and 51

percent did nothing.

Bullying encompasses mistreatment that includes same-sex and same-race harassment. Our research discovered that in only 25 percent of bullying cases does the target have protected group status and thus qualify the offenses as sexual harassment or racial discrimination. A university survey conducted by University of Illinois researchers found a similar dominance of bullying over forms of illegal harassment. The fact that bullying is not illegal makes it easy to ignore even though it is three times more prevalent than its better-recognized, illegal forms.

Women and men are bullies. Women comprise 58 percent of the perpetrator pool, while men represent 42 percent. Our research also shows that when the targeted person is a woman, she is bullied by a woman in 63 percent of cases; when the target is male, he is bullied by a man in 62 percent of incidents. Most bullying is same-sex harassment which is ignored by laws and employer policies. Overall, women comprise the majority of bullied people (80 percent).

In fact, WBTI research shows that half of all bullying is woman-on-woman. Unless the target enjoys protected status based on race, ethnicity, religion or disability, it is not likely that the current laws will provide the target with legal redress. Without laws, employers are reluctant to recognize, let alone correct or prevent, destructive behavior, preferring to minimize it as "personality clashes."

Bullying is nearly invisible. It is non-physical, and nearly always sub-lethal workplace violence. Workplace homicide grabs headlines as vivid rare events even in the violent United States. Corporate decision makers invest heavily in prevention and response processes, complete with zero tolerance policies.

In contrast, bullying is psychological violence, mostly covert and sometimes overt. It is psychological violence, both in its nature and impact. Regardless of how bullying is manifested -- either verbal assaults or strategic moves to render the target unproductive and unsuccessful -- it is the aggressor's desire to control the target that motivates the action. The major risk is psychological damage, but counseling is not offered by employers to complainants who report bullying.

A recent study by the United States Postal Service provided comparative frequencies: physical assaults, 1 in 25; illegal harassment 1 in 8; and verbal abuse 1 in 4. Employers are not interested in the most common negative trend in contemporary workplaces, abusive interpersonal relationships. But changes in related arenas give hope that the silence about bullying is crumbling.

Employers have begun to consider the impact of negative emotional behaviour on work productivity. Depression impacts work and employers are taking notice. Also, thanks to the Corporate Alliance to End

The characteristic common to all bullies is that they are controlling competitors who exploit their cooperative targets. Most bullies would stop if the rules changed and bullying was punished

Partner Violence (CAEPV.org), employers are learning how domestic violence impacts the workplace. First, it is easy for abusive spouses to kill their victims at work. Abused workers miss a great deal of work and are distracted and unproductive. Enlightened CAEPV member firms believe that employers should be sensitive to traumatized victims as injured people deserving human compassion.

Bullying closely resembles the phenomenon of domestic violence. Both were shrouded in silence before being brought to public attention. Partner violence victims initially were blamed for their fate. Eventually the behavior was deemed unacceptable by society as codified in law. Workplace bullying deserves the same evolution from recognition to prohibition. The glaring difference between domestic and workplace psychological violence is that the latter finds the abuser on the employer's payroll.

Damaging people

Bullying impacts targeted employees by causing a host of stress-related health problems. The WBTI 2003

survey polled self-described targets. Stress effects range from severe anxiety (76 percent prevalence), disrupted sleep (71 percent), loss of concentration (71 percent), PTSD (post-traumatic stress disorder, 47%), clinical depression (39%), and panic attacks (32%). Left untreated, and with prolonged exposure, cardiovascular stress-related diseases can result from pathophysiologic changes to the body that transform social factors into damaging biological consequences.

PTSD is a psychological injury. Few blame victims for having it when causes are natural. Yet the experience is just as strong when trauma is induced by intentional human design. Leymann documented Work Trauma as problematic in Sweden, the result of psychosocial workplace stressors. He also estimated that 10 percent of his country's suicides were related to workplace traumatization.

Targets of workplace bullying endure their pain, on average, for 22 months. The attribute common to all targets is that they are unwilling or unable to react to unwarranted aggression with aggression. Research and anecdotal evidence show that it is the emotionally unintelligent perpetrators who escalate their tyrannical misconduct when they feel threatened by, and react in response to, targets' asserted independence, technical and social skills or ethical whistle blowing Targets do not seek to be tormented any more than sexual harassment targets invite undesirable assaults or domestic violence victims seek to be beaten or verbally abused.

In an individualistic culture, people tend to blame victims for the harm they endure and make them responsible for solving their unprovoked problems. Cavalier justifications for accepting psychological injury at work include "that's why they call it work," "capitalism depends on competition," and "get used to him, he's just that way, grow a thicker skin."

For a bullied target, health impairment is coupled with economic setbacks that begin when the bully appears in her life. Bullied targets have a 70 percent chance that they will lose their jobs, either voluntarily or through constructive discharge, after being targeted. If the bullying has stopped, it is because 17 percent of targets transferred. In only 13 percent of cases are perpetrators punished or terminated. Destructive aggression carries few risks for perpetrators.

The bullies

Though bullies torment peers and sometimes those above them in the organization chart, WBTI research shows that 71 percent of bullies outrank their targets. Most bullies are bosses. If strict competition is the operating principle at work, then it is a zero-sum game --personal gains made at the expense of others.

It would be convenient to categorize all bullies as psychopaths. Then, all solutions would be focused on rehabilitating individuals. However, only a small proportion of bullies (approximately 4 percent according to the American Psychiatric Association) may have genuinely disordered personalities--antisocial or narcissistic. The characteristic common to all bullies is that they are controlling competitors who exploit their cooperative targets. Most bullies would stop if the rules changed and bullying was punished.

We sort bullies into four categories, based on the wide range of tactics employed, and which are too numerous to list here.

- The *Screaming Mimi*, the stereotypical bully, controls the emotional tone for everyone else. He toxifies the workplace with mood swings and unpredictable displays of anger. Targets are publicly humiliated to convince witnesses that the bully is to be feared. He usually stops short of physical violence, but this volatile individual poses the violent risk employers fear most.

- The *Constant Critic* is the hyper-critical nitpicker. Her attention to minutiae and obsession over others' performance is the way she hides her own deficiencies and insecurities. This bully resorts to name calling. She loves to complain about everyone else's "incompetence." She invents targets' "errors" to belittle and to confuse them. Though she prefers behind-closed-door settings, she can berate targets in public, too.

- The *Two-Headed Snake* slithers up the organization chart, reserving brutality for those

below. Snakes defame the reputation of targets to boost their own self-image. The Snake spreads rumors and engineers "divide and conquer" schemes within work teams to turn co-workers against the target. His version of events is always believed while the target's perspective is discounted.

- The *Gatekeeper* is obsessed with control. She allocates time, money, staffing and information in ways that ensure her target's failure. Then, she has an excuse to complain about "performance problems." One ludicrous bully actually set office clocks so that everyone seemed to come to work late and leave early.

Solutions should be focused less on personality than on altering the rewards and punishments that would-be aggressors experience as part of a workplace culture.

Characteristics of the bullying-prone workplace

- "Making the numbers," an obsession with outcomes is uncritically adopted
- Recruitment, promotion, and reward systems focus on individuals' "strength of personality" or interpersonal aggressiveness while ignoring emotional intelligence
- Short-term planning, e.g., to meet quarterly investor projections, governs operations.
- Internal conduct codes limit prohibitions to narrowly defined illegal incidents.
- Executives give higher priority to personal friendships than to legitimate business interests.
- Fear is a dominant, desired workplace emotion, whether deliberately engineered or inadvertently created.
- Misuse of performance appraisal processes occur with impunity.

Why employer$ $hould care

In Canada, there exists an implied contract invoking an employer's duty of care for employee safety. Employers are liable for the sexually harassing misconduct of their supervisors. Liability stems from employers' control over the creation and maintenance of the work environment: roles, responsibilities, behavioral expectations, and the workplace culture's health or toxicity.

Here are several reasons why employers should address workplace bullying:

1 It is 3 times more prevalent than sexual harassment. Illegal discrimination and harassment require significant investments of time and money to identify, correct and prevent. Employers already know what to do about harassment.

2 It is costly: Employment practices liability can be substantial. Bullied targets, often the most talented employees, are driven from the workplace. Turnover is expensive. Increased health care utilization can result in heftier premium costs borne by employers.

3 Data to prevent bullying-related losses exist. Because the complaint system gatekeepers (in HR) hear all the stories, the employer has evidence of bullying's prevalence. Everyone knows who the repeat offenders are.

4 Witnesses know when bullying happens, whether or not it was behind closed doors. When a high-performing employee is fired and humiliated by "exit parade"--given a box to take private belongings, escorted by HR and security--or simply disappears without explanation one day, fear dominates the workplace. Fear-driven workplaces with poor morale undermine employee commitment and productivity.

5 Employee recruitment and retention are made more difficult when the employer's reputation suffers from the antics of one or more petty tyrants.

A blueprint for employers

Employers and their representatives should care about bullying for the reasons outlined above. Employer-led, voluntary solutions are the most likely to succeed. Here we suggest four steps for employers to pursue. The system follows a path familiar to any company that has coupled recognition training with a prohibitive policy and enforcement mechanism.

1. Create A new values-driven policy

Ideal provisions in the policy include:

- Declaration of Unacceptability
  The organization must state its displeasure with the misconduct
- Hostile Workplace Protections for Everyone
  To extend rights to everyone regardless of protected group status
  May extend, combine or replace existing anti-violence & anti-harassment policies
- Inescapable Definition
  To reserve prohibitions only for severe incidents, to clarify the threshold for taking action
- Non-Punitive Separation for Safety
  To appropriately place bullying in the health and safety domain
- Documentation of Adverse Impact
  To discourage frivolous complaints or abuse of the policy
  To incorporate perpetrator pattern & practice over time

2. New, credible enforcement processes

- Credible Third-Party Investigation & Adjudication Process
  To foster employee trust, to remove influence of personal relationships
- Progressive Disciplinary Action
  Not zero tolerance, to allow for change in conduct
- Retaliation Prohibition
  To count offenses of retaliation separately, to stop the cycle of violence

3. Restorative interventions for at-risk teams and individuals

- Coaching for identified perpetrators with employment-contingent change contract
- Interviewing affected workteams to identify those most harmed, to provide counseling

4. General and specialized education

- Executive orientation & commitment
- Managerial training
- Specialty preparation for HR, Anti-discrimination Officers, Risk Managers
- All-Hands training coupled with policy implementation

Despite obvious economic advantages of following this blueprint, employers rarely pursue this tack. They face no sanctions for ignoring generalized workplace harassment or bullying. It is easier to stay in denial or to ignore complaints when they surface.

A Legislative Solution

A 1998, a *Washington Post* newspaper editorial called on federal lawmakers to write specific anti-harassment laws without restriction to discrimination against protected groups. The editorial, written in response to Supreme Court decisions extending employer liability for discrimination, stated, that "what bothers people about abusive workplace conduct, after all, is not the fact that it may be discriminatory but that it is abusive in the first place." (Washington Post, March 8, 1998.)

In Quebec, in December, 2002, the province's Labour Standards Act was overhauled. For the first time in Canada, there will be a ban on "psychological harassment" in the workplace. That term is vaguely defined as any "vexatious behaviour in the form of repeated and hostile or unwanted conduct that affects an employee's psychological or physical integrity," including unwanted attitudes, comments and gestures.

Employers have until June, 2004 to prepare for the law's implementation. They need only show they have taken "reasonable action" to prevent or stop the harassment to avoid possible penalties that range from paying the victim's psychological treatment expenses to "punitive and moral damages." The four-step employer Blueprint outlined above would afford adequate protection for conscientious employers.

Starting in June 2004, employees experiencing psychological harassment (bullying according to most of our definition), may begin to file complaints with the Quebec Labour Standards Commission.

The WBTI has sponsored the first U.S. proposed legislation in California, scheduled for consideration in 2004. Its language is more precise than the Quebec law, relying on demonstrated health impairment as the criterion for bringing legal action.

Of course, the real value of having a law in place for bullied employees is to legitimize targets' complaints, compelling employers to correct and prevent "status-blind," health-impairing abusive misconduct. When employers take such steps, the bullies can be held accountable. The Quebec provincial law is a first step. Canadian employees' quality of life at work depends now on conscientious employers.

Selected, Edited, and with Issue Framing Material by:
Alison Alexander, *University of Georgia*
and
Jarice Hanson, *University of Massachusetts—Amherst*

ISSUE

Do Video Games Encourage Violent Behavior?

YES: Craig A. Anderson, from "FAQs on Violent Video Games and Other Media Violence," www .CraigAnderson.org (2009)

NO: Henry Jenkins, from "Reality Bytes: Eight Myths about Video Games Debunked," www.pbs.org (2009)

Learning Outcomes

After reading this issue, you will be able to:

- Describe the differences between Craig Anderson's and Henry Jenkins' perspectives on violent video games.
- Gain an understanding of the potential consequences of video gaming.
- Discuss the ways in which virtual worlds can shape understanding and behavior.
- Apply these concepts to parental and regulatory reactions.

ISSUE SUMMARY

YES: Craig A. Anderson is an expert on the effect of violence in television and film. Based on extensive research, he holds the position that video games prompt young people toward even more aggression and violence than do other media content.

NO: Henry Jenkins tackles a broad array of misconceptions about the place and impact of video games on society. He argues that the primary audience is not children, that violence is not increasing in society, and that concerns about isolation, desensitization, and violence are overblown.

In recent years, the subject of the effect of video games has joined television, films, and recorded music as a topic that provokes strong reactions among individuals who feel that some content may encourage violent, or at least aggressive behavior, among young people. There is less concern about how any type of content affects adults, so most of the attention is focused on how children, adolescents, and young adults use controversial media content. The underlying reason for this is that younger users are assumed to have a lesser sense of moral responsibility and judgment about the relationship of media content and reality, and thus be more vulnerable to its effects. Even though the video game industry voluntarily rates the content of video games (as do the motion picture, television, and recording industries), many parents and critics of media violence feel that video games are a unique form of entertainment that warrants special consideration. Since the games are often played alone, on personal devices, consoles, or computers, the video game user's interaction with the game is engaged and direct. The sophistication of computer graphics has produced images that look even

more realistic than ever before. Linkages drawn between the Columbine shootings and the perpetrators obsession with the game "Doom" in 1999 frightened the general public. The controversy became heated during the summer of 2005 when "Grand Theft Auto" was released and found to contain some hidden sex scenes. In 2011, the Supreme Court struck down Californian law that banned the sale of violent video games to minors on the grounds of freedom of expression. See www.nytimes .com/2011/06/29/arts/video-games/what-supreme-court-ruling-on-video-games-means.html for a spirited discussion of video games and freedom of expression.

Both selections chosen to represent controversial views for this issue cite evidence of research studies that have different conclusions. This raises important problems for us, as readers. How do we decide which studies to believe? How do we weigh the evidence and the credibility of the authors of differing studies? How much of our own experience informs the way we think about some of these types of issues?

As you will see, both Dr. Craig Anderson and Dr. Henry Jenkins offer a series of questions about the effects of video games and purport to debunk them. In the process, they come to opposite conclusions. Dr. Craig Anderson's FAQ list evolves from his years of studying the relationship of media content and violence/aggression. He references decades of research that finds a link between violence and aggression, a conclusion that he has testified to before congressional committees. Less research has examined the concern about the violent content of video games, because most violent games only came to the market in the 1990s. Yet the amount of time spent with games and the high levels of engagement by players lead Craig Anderson, program head of psychology at Iowa State University, to fear that the relationship between violent content and aggressive/violent behavior may be enhanced.

Dr. Henry Jenkins, professor at the University of Southern California and previously head of the comparative media studies program at MIT, offers eight myths about video games. He describes his desire to "challenge the dominant media effects paradigm and call for a more complex understanding of teens' relationship to popular culture." Whether speaking and writing about Columbine or about video games and violence, he argues that the fantasies of children's culture are an important arena to understand how we as a culture are constructing our future.

It may be true that there are few long-term studies of the effect of playing video games now, but this will change in time. There are many longitudinal studies of the way violence and aggression are portrayed in other forms of media. In all of these cases, it is important to consider who sponsors the research and what agenda the sponsoring agency may have. In this edition of *Taking Sides*, you will see several cases for which the attitudes or biases of the authors of certain studies should suggest a critical framework for evaluating their position.

This type of controversy also takes into consideration whether a media industry can adequately control access to questionable material through ratings systems. While ratings on the packages of many games and other content may be somewhat effective as a measure of who may have access to media content, how are those ratings enforced? Is it possible for an industry to monitor use when the bottom line is selling their product? How much regulation should be exercised from outside? Should the government take a stronger role in creating guidelines, or should the bulk of the responsibility be placed on the shoulders of parents and guardians?

As mentioned in the preface to this book, the distribution and appearance of media content has changed dramatically over the years. As mediated images become more realistic through computer enhancement or computer generation, studies of perception will undoubtedly change too. And, as individuals continue to use interactive media, we can expect to see more sophistication in future studies about the effects of media content on audiences of different ages, and in different circumstances.

When asked about the effects of video games on teens, a colleague of mine who studies video games quipped, "They'll have great eye-hand coordination and terrible social skills." Although violence gets much of the attention, his comment reminds us that there are uses and consequences of video game playing other than violent ones. An extensive area of research is emerging on the development of cognitive skills from interactive games. Influence on the development of visual spatial skills, multitasking ability, and attentional skills is being observed. Ironically, finding academic benefits of playing educational games has been more elusive. See Subrahmanyam and Greenfield, referenced in Postscript, for more on these issues. An interesting study detailed in that chapter (p. 81) discusses how action video game skills along with past video game experience predicted laparoscopic surgical skills. It describes the "moral panics" that have erupted during the introduction of almost all new media into society. Parental concerns and media hype have often contributed to concerns about massive negative effects that have ultimately proved to be unwarranted. As you consider the evidence provided by the two positions on this issue, how do you formulate your own position? If you were a parent, would you see things differently? Are video games different from any other form of traditional media content?

YES

Craig A. Anderson

FAQs on Violent Video Games and Other Media Violence

1. For your 2003 article on *The Influence of Media Violence on Youth* you and a distinguished group of media scholars selected by the National Institute of Mental Health reviewed 50 years of research on media violence and aggression. What have been the main research steps, and what are the main conclusions?

Most of the early research focused on two questions:

1. Is there a significant association between exposure to media violence and aggressive behavior?
2. Is this association causal? (That is, can we say that violent television, video games, and other media are directly causing aggressive behavior in our kids?)

The results, overall, have been fairly consistent across types of studies (experimental, cross-sectional, and longitudinal) and across visual media type (television, films, video games). *There is a significant relation between exposure to media violence and aggressive behavior.* Exposing children and adolescents (or "youth") to violent visual media increases the likelihood that they will engage in physical aggression against another person. By "physical aggression" we mean behavior that is intended to harm another person physically, such as hitting with a fist or some object. A single brief exposure to violent media can increase aggression in the immediate situation. Repeated exposure leads to general increases in aggressiveness over time. *This relation between media violence and aggressive behavior is causal.*

2. What have researchers focused on in more recent years? How does exposure to media violence increase later aggressive behavior?

Early aggression researchers were interested in discovering how youth learn to be aggressive. Once they discovered observational learning takes place not only when youth see how people behave in the real world but also when they see characters in films and on television, many began to focus on exactly how watching such violent stories increases later aggression. In other words, more recent research really focused on the underlying psychological mechanisms. *In the last 10 years there also has been a huge increase in research on violent video games.* Based on five decades of research on television and film violence and one decade of research on video games, we now have a

pretty clear picture of how exposure to media violence can increase aggression in both the immediate situation as well as in long term contexts. Immediately after consuming some media violence, there is an increase in aggressive behavior tendencies because of several factors.

1. Aggressive thoughts increase, which in turn increase the likelihood that a mild or ambiguous provocation will be interpreted in a hostile fashion.
2. Aggressive (or hostile) emotion increases.
3. General arousal (e.g., heart rate) increases, which tends to increase the dominant behavioral tendency.
4. Youth learn new forms of aggressive behaviors by observing them, and will reenact them almost immediately afterwards if the situational context is sufficiently similar.

Repeated consumption of media violence over time increases aggression across a range of situations and across time because of several related factors.

1. It creates more positive attitudes, beliefs, and expectations regarding aggressive solutions to interpersonal problems. In other words, youth come to believe that aggression is normal, appropriate, and likely to succeed.
2. It also leads to the development of aggressive scripts, which are basically ways of thinking about how the social world works. Heavy media violence consumers tend to view the world in a more hostile fashion.
3. It decreases the cognitive accessibility of nonviolent ways to handle conflict. That is, it becomes harder to even think about nonviolent solutions.
4. It produces an emotional desensitization to aggression and violence. Normally, people have a pretty negative emotional reaction to conflict, aggression, and violence, and this can be seen in their physiological reactions to observation of violence (real or fictional, as in entertainment media). For example, viewing physical violence normally leads to increases in heart rate and blood pressure, as well as to certain brain wave patterns. Such normal negative emotional reactions tend to inhibit aggressive behavior, and can inspire helping behavior. Repeated consumption of media violence reduces these normal negative emotional reactions.

5. Repetition increases learning of any type of skill or way of thinking, to the point where that skill or way of thinking becomes fairly automatic.

3. Is there a difference between the effects of TV/film violence versus video-games violence?

Most of the research has focused on TV/film violence (so-called "passive" media), mainly because they have been around so much longer than video games. However, the existing research literature on violent video games has yielded the same general types of effects as the TV and cinema research. At a theoretical level, *there are reasons to believe that violent video games may have a larger harmful effect than violent TV and film effects.* This is a very difficult research question, and there currently is no definite answer. But, recent studies that directly compare passive screen media to video games tend to find bigger effects of violent video games.

4. Is that why there have been so many school shootings by kids who play lots of violent video games? Can such games turn a normal, well-adjusted child or adolescent into a school shooter?

No, that would be an overstatement, one that mainstream media violence researchers do not make. The best way to think about this is the risk factor approach. There are three important points to keep in mind.

First, there are many causal risk factors involved in the development of a person who frequently behaves in an aggressive or violent manner. There are biological factors, family factors, neighborhood factors, and so on. Media violence is only one of the top dozen or so risk factors.

Second, extreme aggression, such as aggravated assault and homicide, typically occurs only when there are a number of risk factors present. In other words, none of the causal risk factors are "necessary and sufficient" causes of extreme aggression. Of course, cigarette smoking is not a necessary and sufficient cause of lung cancer, even though it is a major cause of it. People with only one risk factor seldom (I'm tempted to say "never") commit murder.

Third, consumption of media violence is the most common of all of the major risk factors for aggression in most modern societies. It also is the least expensive and easiest risk factor for parents to change. In sum, playing a lot of violent games is unlikely to turn a normal youth with zero or one or even two other risk factors into a killer. But regardless of how many other risk factors are present in a youth's life, playing a lot of violent games is likely to increase the frequency and the seriousness of his or her physical aggression, both in the short term and over time as the youth grows up.

5. Are some social groups more susceptible to the negative effects of violent video games than others? Are some groups immune to these effects?

There is some research suggesting that individuals who are already fairly aggressive may be more affected by consumption of violent video games, but it is not yet conclusive. Similarly, video game effects occasionally appear to be larger for males than females, but such findings are rare. Most studies find that males and females are equally affected, and that high and low aggressive individuals are equally affected. One additional point is worth remembering: Scientists have not been able to find any group of people who consistently appear immune to the negative effects of media violence or video game violence.

6. How important is the distinction between realistic violence versus fantasy violence?

This is an extremely important question because it is so frequently misunderstood. Many people, including psychiatrists and psychologists, tend to think: "Well, it is just a game, this boy (girl) is able to understand the difference between it and reality. Let us not worry about it." *One of the great myths surrounding media violence is this notion that if the individual can distinguish between media violence and reality, then it can't have an adverse effect on that individual.* Of course, the conclusion does not logically follow from the premise. And in fact, most of the studies that have demonstrated a causal link between exposure to media violence and subsequent aggressive behavior have been done with individuals who were fully aware that the observed media violence was not reality. For instance, many studies have used young adult participants who knew that the TV show, the movie clip, or the video game to which they were exposed was not "real." These studies still yielded the typical media violence effect on subsequent aggressive behavior.

7. Aren't there studies of violent video games that have found no significant effects on aggression?

Yes, such studies do exist. *In any field of science, some studies will produce effects that differ from what most studies of that type find.* If this weren't true, then one would need to perform only one study on a particular issue and we would have the "true" answer. Unfortunately, science is not that simple.

As an example, consider the hypothesis that a particular coin is "fair," by which I mean that upon tossing it in the air it is equally likely to come up "heads" as "tails." To test this hypothesis, you toss it 4 times, and it comes up heads 3 times (75% heads). I toss it 4 times and get 2 heads (50%). My two graduate students toss it 4 times each, getting 4 tails and 2 heads (0% heads, 50% heads, respectively). Is the coin fair? Why have different people gotten different results? Well, part of the problem is that each of us has conducted a "study" with a sample size that is much too small to produce consistent results. We each should have tossed the coin at least 100 times. Had we done so, each of us would have had about 50% heads (if the coin was truly a "fair" coin). But we still wouldn't have gotten the exact same results. Chance plays some role in the outcome of any experiment. So even if all the conditions of the test are exactly the same, the results will differ to some extent. Of course, in the real world of science, the situation is much more complex. Each study differs somewhat from every other study, usually in several ways.

Given that scientific studies of the same question will yield somewhat different results, purely on the basis of chance, how should we go about summarizing the results of a set of studies? One way is to look at the average outcome across studies. This is essentially what a meta-analysis does. And when one does a meta-analysis on the video game violence research literature, the clear conclusion is that the results are quite consistent. On average there is a clear effect: exposure to violent video games increases subsequent aggression. This has been found for each of the three major research designs (experimental, cross-sectional, and longitudinal), for youth and for young adults, and for youth in North American, Japan, and Western Europe.

Some of the few contradictory studies can be explained as being the result of poor methods. For example, one frequently cited study that failed to find a video game effect did not actually measure aggressive behavior; instead, it measured arguments with a friend or spouse. That same study also failed to show that participants in the "high video game violence" condition actually played more violent games than participants in the "low video game violence" condition. In fact, when you separate studies into those that were well conducted versus those that had major flaws, you find that the well conducted studies found bigger average effects of violent video games on aggression than did the poorly conducted studies. Some well-conducted and some poorly-conducted studies suffer from a too small sample size. But the main point is that even well conducted studies with appropriate sample sizes will not yield identical results. For this reason, any general statements about a research domain must focus on the pooled results, not on individual studies.

8. But what about the claims made by the media industries and by some other media violence experts, who say that the existing research evidence shows no effects of violent media?

The various entertainment media industries have lots of money to spend on trying to convince the general public and political leaders that there is nothing to worry about. And they do spend large sums on this. Unlike the research community, which has no vested interest in the topic, *the media industry is very concerned about profits* and will do almost anything to protect those profits. A recent book by James Steyer titled "The Other Parent: The Inside Story of the Media's Effect on Our Children," reveals much about how this works in the U.S. I suspect that most people would be shocked by many of the revelations contained in this book. I personally have witnessed media industry lobbyists lie about a factual issue, watched them get caught in that lie, and then seen the same lobbyist deliver the same lie to a different group a year later. So, one must distinguish between real vs. industry supported experts.

9. But haven't other media violence experts also claimed that there is no valid scientific evidence linking media violence to aggression?

Yes, and no. The media industries seek out, promote, and support "experts" who will make such claims. There are several such "experts" who have made their careers by bashing legitimate research. Examining their credentials is quite revealing. Many do not have any research training in an appropriate discipline. Of those who do have advanced degrees in an appropriate discipline (for example, social psychology), almost none of them have ever conducted and published original media violence research in a top-quality peer-reviewed scientific journal. That is, they have never designed, carried out, and published a study in which they gathered new data to test scientific hypotheses about potential media violence effects. In other words, they are not truly experts on media violence research. Again, to get at the truth, one must distinguish between actual vs. self-proclaimed (and often industry-backed) experts.

10. Are there any evaluations of the media violence research literature done by groups who have the appropriate expertise but who are not themselves media violence researchers?

Interestingly, a number of professional organizations have asked their own experts to evaluate the media violence research literature. One of the most recent products of such an evaluation was a "Joint Statement on the Impact of Entertainment Violence on Children," issued by six medical and public health professional organizations at a Congressional Public Health Summit on July 26, 2000. This statement noted that ". . . entertainment violence can lead to increases in aggressive attitudes, values, and behavior, particularly in children." The statement also noted that the research points ". . . overwhelmingly to a causal connection between media violence and aggressive behavior in some children." The six signatory organizations were: American Academy of Pediatrics, American Academy of Child & Adolescent Psychiatry, American Medical Association, American Psychological Association, American Academy of Family Physicians, and the American Psychiatric Association. Along the same line, several reports by the U.S. Surgeon General have concluded that exposure to media violence is a significant risk factor for later aggression and violence. Both the American Academy of Pediatrics and the American Psychological Association have specifically addressed the violent video game issue; both concluded that playing violent video games is a causal risk factor for later aggression against others, and called for a reduction in exposure of youth to this risk factor.

11. The claim has been made that in terms of the general public's beliefs about media violence effects, we are currently in a situation that is very similar to where the public was some 30 years ago in the tobacco/lung cancer issue. In what ways are these two cases similar? Dissimilar?

The medical research community knew that cigarette smoking causes lung cancer long before the general public came to hold such beliefs. In fact, there are still sizable numbers of smokers who don't really believe this to be true. The tobacco industry was quite effective keeping the public confused regarding the true causal effect of tobacco on lung cancer. Among other tactics, they promoted "experts" who claimed that the research was badly done, or was inconsistent, or was largely irrelevant to lung cancer in humans. The media industries have been doing much the same thing, seeking out, promoting, and supporting "experts" willing to bash media violence research.

The tobacco industry successfully defended itself against lawsuits for many years. There have been several lawsuits filed in the U.S. against various video game companies in recent years. As far as I know, none have been successful yet. One big difference between the tobacco industry case and the violent media case is that the main sources of information to the public (e.g., TV news shows, newspapers, magazines) are now largely owned by conglomerates that have a vested interest in denying the validity of any research suggesting that there might be harmful effects of repeated exposure to media violence.

The tobacco industry certainly had some influence on the media, because of their advertising revenues, but the violent media industries are essentially a part of the same companies that own and control the news media. Thus, it is likely to be much more difficult for the general public to get an accurate portrayal of the scientific state of knowledge about media violence effects than it was to get an accurate portrayal of the tobacco/lung cancer state of scientific knowledge. Given that it took 30-some years for the public to learn and accept the tobacco/lung cancer findings, it seems unlikely that we'll see a major shift in the public's understanding of media violence effects. Indeed, a study that my colleague Brad Bushman and I published in 2001 suggests that the media violence/aggression link was firmly established scientifically by 1975, and that news reports on this research have gotten less accurate over time. Another big difference is in the proportion of people who were hooked on these risk factors as children. The vast majority of youth repeatedly consume violent media, well before they turn 18; this was never true of tobacco products. This is important in part because of the "third person effect," a psychological phenomenon in which people tend to **think** that they personally are immune to risk factors that can affect others.

12. The U.S. Senate invited you to deliver an expert's opinion on violent video games in March, 2000. Has anything changed in the video game research literature since then?

Yes, since that time a large number of new video game studies have been published. One of the most important developments is that now there have been several major longitudinal studies of violent video game effects on youth. In such studies, the research gathers information about a child's video game habits and their typical level of aggressiveness at two separate points in time. The two time points may be separated by months or years. Sophisticated statistical techniques are used to answer a simple question: Do those who played lots of violent video games at the first measurement time show larger increases in aggression over time than those who played few violent video games? Such longitudinal studies from North America, Europe, and Japan have all found the same answer: Yes.

In addition, my colleagues and I have done several meta-analyses of all of the video game studies. It is even clearer today than it was at that earlier date that violent video games should be of concern to the general public. That is, even stronger statements can now be made on the basis of the scientific literature.

13. What is your advice concerning public policy towards violent entertainment media, particularly violent video games violence managing?

My colleagues and I try very hard to restrict our role in public policy debate to that of an expert media violence researcher. After all, that's what our training is in, and what we have devoted our careers to doing. So, when the U.S. Senate (or anyone else) asks what the current scientific research literature shows, I tell them as plainly and clearly as possible. There is a "correct" answer to such a question, and I do my best to convey that answer. When asked what society should do about it, well, that's a political question that should (in my view) be publicly debated. There is no single "correct" answer to this public policy question because a host of personal values are relevant to the debate, in addition to the relevant scientific facts. In addition, there are legal issues that differ for different countries.

Nonetheless, I am willing to give a vague answer to the public policy question. Given the scientific evidence that exposure to media violence (and video game violence) increases aggression in both the short-term and the long-term, and given my belief that the level of aggression in modern society could and should be reduced, I believe that we need to reduce the exposure of youth to media violence. My preference for action is to somehow convince parents to do a better job of screening inappropriate materials from their children. It is not always an easy task for parents—in part because of poor ratings systems—and perhaps there are appropriate steps that legislative bodies as well as the media industries could take to make it easier for parents to control their children's media diet. But of course, as long as the media industries persist in denying the scientific facts and persist in keeping the general public confused about those facts, many parents won't see a need to screen some violent materials from their children. Ironically, the industry's success in keeping parents confused and in making parental control difficult is precisely what makes many citizens and legislators willing to consider legislation designed to reign in what they perceive to be an industry totally lacking in ethical values. . . .

14. Does violence sell?

Clearly, violence does sell, at least in the video game market. But it is not clear whether the dominance of violent video games is due to an inherent desire for such games, or whether this is merely the result of the fact that most marketing dollars are spent on promoting violent games instead of nonviolent ones. One great irony in all of this is the industry belief that violence is necessary in their product in order to make a profit. One result of that belief is that most of marketing efforts go into marketing violence. In fact, the media has seemingly convinced many people in the U.S. that they like only violent media products. But nonviolent and low violent products can be exciting, fun, and sell well. *Myst* is a good example of an early nonviolent video game that sold extremely well for quite some time. More recent examples include *The Sims*, many sports and racing games, and many simulation games. Interestingly, in some of our studies college students have to play nonviolent video games. Some of the these students report that they have never played nonviolent games, and are surprised to learn that they like some of the nonviolent ones as much as their violent games.

Even more intriguing is recent research on the psychological motivations that underlie judgments about which games are the most fun and worthy of repeat business. Scholars at the University of Rochester conducted six studies on game players' ratings of game enjoyment, value, and desire for future play. They found that games that give the player a lot of autonomy (lots of choices within the game) and feelings of competence (for example, success in overcoming difficulties with practice) were rated much more positively than games without these characteristics, regardless of whether or not the games included violence. In other words, violent games are so popular mainly because such games tend to satisfy both autonomy needs and competence needs, not because they contain violence.

15. So are video games basically bad for youth?

No, a better summary statement is that a well-designed video game is an excellent teaching tool. But what it teaches depends upon its content. Some games teach thinking skills. Some teach math. Some teach reading, or puzzle solving, or history. Some have been designed to teach kids how to manage specific illnesses, such as diabetes, asthma, and cancer. But all games teach something, and that "something" depends on what they require the player to practice. In short, there are many nonviolent games that are fun, exciting, and challenging. Children and adolescents (and adults) like them and can learn positive things from them. Some even get you to exercise muscles other than those in your hands. *In moderation, such games are good for youth*. But parents and educators need to check the content of the games they are considering for the youth in their care. You can't simply use the game ratings, because many games rated by the industry as appropriate for children and for teens contain lots of violence. But with a bit of parental effort, and some household rules about game-playing, the youth's gaming experience can be fun and positive.

Craig A. Anderson is a Professor in the Department of Psychology, University of Iowa. He has written extensively on human behavior and violence.

Henry Jenkins

Reality Bytes: Eight Myths about Video Games Debunked

A large gap exists between the public's perception of video games and what the research actually shows. The following is an attempt to separate fact from fiction.

1. The Availability of Video Games Has Led to an Epidemic of Youth Violence.

According to federal crime statistics, the rate of juvenile violent crime in the United States is at a 30-year low. Researchers find that people serving time for violent crimes typically consume less media before committing their crimes than the average person in the general population. It's true that young offenders who have committed school shootings in America have also been game players. But young people in general are more likely to be gamers—90 percent of boys and 40 percent of girls play. The overwhelming majority of kids who play do NOT commit antisocial acts. According to a 2001 U.S. Surgeon General's report, the strongest risk factors for school shootings centered on mental stability and the quality of home life, not media exposure. The moral panic over violent video games is doubly harmful. It has led adult authorities to be more suspicious and hostile to many kids who already feel cut off from the system. It also misdirects energy away from eliminating the actual causes of youth violence and allows problems to continue to fester.

2. Scientific Evidence Links Violent Game Play with Youth Aggression.

Claims like this are based on the work of researchers who represent one relatively narrow school of research, "media effects." This research includes some 300 studies of media violence. But most of those studies are inconclusive and many have been criticized on methodological grounds. In these studies, media images are removed from any narrative context. Subjects are asked to engage with content that they would not normally consume and may not understand. Finally, the laboratory context is radically different from the environments where games would normally be played. Most studies found a correlation, not a causal relationship, which means the research could simply show that aggressive people like aggressive entertainment. That's why the vague term "links" is used here. If there is a consensus emerging around this research, it is that violent video games may be one risk factor—when coupled with other more immediate, real-world influences—which can contribute to anti-social behavior. But no research has found that video games are a primary factor or that violent video game play could turn an otherwise normal person into a killer.

3. Children Are the Primary Market for Video Games.

While most American kids do play video games, the center of the video game market has shifted older as the first generation of gamers continues to play into adulthood. Already 62 percent of the console market and 66 percent of the PC market is age 18 or older. The game industry caters to adult tastes. Meanwhile, a sizable number of parents ignore game ratings because they assume that games are for kids. One quarter of children ages 11 to 16 identify an M-Rated (Mature Content) game as among their favorites. Clearly, more should be done to restrict advertising and marketing that targets young consumers with mature content, and to educate parents about the media choices they are facing. But parents need to share some of the responsibility for making decisions about what is appropriate for their children. The news on this front is not all bad. The Federal Trade Commission has found that 83 percent of game purchases for underage consumers are made by parents or by parents and children together.

4. Almost No Girls Play Computer Games.

Historically, the video game market has been predominantly male. However, the percentage of women playing games has steadily increased over the past decade. Women now slightly outnumber men playing Web-based games. Spurred by the belief that games were an important gateway into other kinds of digital literacy, efforts were made in the mid-90s to build games that appealed to girls. More recent games such as *The Sims* were huge crossover successes that attracted many women who had never played games before. Given the historic imbalance in the game market (and among people working inside the game industry), the presence of sexist stereotyping in games is hardly surprising. Yet it's also important to note that female game characters are often portrayed as powerful and independent. In his book *Killing Monsters*, Gerard Jones argues that young girls often build upon these representations of strong women warriors as a means of building up their self confidence in confronting challenges in their everyday lives.

5. Because Games Are Used to Train Soldiers to Kill, They Have the Same Impact on the Kids Who Play Them.

Former military psychologist and moral reformer David Grossman argues that because the military uses games in training (including, he claims, training soldiers to shoot and kill), the generation of young people who play such games are similarly being brutalized and conditioned to be aggressive in their everyday social interactions.

Grossman's model only works if:

- we remove training and education from a meaningful cultural context.
- we assume learners have no conscious goals and that they show no resistance to what they are being taught.
- we assume that they unwittingly apply what they learn in a fantasy environment to real world spaces.

The military uses games as part of a specific curriculum, with clearly defined goals, in a context where students actively want to learn and have a need for the information being transmitted. There are consequences for not mastering those skills. That being said, a growing body of research does suggest that games can enhance learning. In his recent book, *What Video Games Have to Teach Us about Learning and Literacy*, James Gee describes game players as active problem solvers who do not see mistakes as errors, but as opportunities for improvement. Players search for newer, better solutions to problems and challenges, he says. And they are encouraged to constantly form and test hypotheses. This research points to a fundamentally different model of how and what players learn from games.

6. Video Games Are Not a Meaningful Form of Expression.

On April 19, 2002, U.S. District Judge Stephen N. Limbaugh Sr. ruled that video games do not convey ideas and thus enjoy no constitutional protection. As evidence, Saint Louis County presented the judge with videotaped excerpts from four games, all within a narrow range of genres, and all the subject of previous controversy. Over-turning a similar decision in Indianapolis, federal Court of Appeals Judge Richard Posner noted: "Violence has always been and remains a central interest of humankind and a recurrent, even obsessive theme of culture both high and low. It engages the interest of children from an early age, as anyone familiar with the classic fairy tales collected by Grimm, Andersen, and Perrault are aware." Posner adds, "To shield children right up to the age of 18 from exposure to violent descriptions and images would not only be quixotic, but deforming; it would leave them unequipped to cope with the world as we know it." Many early games were little more than shooting galleries where players were encouraged to blast everything that moved. Many current games are designed to be ethical testing grounds. They allow players to navigate an expansive and open-ended world, make their own choices and witness their consequences. *The Sims* designer Will Wright argues that games are perhaps the only medium that allows us to experience guilt over the actions of fictional characters. In a movie, one can always pull back and condemn the character or the artist when they cross certain social boundaries. But in playing a game, we choose what happens to the characters. In the right circumstances, we can be encouraged to examine our own values by seeing how we behave within virtual space.

7. Video Game Play Is Socially Isolating.

Much video game play is social. Almost 60 percent of frequent gamers play with friends. Thirty-three percent play with siblings and 25 percent play with spouses or parents. Even games designed for single players are often played socially, with one person giving advice to another holding a joystick. A growing number of games are designed for multiple players—for either cooperative play in the same space or online play with distributed players. Sociologist Talmadge Wright has logged many hours observing online communities interact with and react to violent video games, concluding that meta-gaming (conversation about game content) provides a context for thinking about rules and rule-breaking. In this way there are really two games taking place simultaneously: one, the explicit conflict and combat on the screen; the other, the implicit cooperation and comradeship between the players. Two players may be fighting to death on screen and growing closer as friends off screen. Social expectations are reaffirmed through the social contract governing play, even as they are symbolically cast aside within the transgressive fantasies represented onscreen.

8. Video Game Play Is Desensitizing.

Classic studies of play behavior among primates suggest that apes make basic distinctions between play fighting and actual combat. In some circumstances, they seem to take pleasure wrestling and tousling with each other. In others, they might rip each other apart in mortal combat. Game designer and play theorist Eric Zimmerman describes the ways we understand play as distinctive from reality as entering the "magic circle." The same action—say, sweeping a floor—may take on different meanings in play (as in playing house) than in reality (housework). Play allows kids to express feelings and impulses that have to be carefully held in check in their real-world interactions. Media reformers argue that playing violent video games can cause a lack of empathy for real-world victims. Yet, a child who responds to a video game the same way he or she responds to a real-world tragedy could be showing symptoms of being severely emotionally disturbed.

Here's where the media effects research, which often uses punching rubber dolls as a marker of real-world aggression, becomes problematic. The kid who is punching a toy designed for this purpose is still within the "magic circle" of play and understands her actions on those terms. Such research shows us only that violent play leads to more violent play.

Henry Jenkins is the Director of the Comparative Media Studies program at MIT. He has co-authored several books, including *Democracy and the New Media* (MIT Press, 2003).

EXPLORING THE ISSUE

Do Video Games Encourage Violent Behavior?

Critical Thinking and Reflection

1. How are the effects of video games suggested in the YES and NO selections different from one another? Do they share any similarities?
2. How can the virtual world influence behaviors and thoughts in the real world? Do games shape values? Are video games different from other types of media content?
3. What are some of the assumptions that underlie social science research? How do they differ from the assumptions that underlie the cultural approach of Jenkins?
4. As a future parent, what rules would you set regarding your teens' use of violent video games?
5. Currently video games are rated. What, if any, other public policy regulations would be appropriate?

Is There Common Ground?

Anderson argues for negative effects on individuals. Jenkins points to a lack of change in the social order due to video games. Can both be true? Dr. Anderson et al. in a 2003 study says "The 14-year-old boy arguing that he has played violent video games for years and has not ever killed anybody is absolutely correct in rejecting the extreme 'necessary and sufficient' position, as is the 45-year-old two-pack-a-day cigarette smoker who notes that he still does not have lung cancer. But both are wrong in inferring that their exposure to their respective risk factors (violent media, cigarettes) has not causally increased the likelihood that they and people around them will one day suffer the consequences of that risky behavior." Perhaps it is in rejecting the extremes of both sides that common ground will be found.

Dramatic anecdotes abound concerning the violent consequences of video games. Yet history shows that moral panics abate as new media or other social changes emerge in the social world and become the target of public concern. Perhaps time gives context and perspective; perhaps it just diverts attention. But issues of importance, such as the impact of media on behavior should not be forgotten.

Create Central

www.mhhe.com/createcentral

Additional Resources

Craig A. Anderson, Douglas A. Gentile, and Katherine E. Buckley, *Violent Video Game Effects on Children and Adolescents: Theory, Research, and Public Policy* (Oxford University Press, 2007)

An edited volume that offers additional studies of violent video game effects. Studies test theories to explain these consequences and then consider public policy.

Peter Vorderer and Jennings Bryant (eds). *Playing Video Games: Motives, Responses, and Consequences* (Wiley, 2006)

This volume offers a multidisciplinary approach to the media psychology of video games.

Bernard Perron and Mark J. P. Wolf (eds). *The Video Game Theory Reader 2* (Routledge, 2008)

These articles address the many ways in which video games are shaping entertainment with a focus on the theories that may help us to understand their importance.

Thomas A. Hemphill. "The Entertainment Industry, Marketing Practices, and Violent Content: Who's Minding the Children?" *Business and Society Review* (vol. 108, pp. 263–277, 2003)

Hemphill examines the way the entertainment industry targets young audiences.

Kaveri Subrahmanyam and Patricia Greenfield, "Digital Media and Youth: Games, Internet and Development," in Singer and Singer (eds), *Handbook of Children and the Media* (Sage, 2011).

The *Handbook* offers extensive coverage of a variety of issues concerning children. Subrahmanyam and Greenfield offer a balanced review of existing issues concerning video games.

Internet References . . .

American Academy of Child & Adolescent Psychiatry

www.aacap.org/AACAP/Families_and_Youth/Facts_
for_Families/Facts_for_Families_Pages/Children_
and_Video_Games_Playing_with_Violence_91.aspx

Entertainment Consumers Association

www.theeca.com/video_games_violence

New York Times

www.nytimes.com/2013/02/12/science/studying-the-
effects-of-playing-violent-video-games.html

Rolling Stone

www.rollingstone.com/culture/pictures/12-horrifyingly-
violent-video-games-20131011

Video Game Addiction

www.video-game-addiction.org/violence.html

Article   Prepared by: Daniel Mittleman, *DePaul University*

The Truth about Video Games and Gun Violence

Aaron Alexis reportedly loved first-person shooters. Does that explain his mass killing at the Washington Navy Yard?

ERIK KAIN

Learning Outcomes

After reading this article, you will be able to:

- Summarize the research on the connection between video game playing and violence.

- Aritculate why it is difficult to research the relationship between video game playing and violence.

- Understand and articulate both the costs and benefits of game playing among a large subset of our population.

It was one of the most brutal video games imaginable—players used cars to murder people in broad daylight. Parents were outraged, and behavioral experts warned of real-world carnage. "In this game a player takes the first step to creating violence," a psychologist from the National Safety Council told the *New York Times*. "And I shudder to think what will come next if this is encouraged. It'll be pretty gory."

To earn points, Death Race encouraged players to mow down pedestrians. Given that it was 1976, those pedestrians were little pixel-gremlins[1] in a 2-D black-and-white universe that bore almost no recognizable likeness to real people.

Indeed, the debate about whether violent video games lead to violent acts by those who play them goes way back. The public reaction to Death Race can be seen as an early predecessor to the controversial Grand Theft Auto[2] three decades later and the many other graphically violent and hyper-real games of today, including the slew of new titles debuting at the E3 gaming[3]summit[3] this week in Los Angeles.

In the wake of the Newtown massacre and numerous other recent mass shootings,[4] familiar condemnations of and questions about these games have reemerged. Here are some answers.

Who's claiming video games cause violence in the real world?

Though conservatives tend to raise it more frequently, this bogeyman plays across the political spectrum, with regular calls for more research, more regulations, and more censorship. The tragedy in Newtown set off a fresh wave:

Donald Trump tweeted:[5] "Video game violence & glorification must be stopped—it's creating monsters!" Ralph Nader likened violent video games to "electronic child molesters."[6] (His outlandish rhetoric was meant to suggest that parents need to be involved in the media their kids consume.) MSNBC's Joe Scarborough asserted that the government has a right to regulate[7] video games, despite a Supreme Court ruling to the contrary.[8]

Unsurprisingly, the most over-the-top talk came from the National Rifle Association:

"Guns don't kill people. Video games, the media, and Obama's budget kill people," NRA Executive Vice President Wayne LaPierre said at a press conference[9] one week after the mass shooting at Sandy Hook Elementary. He continued without irony: "There exists in this country, sadly, a callous, corrupt and corrupting shadow industry that sells and stows violence against its own people through vicious, violent video games with names like Bulletstorm, Grand Theft Auto, Mortal Kombat, and Splatterhouse."

Has the rhetoric led to any government action?

Yes. Amid a flurry of broader legislative activity on gun violence,[10] since Newtown there have been proposals specifically focused on video games. Among them:

State Rep. Diane Franklin, a Republican in Missouri, sponsored a state bill[11] that would impose a 1 percent tax on violent games, the revenues of which would go toward "the treatment of mental-health conditions associated with exposure to violent video games." (The bill has since been withdrawn.) Vice President Joe Biden[12] has also promoted this idea.

Rep. Jim Matheson (D-Utah) proposed a federal bill[13] that would give the Entertainment Software Rating Board's ratings system the weight of the law, making it illegal to sell Mature-rated games to minors, something Gov. Chris Christie (R-N.J.) has also proposed for his home state.[14]

A bill introduced in the Senate by Sen. Jay Rockefeller (D-W.Va.) proposed studying the impact of violent video games on children.[15]

So who actually plays these games and how popular are they?

While many of the top selling games in history have been various Mario and Pokemon titles, games from the the first-person-shooter genre, which appeal in particular to teen boys and young men, are also huge sellers.

The new king of the hill is Activision's Call of Duty: Black Ops II, which surpassed Wii Play as the No. 1 grossing game[16] in 2012. Call of Duty is now one of the most successful franchises in video game history, topping charts year after year and boasting around 40 million active monthly users playing one of the franchise's games over the internet. (Which doesn't even include people playing the game offline.) There is already much anticipation for the release later this year of Call of Duty: Ghosts.

The Battlefield games from Electronic Arts also sell millions of units with each release. Irrational Games' BioShock Infinite, released in March, has sold nearly 4 million units and is one of the most violent games to date. (Read *MoJo*'s interview[17] with Irrational's cofounder and creative director, Ken Levine.)

What research has been done on the link between video games and violence, and what does it really tell us?

Studies on how violent video games affect behavior date to the mid 1980s, with conflicting results. Since then there have been at least two dozen studies[18] conducted on the subject.

"Video Games, Television, and Aggression in Teenagers," published by the University of Georgia in 1984, found that playing arcade games was linked to increases in physical aggression. But a study published a year later by the Albert Einstein College of Medicine, "Personality, Psychopathology, and Developmental Issues in Male Adolescent Video Game Use," found that arcade games have a "calming effect" and that boys use them to blow off steam. Both studies relied on surveys and interviews asking boys and young men about their media consumption.

Studies grew more sophisticated over the years, but their findings continued to point in different directions. A 2011 study found that people who had played competitive games, regardless of whether they were violent or not, exhibited increased aggression. In 2012, a different study found that cooperative playing in the graphically violent Halo II made the test subjects more cooperative even outside of video game playing.

Metastudies—comparing the results and the methodologies of prior research on the subject—have also been problematic.

One published in 2010 by the American Psychological Association, analyzing data from multiple studies and more than 130,000 subjects, concluded that "violent video games increase aggressive thoughts, angry feelings, and aggressive behaviors and decrease empathic feelings and pro-social behaviors." But results from another metastudy showed that most studies of violent video games over the years suffered from publication biases that tilted the results toward foregone correlative conclusions.

Why is it so hard to get good research on this subject?

"I think that the discussion of media forms—particularly games—as some kind of serious social problem is often an attempt to kind of corral and solve what is a much broader social issue," says Carly Kocurek, a professor of Digital Humanities at the Illinois Institute of Technology. "Games aren't developed in a vacuum, and they reflect the cultural milieu that produces them. So of course we have violent games."

There is also the fundamental problem of measuring violent outcomes ethically and effectively.

"I think anybody who tells you that there's any kind of consistency to the aggression research is lying to you," Christopher J. Ferguson, associate professor of psychology and criminal justice at Texas A&M International University, told *Kotaku*.[19] "There's no consistency in the aggression literature, and my impression is that at this point it is not strong enough to draw any kind of causal, or even really correlational links between video game violence and aggression, no matter how weakly we may define aggression."

Moreover, determining why somebody carries out a violent act like a school shooting can be very complex; underlying mental-health issues are almost always present. More than half of mass shooters[20] over the last 30 years had mental-health problems.

But America's consumption of violent video games must help explain our inordinate rate of gun violence, right?

Actually, no. A look at global video game spending per capita in relation to gun death statistics reveals that gun deaths in the United States far outpace those in other countries—including countries with higher per capita video game spending.

A 10-country comparison[21] from the *Washington Post* shows the United States as the clear outlier in this regard. Countries with the highest per capita spending on video games, such as the Netherlands and South Korea, are among the safest countries in the world when it comes to guns. In other words, America plays about the same number of violent video games per capita as the rest of the industrialized world, despite that we far outpace every other nation in terms of gun deaths.

Or, consider it this way: With violent video game sales almost always at the top of the charts,[22] why do so few gamers turn into homicidal shooters? In fact, the number of violent youth offenders in the United States fell by more than half between 1994 and 2010—while video game sales more than doubled since 1996. A working paper from economists on violence and video game sales published in 2011 found that higher rates of violent video game sales in fact correlated with a decrease in crimes, especially violent crimes.

I'm still not convinced. A bunch of mass shooters were gamers, right?

Some mass shooters over the last couple of decades have had a history with violent video games. The Newtown shooter, Adam Lanza, was reportedly "obsessed" with video games. Norway shooter Anders Behring Breivik was said to have played World of Warcraft for 16 hours a day until he gave up the game in favor of Call of Duty: Modern Warfare, which he claimed he used to train with a rifle.[23] Aurora theater shooter James Holmes was reportedly a fan of violent video games[24] and movies such as *The Dark Knight*. (Holmes reportedly went so far as to mimic the Joker by dying his hair prior to carrying out his attack.)

Jerald Block, a researcher and psychiatrist in Portland, Oregon, stirred controversy when he concluded that Columbine shooters Eric Harris and Dylan Klebold carried out their rampage after their parents took away their video games. According to the *Denver Post*,[25] Block said that the two had relied on the virtual world of computer games to express their rage, and that cutting them off in 1998 had sent them into crisis.

But that's clearly an oversimplification. The age and gender[26] of many mass shooters, including Columbine's, places them right in the target demographic for first-person-shooter (and most other) video games. And people between ages 18 and 25 also tend to report the highest rates of mental-health issues.[27] Harris and Klebold's complex mental-health problems have been well documented.[28]

To hold up a few sensational examples as causal evidence between violent games and violent acts ignores the millions of other young men and women who play violent video games and never go on a shooting spree in real life. Furthermore, it's very difficult to determine empirically whether violent kids are simply drawn to violent forms of entertainment, or if the entertainment somehow makes them violent. Without solid scientific data to go on, it's easier to draw conclusions that confirm our own biases.

How is the industry reacting to the latest outcry over violent games?

Moral panic over the effects of violent video games on young people has had an impact on the industry over the years, says Kocurek, noting that "public and government pressure has driven the industry's efforts to self regulate."

In fact, it is among the best when it comes to abiding by its own voluntary ratings system, with self-regulated retail sales of Mature-rated games to minors lower than in any other entertainment field.[14]

But is that enough? Even conservative judges think there should be stronger laws regulating these games, right?

There have been two major Supreme Court cases involving video games and attempts by the state to regulate access to video games. *Aladdin's Castle, Inc. v. City of Mesquite* in 1983 and *Brown v. Entertainment Merchants Association* in 2011.

"Both cases addressed attempts to regulate youth access to games, and in both cases, the court held that youth access can't be curtailed," Kocurek says.

In *Brown v. EMA,* the Supreme Court found that the research simply wasn't compelling enough to spark government action, and that video games, like books and film, were protected by the First Amendment.

"Parents who care about the matter can readily evaluate the games their children bring home," Justice Antonin Scalia wrote when the Supreme Court deemed California's video game censorship bill unconstitutional in *Brown v. EMA*. "Filling the remaining modest gap in concerned-parents' control can hardly be a compelling state interest."

So how can we explain the violent acts of some kids who play these games?

For her part, Kocurek wonders if the focus on video games is mostly a distraction from more important issues. "When we talk about violent games," she says, "we are too often talking about something else and looking for a scapegoat."

In other words, violent video games are an easy thing to blame for a more complex problem. Public policy debates, she says, need to focus on serious research into the myriad factors that may contribute to gun violence. This may include video games— but a serious debate needs to look at the dearth of mental-health care[29] in America, our abundance of easily accessible weapons, our highly flawed background-check system, and other factors.

There is at least one practical approach to violent video games, however, that most people would agree on: Parents should think deliberately about purchasing these games for their kids. Better still, they should be involved in the games their kids play as much as possible so that they can know first-hand whether the actions and images they're allowing their children to consume are appropriate or not.

References

1. www.retrogamer.net/show_image.php?imageID=2833
2. www.theguardian.com/technology/grand-theft-auto
3. www.techradar.com/us/news/gaming/e3-2013-10-things-we-expect-from-the-show-1139138
4. www.motherjones.com/special-reports/2012/12/guns-in-america-mass-shootings
5. https://twitter.com/realDonaldTrump/status/280812064539283457
6. www.politico.com/story/2013/01/nader-inauguration-political-bullsh-t-86479.html?hp=r6
7. www.youtube.com/watch?v=CG1roDmFQAg
8. http://thinkprogress.org/alyssa/2011/06/27/254812/supreme-court-rules-against-video-game-censorship-7-2/
9. http://usnews.nbcnews.com/_news/2013/01/15/16524425-new-practice-range-app-says-its-from-nra-which-blamed-video-games-for-violence?lite
10. www.motherjones.com/mojo/2013/03/crazy-gun-laws-newtown
11. www.polygon.com/2013/1/16/3882840/mo-house-bill-violent-video-game-tax
12. www.geek.com/games/joe-biden-floats-idea-of-a-violent-video-game-tax-1555101/
13. http://venturebeat.com/2013/01/17/deja-vu-new-bill-would-give-esrb-ratings-the-force-of-law/

14. www.motherjones.com/mojo/2013/04/chris-christie-violent-video-games-guns

15. www.huffingtonpost.com/2012/12/19/video-games-sandy-hook_n_2330741.html

16. www.gamespot.com/news/npd-black-ops-ii-is-us-top-selling-game-of-2012-6402271

17. www.motherjones.com/media/2013/05/irrational-games-bioshock-infinite-creator-ken-levine-interview

18. http://kotaku.com/5976781/25-video-game-violence-studies-summarized

19. http://kotaku.com/5976733/do-video-games-make-you-violent-an-in+depth-look-at-everything-we-know-today

20. www.motherjones.com/politics/2012/11/jared-loughner-mass-shootings-mental-illness

21. www.washingtonpost.com/blogs/worldviews/wp/2012/12/17/ten-country-comparison-suggests-theres-little-or-no-link-between-video-games-and-gun-murders/

22. www.guardian.co.uk/world/interactive/2013/apr/30/violence-guns-best-selling-video-games

23. http://news.yahoo.com/norway-killer-sharpened-aim-playing-video-game-213107800.html

24. http://latimesblogs.latimes.com/lanow/2012/07/colorado-shooter-enjoyed-video-games-movies-school-friend-says.html

25. www.denverpost.com/headlines/ci_6300370

26. www.motherjones.com/politics/2012/07/mass-shootings-map

27. www.nimh.nih.gov/statistics/SMI_AASR.shtml

28. www.davecullen.com/columbine/faq.htm

29. www.motherjones.com/politics/2013/04/mental-health-crisis-mac-mcclelland-cousin-murder

Critical Thinking

1. Do we know whether video games cause violence in the real world? What do we actually know about the relationship between video games and violence, and what questions remain unanswered?

2. If someone who commits a violent act is also a video game player, is this evidence that video game playing causes violence? Explain your position.

3. Take a look at the web resources at the end of this article. Do politicians and newscasters accurately portray what we know about the relationship between video game playing and violence? What factors do you think influence those who speak out on this subject?

Create Central

www.mhhe.com/createcentral

Internet References

How Virtual Reality Games Can Impact Society, Encourage Prosperity
www.pbs.org/newshour/bb/business/july-dec13/games_07-11.html

Jane McGonigal: Gaming Can Make a Better World
www.ted.com/talks/jane_mcgonigal_gaming_can_make_a_better_world.html

Lawmakers Neglect Facts on Video Games and Gun Violence
www.psychologytoday.com/blog/talking-about-trauma/201306/lawmakers-neglect-facts-video-games-and-gun-violence

Media Figures Say Guns Don't Kill People, Video Games Do
http://mediamatters.org/blog/2013/09/17/media-figures-say-guns-dont-kill-people-video-g/195921

Navy Yard Shooting & Gun Violence Causes
www.colbertnation.com/the-colbert-report-videos/429165/september-18-2013/navy-yard-shooting—gun-violence-causes

Article   Prepared by: Patricia Hrusa Williams,
                                                                   University of Maine at Farmington

Terrorism in the Home

Eleven myths and facts about domestic violence

VICTOR M. PARACHIN

Learning Outcomes

After reading this article, you will be able to:

- Identify the signs of domestic violence.

- Understand several causes or factors associated with the occurrence of domestic violence.

- Explain strategies which may be effective in reaching out to and assisting victims.

If anything is truly equal opportunity, it is battering. Domestic violence crosses all socioeconomic, ethnic, racial, educational, age, and religious lines.

— K. J. Wilson, *When Violence Begins At Home*

Sadly, a U.S. Department of Justice study indicates that approximately one million violent crimes are committed by former spouses, boyfriends, or girlfriends each year, with 85 percent of the victims being women. For domestic violence to be defeated, it must begin with information. Here are 11 myths and facts about domestic violence.

Myth 1: Domestic violence is only physical.

Fact: Abusive actions against another person can be verbal, emotional, sexual, and physical.
  There are four basic types of domestic violence:
- Physical (shoving, slapping, punching, pushing, hitting, kicking, and restraining)
- Sexual (when one partner forces unwanted, unwelcome, uninvited sexual acts upon another)
- Psychological (verbal and emotional abuse, threats, intimidations, stalking, swearing, insulting, isolation from family and friends, forced financial dependence)
- Attacks against property and pets (breaking household objects, hitting walls, abusing or killing beloved pets)

Myth 2: Domestic violence is not common.

Fact: While precise statistics are difficult to determine, all signs indicate that domestic violence is more common than most people believe or want to believe. Here's one example: due to lack of space, shelters for battered women are able to admit only 10 to 40 percent of women who request admission. Another example is from divorced women. Though they make up less than 8 percent of the U.S. population, they account for 75 percent of all battered women and report being assaulted 14 times more often than women still living with a partner. Whatever statistics are available are believed to be low because domestic violence is often not reported.

Myth 3: Domestic violence affects only women.

Fact: Abuse can happen to anyone! It can be directed at women, men, children, the elderly. It takes place among all social classes and all ethnic groups. However, women are the most targeted victims of domestic violence. Here are some statistics:
- One in four American women report being physically assaulted and/or raped by a current or former spouse, cohabiting partner, or date at some time in their life.
- According to the FBI, a woman is beaten every 15 seconds.
- In 1996, 30 percent of all female murder victims in the United States were slain by their husbands or boyfriends.
- Around the world, at least one in every three women has been beaten, coerced into sex, or otherwise abused in her lifetime.
- While men are victims of domestic abuse, 92 percent of those subjected to violence are women.

Myth 4: Domestic violence occurs only among lower class or minority or rural communities.

Fact: Domestic violence crosses all race and class lines. Similar rates of abuse are reported in cities, suburbs, and rural areas, according to the Bureau of Justice. Abusers can be found living in mansions as well as in mobile homes. Susan Weitzman,

Ph.D., is author of the book *Not to People Like Us: Hidden Abuse in Upscale Marriages*. In her book, Dr. Weitzman presents case-by-case studies of domestic violence in families with higher than average incomes and levels of education.

Myth 5: Battered women can just leave.

Fact: A combination of factors makes it very difficult for the abused to leave. These include: family and social pressure, shame, financial barriers, children, religious beliefs. Up to 50 percent of women with children fleeing domestic violence become homeless because they leave the abuser. Also, many who are abused face psychological ambivalence about leaving. One woman recalls: "My body still ached from being beaten by my husband a day earlier. But he kept pleading through the door. 'I'm sorry. I'll never do that to you again. I know I need help.' I had a 2-week-old baby. I wanted to believe him. I opened the door." Her abuse continued for two more years before she gained the courage to leave.

Myth 6: Abuse takes place because of alcohol or drugs.

Fact: Substance abuse does not cause domestic violence. However, drugs and alcohol do lower inhibitions while increasing the level of violence, often to more dangerous levels. The U.S. Department of Health and Human Services estimates that one-quarter to one-half of abusers have substance abuse issues.

Myth 7: They can just fight back or walk away.

Fact: Dealing with domestic violence is never as simple as fighting back or walking out the door. "Most domestic abusers are men who are physically stronger than the women they abuse," notes Joyce Zoldak in her book *When Danger Hits Home: Survivors of Domestic Violence*. "In the case of elder abuse, the victims' frail condition may limit their being able to defend themselves. When a child is being abused, the adult guardian is far more imposing—both physically and psychologically—than the victim."

Myth 8: The victim provoked the violence.

Fact: The abuser is completely responsible for the abuse. No one can say or do anything which warrants being beaten and battered. Abusers often try to deflect their responsibility by blaming the victim via comments such as: "You made me angry." "You made me jealous." "This would never have happened if you hadn't done that." "I didn't mean to do that, but you were out of control." Victims need to be assured that the abuse is not their fault.

Myth 9: Domestic abuse is a private matter and it's none of my business.

Fact: We all have a responsibility to care for one another. Officials at the National Domestic Violence Hotline offer this advice to people who see or suspect domestic violence: "Yes, it is your business. Maybe he's your friend, your brother-in-law, your cousin, co-worker, gym partner, or fishing buddy. You've noticed that he interrupts her, criticizes her family, yells at her, or scares her. You hope that when they're alone, it isn't worse. The way he treats her makes you uncomfortable, but you don't want to make him mad or lose his friendship. You surely don't want to see him wreck his marriage or have to call the police. What can you do? Say something. If you don't, your silence is the same as saying abuse is OK. He could hurt someone, or end up in jail. Because you care, you need to do something—before it is too late."

Myth 10: Partners need couples counseling.

Fact: It is the abuser alone who needs counseling in order to change behavior. Social Worker Susan Schechter says couples counseling is "an inappropriate intervention that further endangers the woman." Schechter explains her position: "It encourages the abuser to blame the victim by examining her 'role' in his problem. By seeing the couple together, the therapist erroneously suggests that the partner, too, is responsible for the abuser's behavior. Many women have been brutally beaten following couples counseling sessions in which they disclosed violence or coercion. The abuser alone must take responsibility for assaults and understand that family reunification is not his treatment goal: the goal is to stop the violence."

Myth 11: Abusers are evil people.

Fact: "Anyone can find himself or herself in an abusive situation, and most of us could also find ourselves tempted to be abusive to others, no matter how wrong we know it to be," notes Joyce Zoldak. Abusers are people who may be strong and stable in some areas of their lives but weak, unreasonable and out of control in other ways. This does not excuse their behavior, because abuse is always wrong. Abusers need to be held accountable for their actions and encouraged to seek help promptly by meeting with a psychologist, psychiatrist, therapist, or spiritual leader. Abusers can also receive help from The National Domestic Violence Hotline 1-800-799-7233 or via their website: http://www.thehotline.org.

With an informed community, and with the help of family and friends, the cycle of abuse can be broken.

Critical Thinking

1. What are some impediments or reasons why women do not report domestic violence?

2. What are some reasons why domestic violence occurs in couple relationships and in families?

3. Explain why it can be difficult to identify and assist victims.

4. Why do you think some of these myths about domestic violence persist?

5. Given the information in the article, what do you think may be effective strategies which can be used to reach out to and assist victims of domestic violence?

Create Central

www.mhhe.com/createcentral

Internet References

Futures Without Violence
www.futureswithoutviolence.org

National Coalition Against Domestic Violence
www.ncadv.org

National Network to End Domestic Violence
www.nnedv.org

National Resource Center on Domestic Violence
www.nrcdv.org

VICTOR M. PARACHIN writes from Tulsa, Oklahoma.

CHAPTER VII
Violence Against Women

In the past 30 years, research on violence against women has demonstrated that women of all backgrounds have experienced violence, often at the hands of men they love. In fact, the far-ranging physical and emotional consequences of violence against women make it a major public health and criminal justice concern in the United States.[1] Whether in the form of rape, domestic violence, or childhood sexual abuse, violence against women represents an abuse of power in a misogynist culture. When violence occurs in the family, as in the case of domestic violence and incest, a cloak of privacy surrounds it, frequently silencing its victims. The feminist insistence on the political nature of private life enabled women to talk about the experience of violence, revealing how widespread it was and shattering the myths surrounding it.

The roots of domestic violence, sometimes referred to as "intimate partner violence," lie in the soil of the patriarchal family. The belief that a wife is the possession of a male "head of household" who should control the behavior of all other family members is deeply embedded in many social traditions. Women's disadvantaged position in the workforce and their continued responsibility for child raising reinforces their economic dependence on husbands and partners, making it difficult for women to leave abusive relationships. For years, domestic violence eluded the criminal justice system because police were reluctant to interfere in family life. Women who have been trained all their lives to believe that they should accommodate men's needs and fix any problems that arise in their relationships are often trapped in violent relationships by their own feelings of guilt and shame. Many women in abusive relationships have ambivalent feelings about their abuser. It is difficult to believe that a relationship created out of love has become abusive. While women often feel betrayed by men who abuse them, periods of relative harmony can reinforce women's belief that they can reform their abusers and rescue their relationships.

In the past three decades, women have organized to make the criminal justice system more effective in dealing with domestic violence by educating police and changing laws to ensure that women get the protection they need from law enforcement agencies. Because of the pervasiveness of technologies like cell phones and the Internet, shielding women from abusers is, in many cases, made more difficult today. The shelters and "safe houses" that have been created over the past three decades remain a central support system for women fleeing abusive relationships, and, in light of these now-commonplace technologies, vital to protecting women's privacy. Unfortunately, these shelters can temporarily house only a fraction of those who need them.

In 1996 the trial of O. J. Simpson, a star football player charged with the murder of his wife, Nicole Simpson, focused the country's attention on the prevalence of domestic violence as evidence of Simpson's violent treatment of Nicole surfaced during the trial. More recent high-profile instances of intimate partner violence,

---

[1]Patricia Tjaden and Nancy Thoennes, "Full Report of the Prevalence, Incidence, and Consequences of Violence Against Women," U.S. Department of Justice document NCJ 183781, November 2000.

494   *CHAPTER VII: VIOLENCE AGAINST WOMEN*

like the abuse of singer Rihanna at the hands of Chris Brown, reveal that violence against women is more openly discussed than it has been in the recent past, and that victims today are more likely to know where to turn for help. Despite these advances, however, violence remains a part of the lives of far too many women and their children; recent statistics indicate that, every year, approximately 1.3 million U.S. women are physically assaulted by an intimate partner.[2]

Sexual violence affects the lives of all women. Fear of rape shapes women's behavior from girlhood, restricting their movement and limiting their freedom. This fear pervades both public and private spaces. The persistence of street harassment, for example, turns public spaces into hostile environments that exacerbate the fear of sexual violence and, ultimately, inhibit women's freedom. But despite the precautions women learn to take, thousands of women and girls are raped and molested each year. A national survey of women 18 years and older in the United States found that one in six women has been a victim of attempted or completed rape. Additionally, it was estimated that 876,064 women are raped each year in the United States, and the majority of them are raped by men they know (present or former spouse, boyfriend, or date).[3] Rape, however, is a grossly underreported crime. The FBI estimates that only about 16 percent of all rapes are reported. Overall, researchers acknowledge the difficulty of accurately assessing the prevalence of rape and suggest that, depending on how rape is defined, 20 to 27 percent of women have reported being victims of rape or attempted rape.[4]

In spite of its pervasiveness, women's experience of sexual violence was, until the late 1970s, rarely discussed in public. Susan Griffin's 1979 article, "Rape: The All-American Crime," broke the silence about rape and called attention to the ways that images of sexual violence pervade Western culture. Susan Brownmiller's comprehensive study, *Against Our Will*, continued this investigation, tracing the history of rape in Western culture and demonstrating that, far from being a problem of individual "psychopaths," sexual violence against women has been reinforced by our legal and criminal justice system, as well as prevailing ideas about gender and sexuality.[5] The belief that women are the sexual property of men was, until recently, embodied in state legal statutes that exempted married men from prosecution for raping their wives. As a result of pressure on state legislatures by feminist groups, by the late 1980s the last of the state marital rape exemption laws were repealed, making it illegal in all 50 states for a man to rape his wife.[6] The notion that women are responsible for male sexual behavior is reflected in the humiliating questions rape victims are often asked about their sexual histories and contributes to the low rate of conviction in rape trials. Such victim-blaming occurs not only in the courtroom but

[2]Ibid.

[3]Ibid.

[4]Maria Bevacqua, *Rape on the Public Agenda: Feminism and the Politics of Sexual Assault* (Boston: Northeastern University Press, 2000).

[5]Susan Brownmiller, *Against Our Will: Men, Women and Rape* (New York: Simon and Schuster, 1975).

[6]http://www.wellesley.edu/WCW/mrape.html.

also in everyday discourse, making it difficult for many rape survivors to come forward and press charges against their attackers. Feminist activism has resulted in the enactment of "rape shield laws," state statutes that prohibit defense attorneys from bringing the victim's sexual history into the court proceedings, but many state laws include exceptions that allow evidence of sexual relations between the victim and the accused to be presented in court.[7]

Racism has shaped the experience of rape in this culture, from the systematic rape of enslaved African-American women to the false charges of rape that were used as a pretext for lynching African-American men in the South in the late nineteenth and early twentieth century. African-American rape victims are less frequently believed by white juries, and African-American men are more frequently convicted. The popular myth of the black rapist obscures the realities that most rapes are committed by men who are of the same race as their victims, and that the majority of men arrested for rape in 2000 were white.[8]

Among the myriad misconceptions that surround the subject of rape is the notion that most rapes are committed by strangers. In fact, researchers estimate that 60 to 80 percent of all rapes are acquaintance rapes, many of which occur in dating situations. The traditions of sexual conquest, in which women are seen as sexual objects and male sexuality is assumed to be uncontrollable, make it particularly difficult for the victims of date rape to speak out and be taken seriously. Male culture on college campuses, particularly in fraternities, has encouraged the treatment of women as sexual prey and has celebrated male lust and conquest. The proliferation of drug-induced rape via Rohypnol, the "date rape drug," has increased women's fears of acquaintance rape. Wherever it occurs, rape is a powerful expression of women's subordinate status. To combat it demands asserting that women have a right to say no to unwanted sex and to be seen as sexual actors, not objects.

The sexual abuse of young girls by a trusted adult is another form of sexual violence that has surfaced in shocking proportions in recent years. Researchers estimate that one in four girls is a victim of childhood sexual abuse. Girls are often painfully confused when molested by an adult from whom they crave attention and approval. Feelings of betrayal often follow young women into adulthood, as they attempt to deal with the emotional consequences of abuse. Like the other forms of sexual violence, the molestation of girl children is an egregious violation of female bodily integrity and a cruel, abusive exercise of power.

Because they confront us with some of the most horrifying consequences of gender inequity, the essays and stories in this chapter are upsetting. But silence about these issues has never served women well; only by hearing women's stories and engaging in feminist research can we understand the nature of violence against women and take action against it.

---

[7]Gloria Allred and Margery Summers, "Rape Shield Laws," *Ms.*, Spring 2004.
[8]FBI Uniform Crime Reports, *Forcible Rape,* 2000.

Violence in Intimate Relationships

Physical violence directed at women by their intimate partners has made the home a frightening and dangerous place for the millions of women who are abused each year. While the seven pieces in this section examine violence by intimate partners from a variety of perspectives, the first selection, "Understanding Intimate Partner Violence" by Michele McKeon, details and dispels the "myths and misperceptions" that prevent many people from understanding the experiences of battered women and the reasons that they stay in abusive relationships. Some people assume that if "it really was that bad" women would just leave. Others think that "if she learned to stay out of the way, she wouldn't get hurt." These misconceptions hinder our ability to see partner abuse as a social problem, intimately connected to power relationships within and outside of the home. The pieces in this section demonstrate that social and economic realities often deter battered women from leaving abusive relationships, and cultural norms make it difficult for women to get support from their communities. Some women, though, do manage to leave abusive relationships, as demonstrated by the courageous woman in "The Club," by Mitsuye Yamada.

Violence against women comes in varied forms; sometimes, as in "La Princesa," it happens to women who are successful and independent; sometimes, as bell hooks points out, it is only an occasional incident. Women in some immigrant communities, such as those discussed by Margaretta Wan Lin and Cheng Imm Tan in "Holding Up More Than Half the Heavens," find it difficult to resist violent men, whose "right" to abuse their wives is condoned by the traditions of their cultures. While culture certainly shapes women's experiences of intimate partner violence, Sharmila Lodhia, in "Selective Storytelling," argues that the role of culture is often erroneously elevated in U.S. media coverage of women living in the Global South.

Both locally and globally, there is resistance to domestic violence. But unfortunately, when women do seek help, they often face numerous obstacles at shelters for battered women and law enforcement agencies. Despite these obstacles, many shelters, like the one described by Colleen Farrell, do offer hope to countless women fleeing violent relationships.

🌿 133

Understanding Intimate Partner Violence

MICHELE MCKEON

Each day across the country you can watch the news or pick up a newspaper and read about a horrific story of domestic violence. On average, four women a day are killed by their intimate partner. We know the more notorious stories, like Nicole Brown Simpson or Rhianna, but each and every day anonymous women are battered and abused far from the spotlight. For many years, domestic violence lived under the guise that it was just a private family matter. Nothing could be further from the truth. Domestic violence, otherwise known as intimate partner violence, is a crime.[1]

Up until the mid-1970s, intimate partner violence was a family secret not discussed in public. Springing from the civil rights movement, the battered women's movement pressured national, state, and local leaders to begin to recognize this growing problem. By the mid-1980s, programs and shelters were opened in communities across the country. In 1994 the Violence Against Women Act was passed, revolutionizing programs, services, and funding for individuals affected by intimate partner violence and their families.

Today the movement against intimate partner violence continues to adapt to the ever-changing needs of victims and their children. We advocate for policies and legislation to enhance safety and hold offenders accountable for the crimes they commit against their intimate partners. Though much work has been done, there is a tremendous amount of work left to do. There can be true safety for victims only with the commitment of the entire community and a complete understanding of the dynamics and long-standing effects of intimate partner violence.

WHAT IS INTIMATE PARTNER VIOLENCE?

Intimate partner violence is a pattern of coercive tactics used to maintain power and control over an intimate partner. These tactics can be any combination of the following: physical abuse, which includes slapping, hitting, punching, kicking, shoving; verbal abuse; emotional or mental abuse; sexual abuse; and financial abuse. While intimate partner violence is a criminal justice issue, it is also a major public health epidemic, crossing over into social and human services as well. The Centers for Disease Control and Prevention found that 1,181 women were murdered by their intimate partners in 2005; two million women experience injuries at the hands of their intimate partner annually; and that one in four women experience intimate partner violence in their lifetime.[2]

According to the Family Violence Prevention Fund, women are more likely than men to be victimized.[3] Eighty-four percent of spousal abuse victims are women, and 86 percent of victims at the hands of a dating partner are women. Three-fourths of people who commit family violence are male.[4]

Although women are the majority of victims and men are the primary perpetrators, men can also be victims of violence. According to LAMBDA, domestic violence occurs in approximately 30 to 40 percent of gay and lesbian relationships as well. Furthermore, intimate partner violence crosses socioeconomic, educational, religious, race, and ethnic boundaries.[5]

To establish power and control over an intimate partner, a batterer can use a variety of tools, including intimidation, coercion, or threats, threatening harm to children or pets, minimizing or denying abuse, using male privilege, and isolation. All of these can have a paralyzing effect on a victim. Isolation is frequently the most-used tool in a batterer's arsenal. In order to gain control over their intimate partner, it's necessary to isolate them from support networks. Removing support networks from a victim may be a slow process. It may begin with the batterer telling the victim that her friends and family do not like him. He may remove himself from social situations and convince her that "everyone is against him." Her loyalty to him may force her to choose between family and friends or her relationship. It may then progress from simple coercion to a demand for loyalty to him and, finally, forced isolation through threats and intimidation. Victims may also isolate themselves from friends and family

498   *CHAPTER VII: VIOLENCE AGAINST WOMEN*

for fear of their safety or out of embarrassment. It might not be possible to explain away visible injuries such as bruising, lacerations, or broken bones, or explanations may become implausible to family and friends, and victims may resist or feel unsafe disclosing what is happening to them.

In a well-publicized case, Susan Still speaks about how her husband slowly isolated her from her family and friends, forced her to quit her job, and left her with no outlet and no support outside her home. But Susan eventually went back to work in order to singlehandedly support the household. That outside contact would eventually help Susan leave her abusive husband, for it was Susan's boss who began to notice her bruises and keep a log of her injuries. After nearly a year of quiet support, Susan reached out to her boss, who was able to assist in the prosecution of her husband. Ulner Still was sentenced to a 36-year prison term, the longest prison term without a fatality attached to it. Support systems for victims of intimate partner violence are vital.

There is no stereotypical victim of intimate partner violence, nor is there a one-size-fits-all batterer. While it would be easy to say that all victims are lacking in self-esteem and all batterers are out-of-control rage-aholics, neither of those pictures holds true in every case. Individuals who experience intimate partner violence may end up with low self-esteem, but they don't necessarily start out that way. Batterers use a cycle of tactics that tear at the fabric of their victims over time. Rarely does a batterer show his or her true colors on a first date. Many women tell advocates that it would have been much easier to spot an abuser if their date had punched them at the end of the first date rather than ending the date with a kiss.

Although women of all ages are at risk of intimate partner violence, women are at the greatest risk between the ages 20 and 24. Teens are also a growing population of victims. According to the Family Violence Prevention Fund, one in three teenage girls report being victims of physical, verbal, or emotional abuse, a figure that "far exceeds victimization rates for other types of violence affecting youth."[6] In their article "Dating Violence Against Adolescent Girls and Associated Substance Use, Unhealthy Weight Control, Sexual Risk Behavior, Pregnancy, and Suicidality,"

Silverman, Raj et al. note that teen victims of physical dating violence are more likely than their nonabused peers to smoke, use drugs, engage in unhealthy diet behaviors (taking diet pills or laxatives and vomiting to lose weight), engage in risky sexual behaviors, and attempt or consider suicide.[7] While most services are still tailored to adults seeking services, since 2002 the CDC has funded 14 projects around the country aimed at primary prevention, with one focus being teen dating violence prevention programming.[8]

Technology has also left its mark in the area of intimate partner violence. The prevalence of cell phones, computers, social networking sites, and GPS all make it much easier for us to have access to one another. In healthy relationships, such technologies are used as tools of communication. But in the hands of someone with a need to have complete control over a partner, these technologies are used as tracking devices. Instant communication provides instant access for batterers. Numerous victims report being tracked through their phones, computers, and social networking sites. There are smart phone applications and computer software that can catch every keystroke an individual types or gain access to private e-mail accounts. For as little as $30, spoofcards can change the number, identity, and voice of someone calling. This ever-changing technology makes it even more difficult for victims to find safety from anyone who is interested in stalking and terrorizing them.

MYTHS AND MISPERCEPTIONS

Many people assume that intimate partner violence is caused by an anger management issue or a lack of control. But perpetrators are very specific about where, when, and at whom they lose control. If intimate partner violence were just a matter of anger management, then it would make sense that perpetrators wouldn't be able to control their rage. But in reality, batterers are able to contain their anger and then direct it at their intimate partner behind closed doors. One client shared a story of an incident when her husband assaulted her in a parking lot after a company party. During the party she was at the buffet table with some of her husband's co-workers sharing stories about the office and laughing. She happened to catch her husband's eye and realized he seemed upset about something. She excused herself from the other guests and spent the rest of the evening at her husband's side. Several hours later, as they were getting into the car, he punched her in the face. He accused her of flirting with his co-workers and laughing at him. With a closer look, it's clear that this man didn't lose control. He had perfect control. He had the control to wait three hours until they were alone in an empty parking lot to strike his wife. Intimate partner violence is not an anger management issue; it's an issue of power and control.

Additionally, some people believe that alcohol, drugs, mental illness, poverty, stress, and lack of education cause intimate partner violence. While each of these may be a contributing factor or exacerbate the situation, none of these, in combination or alone, cause the violence. If a batterer has a substance abuse issue and batters his partner, then he has two issues. But substance abuse is not the cause of intimate partner violence.

Treatment for batterers is a murky area, as data do not seem to indicate that one treatment alone works to treat or rehabilitate a batterer. Batterer Intervention Programs operate across the country and vary in approach from clinical treatment to accountability models. Other programs include couples counseling, mediation, as well as anger management. But these methods do not address the issue of power and control in relationships. If the violence is not about anger, but about power and control, then how would an anger management program address the issue? Just as lust management programs are not used as treatment for sex offenders, anger management programs would be ineffectual treatment for batterers.

While it is true that a majority of batterers are men, it's important to remember that not all men are violent with their intimate partners. Most men are respectful and loving to their partners, and it is important to engage these good men in the commitment to ending violence against women. This is not just a women's issue; it is an issue for society as a whole.

VICTIM BLAMING: WHY DOES SHE STAY?

When a story of intimate partner violence is in the news, this question is often posed: Why didn't she leave? This question shifts the blame from the batterer to the victim. If intimate partner violence is a crime, how could the victim participate in its occurrence? Rarely is the victim of a drunk driver asked what they were doing driving on the night of an accident. They are no more responsible than someone attacked in their home by their intimate partner. In cases of intimate partner violence or sexual assault, it is seemingly easier to examine the actions of the victim, rather than look at the factors that led to the abuse in the first place. The most appropriate question to ask is: Will the batterer be held accountable for his actions?

The reality is that people stay in abusive relationships for a whole host of reasons, including family pressure, religious or cultural considerations, socio-economic anxiety, a desire to keep the family as a whole unit, and a fear of homelessness and poverty. A fear of safety for themselves and their children is also often a significant reason victims do not leave relationships. According to the U.S. Department of Justice *National Crime Victim Survey, 1995,* the most dangerous time for a victim is right after they leave or as they are preparing to leave.

SYSTEM RESPONSES

Over the years, law enforcement has improved its responses to intimate partner violence. Long gone are the days when the police response would include separating the parties and asking the offender to "go take a walk and cool off." Many communities now have a mandatory arrest policy and/or a predominant aggressor policy. These tools have been put in place to enhance victim safety and increase offender accountability. Some states have specific domestic violence laws, while others use existing laws to further enhance consequences for batterers. Continuous training and collaboration with service providers increase the response to intimate partner violence and therefore coordinate the service provision to victims.

Although the criminal justice response has improved, a criminal justice approach is merely one system that a victim may access. Many victims do not feel comfortable using the criminal justice system, for a variety of reasons, including immigration fears, an acknowledgment of their own criminal

500 *CHAPTER VII: VIOLENCE AGAINST WOMEN*

activity, and a distrust of law enforcement. Tricia Bent Goodley notes that racial loyalty is a barrier to African-American women seeking services. She defines racial loyalty as an African-American woman's ability "to withstand abuse and make a conscious self-sacrifice for what she perceives as the greater good of the community but to her own physical, psychological, and spiritual detriment."[9]

Without the criminal justice system, where do victims turn? Victims respond by using a variety of systems and services, including local departments of social services, medical and mental health agencies, child care organizations, and of course, local domestic violence service providers. Across the country nearly every community has a domestic violence service agency. These agencies are designed to provide emergency shelter, safety, support groups, 24-hour emergency hotlines, and comprehensive advocacy services. Most services are free of charge and work to help victims find safety and support. While these services are vital and lifesaving, they are not necessarily meeting all the needs of victims as they access them. Since programs were first created in the mid- to late 1970s, services have adapted to the changing needs of clients. Over the past few years, agencies have begun to offer economic empowerment classes, legal services, as well as clinical services. There is an emerging understanding that emergency services are crucial but they are not necessarily enough. Economic and physical stability and safety are just as important to victims. A combination of services is critical for long-term safety for victims.

THE ROLE OF THE COMMUNITY

What role does the community play in responding to intimate partner violence? How do we heighten awareness, reduce victim blaming, hold offenders appropriately accountable, and provide quality services for those affected by intimate partner violence and their families? A community must demand justice and safety for victims and have a desire to hold batterers accountable for their crimes. Judges, prosecutors, police officers, and advocates must work together to provide an effective, coordinated community response. And because all of us need to be aware of the warning signs, public awareness campaigns must be targeted to the entire community.

Another important aspect of public awareness is helping to guide community members to provide assistance to someone they suspect is being battered. Parents, siblings, friends, and co-workers call domestic violence programs every day to ask for guidance in addressing the abuse of someone they care about. Advocates review the warning signs of withdrawal, bruises, fear, isolation, and unexplained absences at school or work, and they provide information and referrals to be shared with victims when they are ready to access services.

It's also important that prevention and awareness be brought into our schools at an early age so that tweens and teens are able to identify and recognize what healthy relationships look like. Whether it's Chris Brown assaulting Rhianna, the obsessive-stalking nature of the highly popular Twilight books, or the relationships that play out on hit MTV reality shows, teens and tweens are overwhelmed with a false sense of what relationships should be modeled after. They need to be taught at a young age that dating relationships should not hurt emotionally or physically, and that healthy relationships are based on respect and trust. Parents, schools, and community organizations should work together to counteract these negative images that disrespect and devalue women. Prevention and awareness have grown over the past three decades, as has the availability of programs, services, and assistance. But there is still more to be done. Until victims are not forced to flee their homes for the safety of shelters and batterers are held appropriately accountable for their actions, the work against intimate partner violence will continue until every home is a safe home. [2011]

NOTES

1. The terms "domestic violence" and "intimate partner violence" are used interchangeably throughout this article.
2. Shannan Catalano, *Intimate Partner Violence in the United States,* U.S. Department of Justice, Bureau of Justice Statistics (2007), http://www.ojp.usdoj.gov/bjs/intimate/ipv.htm.
3. *National Crime Victimization Survey: Criminal Victimization, 2007*, U.S. Department of Justice, Bureau of Justice Statistics (2008), http://www.ojp.usdoj.gov/bjs/pub/pdf/cv07.pdf.

4. Family Violence Statistics: Including Statistics on Strangers and Acquaintances (2005). U.S. Department of Justice, Bureau of Justice Statistics. Available at http://www.ojp.usdoj.gov/bjs/pub/pdf/fvs.pdf.
5. Barnes, "It's Just a Quarrel," *American Bar Association Journal* (February 1998): 25.
6. Antoinette Davis, *Interpersonal and Physical Dating Violence Among Teens,* National Council on Crime and Delinquency Focus (2008), http://www.nccdcrc.org/nccd/pubs/Dating%20Violence%20Among%20Teens.pdf.
7. Jay G. Silverman, Anita Raj, et al., "Dating Violence Against Adolescent Girls and Associated Substance Use, Unhealthy Weight Control, Sexual Risk Behavior, Pregnancy, and Suicidality," *JAMA* 286 (2001): 572–79, http://jama.ama-assn.org/cgi/reprint/286/5/572.
8. Domestic Violence Prevention Enhancement and Leadership Through Alliances (DELTA), CDC website, 2008.
9. Tricia Bent Goodley, "Perceptions of Domestic Violence: A Dialogue with African American Women," *Health Soc Work* 29, no. 4 (November 2004): 323.

134

The Club

MITSUYE YAMADA

He beat me with the hem of a kimono
worn by a Japanese woman
this prized
painted
wooden statue
carved to perfection
in Japan or maybe Hong Kong.

She was usually on display
in our living room atop his bookshelf
among his other overseas treasures
I was never to touch.
She posed there most of the day
her head tilted
her chin resting lightly
on the white pointed fingertips
of her right hand
her black hair
piled high on her head
her long slim neck bared
to her shoulders.
An invisible hand

under the full sleeve
clasped her kimono
close to her body
its hem flared
gracefully around her feet.

That hem
made fluted red marks
on these freckled arms
my shoulders
my back.

That head
inside his fist
made camel
bumps
on his knuckles.
I prayed for her
that her pencil thin neck
would not snap
or his rage would be unendurable.
She held fast for me
didn't even chip or crack.

One day, we were talking
as we often did the morning after.
Well, my sloe-eyed beauty, I said
have you served him enough?
I dared to pick her up with one hand
I held her gently by the flowing robe
around her slender legs.
She felt lighter than I had imagined.
I stroked her cold thighs
with the tips of my fingers
and felt a slight tremor.

I carried her into the kitchen and wrapped her
in two sheets of paper towels
We're leaving
I whispered
you and I
together.

I placed her
between my clothes in my packed suitcase.
That is how we left him
forever.   [1989]

🦎 135

La Princesa

LATINA ANÓNIMA

His car pulled into the driveway. I was crouching behind my neighbor's car, waiting for him to enter the house. As soon as I heard the door slam shut, my heart racing, I ran to the end of the block. I remember feeling the wind in my face and my backpack, carrying students' exams, slumped against my right shoulder. All my senses were alert. It was past dusk and all I could think of was "Where can I go?"

I spotted a bus and jumped on it, shaking, as I slipped some coins into the box, trying to pretend—that everything was fine.

I had finally left him for good. Memories jarred my otherwise numb state.

It was Christmas Eve. We were celebrating it quietly, with a roaring fire, a small "charlie brown" kind of tree, and an abundance of gifts to exchange. I opened package after package—of clothes he had picked out for me. Meanwhile, I lost count of his drinks. Later that evening, I soaked the sleeve of my new coat, stained with blood from the busted lip he had added to my evening's "gifts." I wondered how I would hide the bruises on my left temple and the cuts on the lower left corner of my lip from the friends coming over the next day for tamales. I remember, most of all, looking in the mirror the next morning, not recognizing my own eyes. They were completely vacant of all emotion.

As the bus made stop after stop, I remembered the two years' worth of incidents, apology after apology, promise after promise. I clung to the memory of when I finally snapped, of the moment I knew I would *plan my escape*. It was toward the end of the relationship. By this time I was getting "bold," verbally challenging him when he questioned me, not caring if what I said provoked him. By that time I had finally figured out that no matter what I did, he would find reason for violence.

I entered the house, carrying bags of groceries, placing them on the table. He questioned me, asking me why I had gotten the wrong kind of sausage. He had asked for hot links and I had bought Italian sausage.

He wanted me to return to the store and get the ones he wanted. I didn't like the fact that his tone of voice was in the form of an order. "Go back to the store and get the RIGHT kind," he screamed. I refused and told him, "I'm not going." He shoved me, from one room to another, beginning his tirade of intimidation. When we entered the living room, he pushed me to the floor. I feigned that he had hurt my back, as a way of keeping him from continuing. Not knowing whether he had really hurt me, he kicked me. He kicked me while I was down on the floor. I was no better than a dog. That's when I snapped.

That's when I knew that whatever it took I would leave this animal and keep him out of my life forever.

Over the next few months, as I recovered in the safety of my mother's home, I kept asking myself, How could this happen to me? Only a few years before, I had been special. My picture made Spanish-speaking newspapers, announcing my fellowship award to attend graduate school. My entire history, up until this point, had been laced with validation, awards, and recognition for my academic achievements. And at home, I had been loved and cherished. How could I have reached the point that I would accept the slightest form of physical or emotional violence to my person? The question remains today.

As I sought ways to heal and understand, I did what every good academic does. I went to the library. I punched in the words "battery," "domestic violence," and "women" into the computer. Based on her research and interviews in *The Battered Woman*, Lenore Walker developed a typology of characteristics and types of women who tend to become victims of domestic violence. In these pages, I found a description of "the princess syndrome." The princess, Walker explains, is shocked by her confrontation with violence. So sheltered, protected, and revered has she been and so unexposed to any kind of violence in her life that when she encounters someone violent, she is in a state of shock. With no experience of invalidation and feeling intense personal criticism for the first time in her life, the princess believes she can "do right" by the perpetrator and change his opinion of her. Like the other types of women, she endures all the typical cycles before leaving the batterer.

With hindsight, in contextualizing my circumstances, it would be an understatement to say that

Violence in Intimate Relationships: A Feminist Perspective

BELL HOOKS

Given the nature of patriarchy, it has been necessary for feminists to focus on extreme cases to make people confront the issue, and acknowledge it to be serious and relevant. Unfortunately, an exclusive focus on extreme cases can and does lead us to ignore the more frequent, more common, yet less extreme case of occasional hitting. Women are also less likely to acknowledge occasional hitting for fear that they will then be seen as someone who is in a bad relationship or someone whose life is out of control. Currently, the literature about male violence against women identifies the physically abused woman as a "battered woman." While it has been important to have an accessible terminology to draw attention to the issue of male violence against women, the terms used reflect biases because they call attention to only one type of violence in intimate relationships. The term "battered woman" is problematical. It is not a term that emerged from feminist work on male violence against women; it was already used by psychologists and sociologists in the literature on domestic violence. This label "battered woman" places primary emphasis on physical assaults that are continuous, repeated, and unrelenting. The focus is on extreme violence, with little effort to link these cases with the everyday acceptance within intimate relationships of physical abuse that is not extreme, that may not be repeated. Yet these lesser forms of physical abuse damage individuals psychologically and, if not properly addressed and recovered from, can set the stage for more extreme incidents.

Most importantly, the term "battered woman" is used as though it constitutes a separate and unique category of womanness, as though it is an identity, a mark that sets one apart rather than being simply a descriptive term. It is as though the experience of being repeatedly violently hit is the sole defining characteristic of a woman's identity and all other aspects of who she is and what her experience has been are submerged.

. . . Women who are hit once by men in their lives, and women who are hit repeatedly do not want to be placed in the category of "battered woman" because it is a label that appears to strip us of dignity, to deny that there has been any integrity in the relationships we are in. A person physically assaulted by a stranger or a casual friend with whom they are not intimate may be hit once or repeatedly but they do not have to be placed into a category before doctors, lawyers, family, counselors, etc., take their problem seriously. Again, it must be stated that establishing categories and terminology has been part of the effort to draw public attention to the seriousness of male violence against women in intimate relationships. Even though the use of convenient labels and categories has made it easier to identify problems of physical abuse, it does not mean the terminology should not be critiqued from a feminist perspective and changed if necessary.

[1989]

504   *CHAPTER VII: VIOLENCE AGAINST WOMEN*

there were competing tensions in my life at the time. They culminated to create ripe conditions—even for a former homecoming "princess," literally—to enter and come to know a sphere of violence far too many women experience. Ideologically, I had failed to reconcile the family expectation that I marry and have children with my pursuit of an advanced degree and my identity as a Chicana feminist (the ironies prevail). I thought I could have both. Hence, when I connected with this man I was still trying to be a "good girl" and find that husband everyone expected. Yet I was in a graduate program that was brutally competitive, alienating, and disempowering. Looking back, I realize that my self-esteem was at an all-time low with respect to my graduate studies and that I was no longer looking to the institution, or academic processes, to nourish my sense of self. Thus, it was no surprise that when I met this man I foolishly looked to him as someone who would make me feel that I was special.

During pensive moments, I've developed a theory for *princesas* of color. *Earned privileges* in a given life cycle only buy us time. The structures of subordination will get even the achievers. Those who think they might have escaped find themselves—like countless other *princesas* of color—treated just as women. Today the memories of this time in my life seem surreal. I do not identify, much less connect, with the experiences I've just recounted. It's as if they belong to someone else. But they don't, and instead they are tucked away in what I like to call my *caja de llagas,* my box of scars. I do, however, use the memories to move myself into using my voice. By remembering the contents, I remember to speak.   [2001]

🌿 136

Holding Up More Than Half the Heavens

MARGARETTA WAN LIN
and CHENG IMM TAN

Because of the barriers of language, culture, and economic disparities and the vagaries of racism and sexism, Asian Pacific American (APA) victims of domestic violence suffer revictimization at the hands of institutions designed to serve battered women. According to the 1990 U.S. Census, Asians and Pacific Islanders are the fastest growing minority group, totalling nearly seven million. And yet, in the entire United States only two shelters exist for APA women, one safe-home network and one advocacy group that provides culturally sensitive programs and counseling.[1] Of the domestic violence resources available—police, shelters, hotlines, human services programs—few have staff who speak Asian Pacific languages. Given the highly sensitive nature of addressing domestic violence, it is unacceptable not to have linguistically accessible resources. The language barrier, in effect, shuts out most refugee and immigrant women. In addition, many battered women's shelters turn away APA women because of language and cultural difficulties or sheer racism. Economic concerns present yet another obstacle. Most women who are victims of domestic violence do not have control of the family's money. Many leave their homes with little besides the clothes on their backs. This means that many battered APA women who have gathered up the strength and courage to flee the violence in their homes must then return there because they have no other viable options. Legal protection is also often both inaccessible because of cultural and linguistic barriers and unavailable because of institutionalized racism and sexism. There are too many examples of the revictimization of battered APA women by institutionalized forces; it would require another whole book just to document the abuses we have seen. Consider the story of Ling.

One evening as Ling was cleaning some fish for dinner her husband, who had beaten her repeatedly for the past eight years, and had given her concussions, a broken hip, and a broken jaw, began to pick a fight. Ling did not answer any of his accusations and her enduring silence made him even angrier. He picked up a chair to strike her. She sidestepped the impending blow and screamed at him to stop. The chair broke against the door and he lunged at her, more enraged than before. Ling tried to ward him off by waving the knife that she had been using to clean the fish for dinner that evening. He continued to lunge at her and in attempting to get the knife, fell upon the knife and cut himself. He continued to strike out at Ling.

Terrified, Ling ran to a nearby store to call the police. When the police came, her husband who spoke good English, accused Ling of attacking him. Ling's English was not enough to defend herself. The police whom she called arrested Ling and put her in jail. They set her bond at $2,500. The case against Ling is still pending. This is how our justice system works to protect battered women.

THE PRIMACY OF FEAR OF RACIST ATTACKS, THE SACRIFICE OF OUR SISTERS

Within each ethnic group, male control and domestic violence take on culturally specific expressions. APA communities have tolerated and overlooked domestic violence for some of the same reasons that mainstream society has tolerated and overlooked it for so long—the unquestioning acceptance of patriarchy, of male control and privilege. Some APA activists worry that bringing domestic violence into the open will confirm negative stereotypes about the community, and further fuel the fires of anti-Asian sentiment. To expose the problem within APA communities is not a statement about the greater violence or misogyny in Asian Pacific culture. Instead, the sad reality is that Asian men, like all other men, live in a male-dominated culture that views women as property, objects they must control and possess. Compounding this reality, or underlying it, are cultures that view violence as an acceptable solution to problems.

As a reaction to the pervasive racism and cultural imperialism that threaten to undermine our cultural integrity, APA activists and community leaders have been reluctant to look self-critically at traditional misogynistic attitudes and practices for fear that it would reinforce racist stereotypes about Asian Pacific Americans. This attitude of denial, however, does not keep racism at bay. Instead, it is at odds with cherished notions of our rights as humans and citizens.

The same reasons that inspire the unequivocal and emphatic support of APA activists to identify crimes motivated by race, color, and/or national origin as hate crimes hold for crimes motivated by gender. As with crimes of racist hate, statistics on domestic violence are inadequate; elected officials will not fund programs until we fully document the violence; keeping such statistics would encourage more public awareness and debate on the crimes.

While there is an emerging effort on the part of APA women activists to include domestic violence as a hate crime, APA civil rights and advocacy groups have not supported their work. We believe that along with sexist motivations, fear of betraying our brothers, of adding to their oppression, plays a role in the glaring absence of their support. Such fear causes APA activists to overlook and ignore domestic violence. It has meant sacrificing the lives of our sisters.

A heinous example of this is Dong Lu Chen's murder of his wife, Jian Wan Chen, and his successful use of the cultural defense. On September 7, 1987, Jian Wan Chen's husband smashed her skull in with a claw hammer after she allegedly admitted to having an affair. Chen's teenage son discovered her body in the family's Brooklyn apartment. The trial judge sentenced Dong to five years probation on a reduced manslaughter charge after concluding, based on the testimony of an anthropologist, that Dong was driven to violence by traditional Chinese values about adultery and loss of manhood. APA activists came out in support of the cultural defense as a necessary tool to protect immigrants in U.S. courtrooms.

Does this mean that Jian Wan Chen's immigrant status is negligible, or that such activists believe that Asian men are traditionally more violent and misogynistic than their white counterparts? Does it mean that the status of Jian Wan Chen as an Asian sister, as a human being, is negligible when weighed against the crime of her husband? And what are the repercussions of such outrage? Domestic violence counselors have reported that the case has convinced many battered APA women that they have no protection, period. As for the lawyers, they feel "empowered" to use the cultural defense at any

506   *CHAPTER VII: VIOLENCE AGAINST WOMEN*

opportunity.[2] What does this say about our society, about our value of human life, about our perception of justice?   [1994]

NOTES

1. Centers in San Francisco, Los Angeles, and New York City provide programs for Chinese, Korean, Philippine, Japanese, Indonesian, Laotian, Vietnamese, and Cambodian women, and are staffed with multilingual abuse-hotlines. A program in Boston provides counseling and advocacy services for Vietnamese, Cambodian, and Chinese women. Bilingual hotlines are available for Koreans in Honolulu and Chicago and for Indians in New Brunswick, New Jersey.
2. Alexis Jetter, "Fear is Legacy of Wife Killing in Chinatown," *Newsday*, November 26, 1989.

137

Selective Storytelling: A Critique of U.S. Media Coverage Regarding Violence Against Indian Women

SHARMILA LODHIA

In July 2003, Guljit Sandhu was shot and killed by her husband, Inderpreet Sandhu, in Milpitas, California. He killed himself minutes later. After the crime was committed, a family member was quoted as saying that Inderpreet had no choice but to kill his wife, who was attempting to leave him, because his "culture didn't allow divorce."[1] The local media latched onto this statement, and its coverage of the crime focused overwhelmingly on this unchecked assertion about a "cultural" prohibition on divorce as a justification for this violence.[2] News accounts presented the crime as a foreseeable outcome in a community where "marriages are arranged" and women are "second-class citizens."

In October 2003, Nisha Sharma, a woman from India, made international headlines when she had her would-be husband arrested for demanding $25,000 dollars as a dowry payment from her family shortly before their wedding was to take place. While her act was brave and has inspired other young women to challenge dowry demands, news coverage of the event was similarly riddled with generalizations about the so-called "status of women in India" and the motivations for the violence committed against them. In particular, a *60 Minutes* story by CBS correspondent Christiane Amanpour was filled with magnified accounts of the links between marriage, dowry harassment, and a form of domestic violence commonly referred to in India as "bride burning."[3]

In January 2004, Oprah Winfrey began her show with the following statement: "I always say that if you are a woman born in the United States, you are one of the luckiest women in the world. Did you know that? Well, if you didn't know that, you're really going to believe me after this show. . . . Today I wanted to take you to the other side of the globe, so to all of you soccer moms out there, here's a chance to go places you'd never normally see and have an opportunity to meet women you'd never meet."[4] What followed was a montage of images of violence inflicted upon women in the Global South that included, not surprisingly, a highly disturbing journey into the "horror of bride burning in India" that Winfrey warned her audience was "right out of the Dark Ages."[5] The show not only relied on oversimplifications that distorted many aspects of these forms of violence, but also noticeably ignored the very tangible similarities between these crimes and parallel crimes of domestic-violence-related homicide in the United States—similarities that might have raised doubts about how "lucky" American women really are.

These examples are indicative of the limited ways in which ideas about foreign violence against women get imported into the dominant Western imagination. In these storylines, "culture" is presented as monolithic, and religious diversity is disregarded in favor of distorted versions of what gendered violence signifies within the Indian community.[6]

It is much easier for reporters to make claims that leave concepts like culture and race unproblematized and to focus instead on the heightened drama of "the burning bride."[7] What I find especially discouraging is the fact that, in these reports, the Indian community is faulted not only for its particular brand of domestic violence, but also for things like arranged marriages, lavish weddings, and rising consumerism—as if these phenomena have no parallels in the West. I suppose that those who come from the land of speed dating, bridezillas, and millionaire-seeking bachelorettes are insulated from allegations of this kind of "cultural" deviance.[8]

These media reports reinforce the belief that Indian women are at risk of a unique incarnation of patriarchal violence that Uma Narayan describes as "death by culture."[9] Crimes such as "dowry deaths" and "bride burnings" can thus continue to be distinguished from other forms of domestic violence.

Wester audiences seem to derive a kind of voyeuristic pleasure in imagining the spectacle of "burning brides" and hearing lurid tales of deadly mothers-in-law, both of which are perceived as far more intriguing than acts of domestic violence that occur locally. In fact, if these reporters were to look more critically at the issues involved in these cases, they would not only gain a far more complete picture of why these kinds of crimes occur, but they would be forced to notice the striking similarities between these acts and those committed against women in the United States.[10] The weapons may differ, but the fact remains that women in many parts of the world are more likely to die at the hands of a boyfriend or husband than of a stranger. To single out the particular embodiment of lethal violence that one finds in the Indian context is to willfully blind oneself to this tragic reality.

Choosing to invoke ideas about culture exclusively within the context of violence against non-Western women performs several critical functions. One key historical function in the case of India was the desire to advance the goals and objectives of the British Empire. By focusing overwhelmingly on issues such as female infanticide, *sati*, and dowry deaths, the British could present the diverse Indian subcontinent as so steeped in backwardness as to require salvation.[11] This enabled the British to take control of local economies and to masculinize property rights in a way that historian Veena Oldenberg has argued did far more to damage the social position of Indian women than the supposed "traditions" on which these societal ills were blamed.[12]

Elevating the role of "culture" allows for distinctions to be made between violence against "third world women" and violence against women from Western communities. "Women in the third world are portrayed as victims of their culture, which reinforces stereotyped and racist representations of that culture and privileges the culture of the West."[13] . . .

Uma Narayan's critical analysis of what happens when violence travels across borders and becomes decontextualized should inform our thinking about comparisons between the United States and India.[14] In her work she examines how the national contexts of India and the United States differently shaped these violence discourses. In addition to pointing out the difficulty of comparing statistics when definitions of domestic violence are so varied, she also notes that while "there is a *visible category* of 'dowry-murder' that picks out a lethal form of domestic violence in the Indian context, there is no similar, readily available category that specifically picks out *lethal instances* of domestic violence in the United States."[15] In critiquing the popular construction of these crimes, she notes that "Indian women's murder-by-fire seems mysterious, possibly ritualistic, and one of those factors that is assumed to have something to do with 'Indian culture.'"[16]

What scholars like Narayan and Oldenberg have pointed out, however, is that fire is simply more accessible in Indian households than other weapons, and that the use of fire to kill is "forensically expedient," because all evidence is destroyed.[17] Interestingly this exoticized violence seems to garner far more interest and support from feminists who are eager to "expose" the dismal conditions of women internationally, yet who are conspicuously absent in the activism being engaged in by women of color who experience violence within their own countries.

In reality many women in the United States are victims of domestic violence. The U.S. Department of Justice has found that women recently divorced or who have left battering relationships are at greater risk of fatal violence.[18] Pregnant women and women who have been pregnant recently are also more likely to be victims of homicide than to die by other causes, and evidence suggests that a

508   *CHAPTER VII: VIOLENCE AGAINST WOMEN*

large number of these women are killed by their intimate partners.[19] Women are also far more likely than men to be victims of rape, attempted rape, and stalking in their lifetimes.[20]

These figures indicate a serious problem of violence in the United States, and the fact that there is an increased likelihood of violence when a woman tries to leave a relationship or gets pregnant suggests that similar issues of pride, honor, patriarchy, and—dare I say it even—"culture" may be operating in these cases. We never use such language to describe these crimes, however, and instead these cases are viewed as anomalous breakdowns within a family. Law professor Leti Volpp has noted that while the culture of the "Other" is always described in very limited and ahistorical ways, Western culture is never singled out in the same manner. She argues that because "we tend to perceive white Americans as 'people without culture,' when white people engage in certain practices, we do not associate their behavior with a racialized conception of culture, but rather construct other, noncultural explanations."[21] These problematic "*bad behaviors*" are thus only inscribed on "the bodies of racialized immigrant subjects."[22]

THE REAL STORY: IN INDIA

In September 2005, after years of dedicated advocacy by women's groups, the Indian government passed the Protection for Women from Domestic Violence Act of 2005, and it went into effect in October 2006. This pioneering law covers not only wives but *any* woman residing in a shared household. This includes not only women in live-in relationships, but also sisters, mothers, daughters, widows, divorced women, and women in marriages that the law views as invalid.[23] One of the other striking features of the recently enacted civil law is its broad conceptualization of "domestic violence," which includes physical, sexual, verbal, emotional, and economic abuse. In addition, the law establishes a unique remedial framework for safeguarding the rights of women who are victims of violence, including a unique "right of residency" provision that allows a woman to remain within the family home, regardless of whether she

has a legal claim or share in the property. The enactment of this law was a significant milestone in antiviolence activism for women in India, though critical questions remain about how well it will be implemented.

Beyond efforts toward legal reform, advocates in India have worked to develop a range of innovative nonlegal responses to violence against women in both urban and rural parts of India. In some areas, All-Women Police Stations have been established in an effort to make the police more accessible to women and in the hope of creating greater sensitivity around gender-based crimes.[24] Another distinct response to violence is the "Self-Help Collectives" or "Village Sanghas." These small and self-governed women's groups focus their efforts on improving women's opportunities to gain economic and political power. "The hope . . . is that if women are given increased educational, economic, and political status through these village collectives, or *sanghas*, they will be in a better position to take a stand against domestic violence."[25]

These alternative methods are interesting, because they seek to create an integrated and multilayered approach to the problem of violence within the family. They offer hope for advocacy that extends beyond the boundaries of the criminal justice system and that seeks to address the critical social and economic dimensions of these crimes. The insights about Indian activism, obtained through regional research in India, are extremely valuable and might well inform U.S.-based responses to violence against women, particularly efforts aimed at women whose experiences of violence are magnified by factors such as race, class, or immigrant status. Examinations of violence that occurs outside the United States should not be undertaken in order to convince ourselves that we are more "safe" than other women, but rather in an effort to understand the complex reasons why violence against women persists globally, despite myriad efforts to address it. I would argue that only when we redirect our attention away from culture and focus instead on how violence against women is linked to issues such as globalization, reassertions of state power, shifting racializations, religious fundamentalisms, and increased militarism worldwide can we really begin to understand the true magnitude of this multifaceted problem. [2008]

NOTES

1. Sue Hutchinson, "Again, Abuse Masquerades as Love and a Woman Dies," *San Jose Mercury News*, August 1, 2003.
2. Julie Patel, "When Culture Rejects Divorce: For Indo-Americans, Breakup Can Be Risky," *San Jose Mercury News*, August 3, 2003; Roxanne Stites, "Milpitas Husband Kills Estranged Wife, Self; Man Distraught Over Breakup of Arranged Marriage," *San Jose Mercury News*, July 22, 2003.
3. Christiane Amanpour, *For Love of Money*, CBSNews.com, October 5, 2003, www.cbsnews.com/stories/2003/10/03/60minutes/main576466.shtml.
4. "Lisa Ling Investigates Dowry Deaths," *The Oprah Winfrey Show*. ABC, January 16, 2004.
5. Ibid.
6. Narayan, *Dislocating Cultures;* Sonia N. Lawrence, "Cultural (in)Sensitivity: The Dangers of a Simplistic Approach to Culture in the Courtroom," *CJWL/RFD* 13 (2001); Leti Volpp, "Symposium: On Culture, Difference, and Domestic Violence," *American University Journal of Gender, Social Policy and the Law* 11 (2003).
7. Parameswaran, Radhika (1996). Coverage of Bride Burning in the *Dallas Observer: A cultural analysis of the other*. Frontiers, 16 (2–3), page 69.
8. Leti Volpp, "Essay: Blaming Culture for Bad Behavior," *Yale Journal of Law and the Humanities* 12 (2000); Parameswaran, "Coverage of Bride Burning."
9. Narayan, *Dislocating Cultures*, 100–17.
10. Ibid.
11. Lata Mani, *Contentious Traditions: The Debate on* Sati *in Colonial India* (Berkeley: University of California Press, 1998).
12. Oldenburg, Veena Talwar (2002). *Dowry Murders: The imperial origins of a cultural crime*. Oxford University Press: Oxford, England.
13. Kapur, Ratna.The Tragedy of Victimization Rhetoric: Resurrecting the "Native" Subject in International/Post-Colonial Feminist Legal Politics. *Harvard Human Rights*, Journal, 15 (2002), page 6.
14. Narayan, *Dislocating Cultures*.
15. Ibid., 95.
16. Ibid., 101–2.
17. Narayan, *Dislocating Cultures;* Oldenburg, *Dowry Murder*.
18. U. S. Department of Justice, Bureau of Justice Statistics, Special Report, Intimate Partner Violence, NCJ 178247, May 2000.
19. I. Horon and D. Cheng, "Enhanced Surveillance for Pregnancy-Associated Mortality—Maryland, 1993–1998," *Journal of the American Medical Association*, 11 (2001).
20. Patricia Tjaden and Nancy Thoennes, "Full Report of the Prevalence, Incidence and Consequences of Violence against Women: Findings from the National Violence against Women Survey" Pub. No. NCJ 183781, Washington: Department of Justice, 2000.
21. Volpp, "Essay: Blaming Culture for Bad Behavior," 89.
22. Ibid., 90.
23. *The Protection of Women from Domestic Violence Act*, No. 43 (2005).
24. Mangai Natarajan, "Women's Police Stations as a Dispute Processing System: The Tamil Nadu in Experience in Dealing with Dowry-related Domestic Violence Cases," *Women and Criminal Justice* 16.1/2 (2005).
25. Visaria, et al., "Domestic Violence in India: A Summary Report of Three Studies," 36.

🌿 138

Bringing Women's Studies to a Battered Women's Shelter

COLLEEN FARRELL

I was in my midthirties and at a point in my life where I truly felt I was ready to make a change. I returned to college as a women's studies major. That turned out to be the best decision of my life. The curriculum offered through the women's studies program enabled me to see how society's widespread notions, perceptions, and thoughts have had a major impact on my life.

All that I have learned I bring daily to my work as a Domestic Violence Advocate. My women's studies education has helped me to realize that every woman is at risk for becoming a victim of violence. I share with the women with whom I work how violence against women has been accepted and even condoned throughout history. Violence happens regardless of socioeconomic status, race, ethnicity, age, education, sexual orientation, or childhood history. In fact, being female is the only significant risk factor for being a victim of violence. Violence against women is not just a woman's problem. Violence against women is a social problem.

Many of the women who attend the Battered Women's Support Group that I facilitate talk about how they have been called lesbians by their abusers. It is at this time that I explain how society perceives a lesbian as someone who has stepped

510   *CHAPTER VII: VIOLENCE AGAINST WOMEN*

out of line and how the word lesbian has been used to hurt all women. Many women are also forced to stay in abusive and dangerous relationships because they can't support themselves and their children. My feminist perspective and women's studies background allow me to point out to the members of the support group the common elements of oppressions (sexism, racism, heterosexism, classism, etc.) and how they are linked by economic power and control.

I have also started a newsletter for my co-workers that centers on information about the history of women and women's issues such as heterosexism and sexism, titled "The Lily" (a tribute to the nineteenth century women's newspaper edited by Amelia Bloomer). And finally, I remind myself every day of the most important lesson I have taken with me from my time as a women's studies major at SUNY New Paltz. Never judge other women too harshly—for they too have traveled a long and difficult road. In order to end the devaluation of women and girls in our culture, we must begin to value other women as well as ourselves.   [2003]

Sexual Violence

Whether or not one has personally experienced sexual assault or abuse, the threat of violence shadows the lives of women and girls. The pieces in this section make connections between sexual violence and the celebration of male sexual conquest that prevails in most of the world. From childhood sexual abuse to the rape of women by conquering armies, women are seen as sexual prey. Susan Griffin's 1971 article "Rape: The All-American Crime" drew rape out of the realm of inexplicable atrocities and placed it squarely in the context of patriarchal traditions that entitle men to control women's bodies. The threat of sexual violence looms large for women and girls, curtailing a sense of safety and belonging and made worse, as Holly Kearl argues, by harassment in the streets. Kearl suggests that one of the ways we can begin to take back our public spaces is by encouraging men to find ways to stop street harassment.

While public spaces are often not safe places for women, the myth of the rapist as a stranger lurking in the bushes was further challenged in the 1980s by studies that revealed the extent of acquaintance rape. Peggy Reeves Sanday's groundbreaking article synthesizes these studies and draws attention to the role of fraternities in perpetuating gang rapes on college campuses. Recent high-profile cases have trained the spotlight on the culture of entitlement and misogyny that prevails in the world of competitive male sports.

In a wide variety of ways, women and girls have challenged what some have called a "rape culture." They have reached out to each other, as Rachel did in the "High-School Gauntlet," ending the silence, passivity, and isolation that enable boys to sexually humiliate girls. College women who have been raped by acquaintances are speaking out and taking their rapists to court. Survivors of sexual abuse are using their own experience to help other survivors reclaim their lives, and activists are challenging a criminal justice system that protects male abusers of children. In the past 15 years, women from around the world have worked together to force the international community to recognize rape as a war crime. Several of these essays tell the stories of women who are challenging a culture that supports rape and defending their autonomy as human beings.

512 *CHAPTER VII: VIOLENCE AGAINST WOMEN*

139

With No Immediate Cause

NTOZAKE SHANGE

every 3 minutes a woman is beaten
every five minutes a
woman is raped/every ten minutes
a lil girl is molested
yet i rode the subway today
i sat next to an old man who
may have beaten his old wife
3 minutes ago or 3 days/30 years ago
he might have sodomized his
daughter but i sat there
cuz the young men on the train
might beat some young women
later in the day or tomorrow
i might not shut my door fast
enuf/push hard enuf
every 3 minutes it happens
some woman's innocence
rushes to her cheeks/pours from her mouth
like the betsy wetsy dolls have been torn
apart/their mouths
mensis red & split/every
three minutes a shoulder
is jammed through plaster & the oven door/
chairs push thru the rib cage/hot water or
boiling sperm decorate her body
i rode the subway today
& bought a paper from a
man who might
have held his old lady onto
a hot pressing iron/i dont know
maybe he catches lil girls in the
park & rips open their behinds
with steel rods/i cdnt decide
what he might have done i only
know every 3 minutes
every 5 minutes every 10 minutes/so
i bought the paper
looking for the announcement
there has to be an announcement

of the women's bodies found
yesterday/the missing little girl
i sat in a restaurant with my
paper looking for the announcement
a yng man served me coffee
i wondered did he pour the boiling
coffee/on the woman cuz she waz stupid/
did he put the infant girl/in
the coffee pot/with the boiling coffee/cuz she cried
    too much
what exactly did he do with hot coffee
i looked for the announcement
the discovery/of the dismembered
woman's body/the
victims have not all been
identified/today they are
naked & dead/refuse to
testify/one girl out of 10's not
coherent/i took the coffee
& spit it up/i found an
announcement/not the woman's
bloated body in the river/floating
not the child bleeding in the
59th street corridor/not the baby
broken on the floor/
    "there is some concern
    that alleged battered women
    might start to murder their
    husbands & lovers with no
    immediate cause"
i spit up   i vomit   i am screaming
we all have immediate cause
every 3 minutes
every 5 minutes
every 10 minutes
every day
women's bodies are found
in alleys & bedrooms/at the top of the stairs
before i ride the subway/buy a paper/drink
coffee/i must know/
have you hurt a woman today
did you beat a woman today
throw a child cross a room
    are the lil girl's panties
    in yr pocket
did you hurt a woman today

i have to ask these obscene questions
the authorities require me to
establish
immediate cause

every three minutes
every five minutes
every ten minutes
every day   [1970]

🌿 140

Rape:
The All-American Crime

SUSAN GRIFFIN

I

I have never been free of the fear of rape. From a very early age I, like most women, have thought of rape as part of my natural environment—something to be feared and prayed against like fire or lightning. I never asked why men raped; I simply thought it one of the many mysteries of human nature.

I was, however, curious enough about the violent side of humanity to read every crime magazine I was able to ferret away from my grandfather. Each issue featured at least one "sex crime," with pictures of a victim, usually in a pearl necklace, and of the ditch or the orchard where her body was found. I was never certain why the victims were always women, nor what the motives of the murderer were, but I did guess that the world was not a safe place for women. I observed that my grandmother was meticulous about locks, and quick to draw the shades before anyone removed so much as a shoe. I sensed that danger lurked outside.

At the age of eight, my suspicions were confirmed. My grandmother took me to the back of the house where the men wouldn't hear, and told me that strange men wanted to do harm to little girls. I learned not to walk on dark streets, not to talk to strangers, or get into strange cars, to lock doors,

and to be modest. She never explained why a man would want to harm a little girl, and I never asked.

If I thought for a while that my grandmother's fears were imaginary, the illusion was brief. That year, on the way home from school, a schoolmate a few years older than I tried to rape me. Later, in an obscure aisle of the local library (while I was reading *Freddy the Pig*) I turned to discover a man exposing himself. Then, the friendly man around the corner was arrested for child molesting.

My initiation to sexuality was typical. Every woman has similar stories to tell—the first man who attacked her may have been a neighbor, a family friend, an uncle, her doctor, or perhaps her own father. And women who grow up in New York City always have tales about the subway. . . .

When I was very young, my image of the "sexual offender" was a nightmarish amalgamation of the bogey man and Captain Hook: he wore a black cape, and he cackled. As I matured, so did my image of the rapist. Born into the psychoanalytic age, I tried to "understand" the rapist. Rape, I came to believe, was only one of many unfortunate evils produced by sexual repression. Reasoning by tautology, I concluded that any man who would rape a woman must be out of his mind.

Yet, though the theory that rapists are insane is a popular one, this belief has no basis in fact. According to Professor Menachem Amir's study of 646 rape cases in Philadelphia, *Patterns in Forcible Rape*, men who rape are not abnormal. Amir writes, "Studies indicate that sex offenders do not constitute a unique or psychopathological type; nor are they as a group invariably more disturbed than the control groups to which they are compared." Alan Taylor, a parole officer who has worked with rapists in the prison facilities at San Luis Obispo, California, stated the question in plainer language, "Those men were the most normal men there. They had a lot of hang-ups, but they were the same hang-ups as men walking out on the street."

Another canon in the apologetics of rape is that, if it were not for learned social controls, all men would rape. Rape is held to be natural behavior, and not to rape must be learned. But in truth rape

514   *CHAPTER VII: VIOLENCE AGAINST WOMEN*

is not universal to the human species. Moreover, studies of rape in our culture reveal that far from being impulsive behavior, most rape is planned. Professor Amir's study reveals that in cases of group rape (the "gangbang" of masculine slang), 90 percent of the rapes were planned; in pair rapes, 83 percent of the rapes were planned; and in single rapes, 58 percent were planned. These figures should significantly discredit the image of the rapist as a man who is suddenly overcome by sexual needs society does not allow him to fulfill.

Far from the social control of rape being learned, comparisons with other cultures lead one to suspect that, in our society, it is rape itself that is learned. (The fact that rape is against the law should not be considered proof that rape is not in fact encouraged as part of our culture.)

This culture's concept of rape as an illegal, but still understandable, form of behavior is not a universal one. In her study *Sex and Temperament,* Margaret Mead describes a society that does not share our views. The Arapesh do not ". . . have any conception of the male nature that might make rape understandable to them." Indeed our interpretation of rape is a product of our conception of the nature of male sexuality. A common retort to the question, why don't women rape men, is the myth that men have greater sexual needs, that their sexuality is more urgent than women's. And it is the nature of human beings to want to live up to what is expected of them.

And this same culture which expects aggression from the male expects passivity from the female. Conveniently, the companion myth about the nature of female sexuality is that all women secretly want to be raped. Lurking beneath her modest female exterior is a subconscious desire to be ravished. The following description of a stag movie, written by Brenda Starr in Los Angeles' underground paper, *Everywoman,* typifies this male fantasy. The movie "showed a woman in her underclothes reading on her bed. She is interrupted by a rapist with a knife. He immediately wins her over with his charm and they get busy sucking and fucking." An advertisement in the *Berkeley Barb*

reads, "Now as all women know from their daydreams, rape has a lot of advantages. Best of all it's so simple. No preparation necessary, no planning ahead of time, no wondering if you should or shouldn't; just whang! bang!" Thanks to Masters and Johnson even the scientific canon recognizes that for the female, "whang! bang!" can scarcely be described as pleasurable.

Still, the male psyche persists in believing that, protestations and struggles to the contrary, deep inside her mysterious feminine soul, the female victim has wished for her own fate. A young woman who was raped by the husband of a friend said that days after the incident the man returned to her home, pounded on the door and screamed to her, "Jane, Jane. You loved it. You know you loved it."

The theory that women like being raped extends itself by deduction into the proposition that most or much of rape is provoked by the victim. But this too is only myth. Though provocation, considered a mitigating factor in a court of law, may consist of only "a gesture," according to the Federal Commission on Crimes of Violence, only 4 percent of reported rapes involved any precipitative behavior by the woman.

The notion that rape is enjoyed by the victim is also convenient for the man who, though he would not commit forcible rape, enjoys the idea of its existence, as if rape confirms that enormous sexual potency which he secretly knows to be his own. It is for the pleasure of the armchair rapist that detailed accounts of violent rapes exist in the media. Indeed, many men appear to take sexual pleasure from nearly all forms of violence. Whatever the motivation, male sexuality and violence in our culture seem to be inseparable. James Bond alternately whips out his revolver and his cock, and though there is no known connection between the skills of gun-fighting and love-making, pacifism seems suspiciously effeminate. . . .

In the spectrum of male behavior, rape, the perfect combination of sex and violence, is the penultimate act. Erotic pleasure cannot be separated from culture, and in our culture male eroticism is wedded to power. Not only should a man be taller and stronger than a female in the perfect love-match, but he must also demonstrate his superior strength in gestures of dominance which are perceived as amorous. Though the law attempts to make a clear division between rape and sexual intercourse, in fact the courts find it difficult to distinguish between a case where the decision to copulate was mutual and one where a man forced himself upon his partner.

The scenario is even further complicated by the expectation that, not only does a woman mean "yes" when she says "no," but that a really decent woman ought to begin by saying "no," and then be led down the primrose path to acquiescence. Ovid, the author of Western civilization's most celebrated sex-manual, makes this expectation perfectly clear:

> . . . and when I beg you to say "yes," say "no."
> Then let me lie outside your bolted door. . . . So
> Love grows strong. . . .

That the basic elements of rape are involved in all heterosexual relationships may explain why men often identify with the offender in this crime. But to regard the rapist as the victim, a man driven by his inherent sexual needs to take what will not be given him, reveals a basic ignorance of sexual politics. For in our culture heterosexual love finds an erotic expression through male dominance and female submission. A man who derives pleasure from raping a woman clearly must enjoy force and dominance as much or more than the simple pleasures of the flesh. Coitus cannot be experienced in isolation. The weather, the state of the nation, the level of sugar in the blood—all will affect a man's ability to achieve orgasm. If a man can achieve sexual pleasure after terrorizing and humiliating, the object of his passion, and in fact while inflicting pain upon her, one must assume he derives pleasure directly from terrorizing, humiliating and harming a woman. According to Amir's study of forcible rape, on a statistical average the man who has been convicted of rape was found to have a normal sexual personality,

tending to be different from the normal, well-adjusted male only in having a greater tendency to express violence and rage.

And if the professional rapist is to be separated from the average dominant heterosexual, it may be mainly a quantitative difference. For the existence of rape as an index to masculinity is not entirely metaphorical. Though this measure of masculinity seems to be more publicly exhibited among "bad boys" or aging bikers who practice sexual initiation through group rape, in fact, "good boys" engage in the same rites to prove their manhood. In Stockton, a small town in California which epitomizes silent-majority America, a bachelor party was given last summer for a young man about to be married. A woman was hired to dance "topless" for the amusement of the guests. At the high point of the evening the bridegroom-to-be dragged the woman into a bedroom. No move was made by any of his companions to stop what was clearly going to be an attempted rape. Far from it. As the woman described, "I tried to keep him away—told him of my *herpes genitalis*, et cetera, but he couldn't face the guys if he didn't screw me." After the bridegroom had finished raping the woman and returned with her to the party, far from chastising him, his friends heckled the woman and covered her with wine.

It was fortunate for the dancer that the bridegroom's friends did not follow him into the bedroom for, though one might suppose that in group rape, since the victim is outnumbered, less force would be inflicted on her, in fact, Amir's studies indicate, "the most excessive degrees of violence occurred in group rape." Far from discouraging violence, the presence of other men may in fact encourage sadism, and even cause the behavior. In an unpublished study of group rape by Gilbert Geis and Duncan Chappell, the authors refer to a study by W. H. Blanchard which relates, "The leader of the male group . . . apparently precipitated and maintained the activity, despite misgivings, because of a need to fulfill the role that the other two men had assigned to him. 'I was scared when it began to happen,' he says. 'I wanted to leave but I didn't want to say it to the other guys—you know—that I was scared.'"

Thus it becomes clear that not only does our culture teach men the rudiments of rape, but society, or more specifically other men, encourage the practice of it.

II

Every man I meet wants to protect me. Can't figure out what from.

—Mae West

. . . According to the male mythology which defines and perpetuates rape, it is an animal instinct inherent in the male. The story goes that sometime in our prehistorical past, the male, more hirsute and burly than today's counterparts, roamed about an uncivilized landscape until he found a desirable female. (Oddly enough, this female is *not* pictured as more muscular than the modern woman.) Her mate does not bother with courtship. He simply grabs her by the hair and drags her to the closest cave. Presumably, one of the major advantages of modern civilization for the female has been the civilizing of the male. We call it chivalry.

But women do not get chivalry for free. According to the logic of sexual politics, we too have to civilize our behavior. (Enter chastity. Enter virginity. Enter monogamy.) For the female, civilized behavior means chastity before marriage and faithfulness within it. Chivalrous behavior in the male is supposed to protect that chastity from involuntary defilement. The fly in the ointment of this otherwise peaceful system is the fallen woman. She does not behave. And therefore she does not deserve protection. Or, to use another argument, a major tenet of the same value system: what has once been defiled cannot again be violated. One begins to suspect that it is the behavior of the fallen woman, and not that of the male, that civilization aims to control.

The assumption that a woman who does not respect the double standard deserves whatever she gets (or at the very least "asks for it") operates in the courts today. While in some states a man's previous rape convictions are not considered admissible evidence, the sexual reputation of the rape victim is considered a crucial element of the facts upon which the court must decide innocence or guilt. . . .

According to the double standard, a woman who has had sexual intercourse out of wedlock cannot be raped. Rape is not only a crime of aggression against the body; it is a transgression against chastity as defined by men. When a woman is forced into a sexual relationship, she has, according to the male ethos, been violated. But she is also defiled if she does not behave according to the double standard, by maintaining her chastity, or confining her sexual activities to a monogamous relationship.

One should not assume, however, that a woman can avoid the possibility of rape simply by behaving. Though myth would have it that mainly "bad girls" are raped, this theory has no basis in fact. Available statistics would lead one to believe that a safer course is promiscuity. In a study of rape done in the District of Columbia, it was found that 82 percent of the rape victims had a "good reputation." Even the Police Inspector's advice to stay off the streets is rather useless, for almost half of reported rapes occur in the home of the victim and are committed by a man she has never before seen. Like indiscriminate terrorism, rape can happen to any woman, and few women are ever without this knowledge.

But the courts and the police, both dominated by white males, continue to suspect the rape victim, *sui generis,* of provoking or asking for her own assault. According to Amir's study, the police tend to believe that a woman without a good reputation cannot be raped. The rape victim is usually submitted to countless questions about her own sexual mores and behavior by the police investigator. This preoccupation is partially justified by the legal requirements for prosecution in a rape case. The rape victim must have been penetrated, and she must have made it clear to her assailant that she did not want penetration (unless of course she is unconscious). A refusal to accompany a man to some isolated place to allow him to touch her does not in the eyes of the court, constitute rape. She must have said "no" at the crucial genital moment. And the rape victim, to qualify as such, must also have put up a physical struggle—unless she can prove that to do so would have been to endanger her life.

But the zealous interest the police frequently exhibit in the physical details of a rape case is only partially explained by the requirements of the court. A woman who was raped in Berkeley was asked to tell the story of her rape four different times "right out in the street," while her assailant was escaping. She was then required to submit to a pelvic examination to prove that penetration had taken place. Later, she was taken to the police station where she was asked the same questions again: "Were you forced?" "Did he penetrate?" "Are you sure your life was in danger and you had no other choice?" This woman had been pulled off the street by a man who held a 10-inch knife at her throat and forcibly raped her. She was raped at midnight and was not able to return to her home until five in the morning. Police contacted her twice again in the next week, once by telephone at two in the morning and once at four in the morning. In her words, "The rape was probably the least traumatic incident of the whole evening. If I'm ever raped again, . . . I wouldn't report it to the police because of all the degradation. . . ."

If white women are subjected to unnecessary and often hostile questioning after having been raped, Third World women* are often not believed at all. According to the white male ethos (which is not only sexist but racist), Third World women are defined from birth as "impure." Thus the white male is provided with a pool of women who are fair game for sexual imperialism. Third World women frequently do not report rape and for good reason. When blues singer Billie Holliday was 10 years old, she was taken off to a local house by a neighbor and raped. Her mother brought the police to rescue her, and she was taken to the local station crying and bleeding:

---

*Editor's note: "Third World" was used to describe women of color in the United States at the time this article was written.

When we got there, instead of treating me and Mom like somebody who called the cops for help, they treated me like I'd killed somebody. . . . I guess they had me figured for having enticed this old goat into the whorehouse. . . . All I know for sure is they threw me into a cell . . . a fat white matron . . . saw I was still bleeding, she felt sorry for me and gave me a couple glasses of milk. But nobody else did anything for me except give me filthy looks and snicker to themselves.

After a couple of days in a cell they dragged me into a court. Mr. Dick got sentenced to five years. They sentenced me to a Catholic institution.

Clearly the white man's chivalry is aimed only to protect the chastity of "his" women.

As a final irony, that same system of sexual values from which chivalry is derived has also provided womankind with an unwritten code of behavior, called femininity, which makes a feminine woman the perfect victim of sexual aggression. If being chaste does not ward off the possibility of assault, being feminine certainly increases the chances that it will succeed. To be submissive is to defer to masculine strength; is to lack muscular development or any interest in defending oneself; is to let doors be opened, to have one's arm held when crossing the street. To be feminine is to wear shoes which make it difficult to run; skirts which inhibit one's stride; underclothes which inhibit the circulation. Is it not an intriguing observation that those very clothes which are thought to be flattering to the female and attractive to the male are those which make it impossible for a woman to defend herself against aggression?

Each girl as she grows into womanhood is taught fear. Fear is the form in which the female internalizes both chivalry and the double standard. Since, biologically speaking, women in fact have the same if not greater potential for sexual expression as do men, the woman who is taught that she must behave differently from a man must also learn to distrust her own carnality. She must deny her own feelings and learn not to act from them. She fears herself. This is the essence of passivity, and of course, a woman's passivity is not simply sexual

518 *CHAPTER VII: VIOLENCE AGAINST WOMEN*

but functions to cripple her from self-expression in every area of her life.

Passivity itself prevents a woman from ever considering her own potential for self-defense and forces her to look to men for protection. The woman is taught fear, but this time fear of the other; and yet her only relief from this fear is to seek out the other. Moreover, the passive woman is taught to regard herself as impotent, unable to act, unable even to perceive, in no way self-sufficient, and, finally, as the object and not the subject of human behavior. It is in this sense that a woman is deprived of the status of a human being. She is not free to be. . . .

III

If the basic social unit is the family, in which the woman is a possession of her husband, the super-structure of society is a male hierarchy, in which men dominate other men (or patriarchal families dominate other patriarchal families). And it is no small irony that, while the very social fabric of our male-dominated culture denies women equal access to political, economic, and legal power, the literature, myth, and humor of our culture depict women not only as the power behind the throne, but the real source of the oppression of men. The religious version of this fairy tale blames Eve for both carnality and eating of the tree of knowledge, at the same time making her gullible to the obvious devices of a serpent. Adam, of course, is merely the trusting victim of love. Certainly this is a biased story. But no more biased than the one television audiences receive today from the latest slick comedians. Through a media which is owned by men, censored by a State dominated by men, all the evils of this social system which make a man's life unpleasant are blamed upon "the wife." The theory is: were it not for the female who waits and plots to "trap" the male into marriage, modern man would be able to achieve Olympian freedom. She is made the scapegoat for a system which is in fact run by men.

Nowhere is this more clear than in the white racist use of the concept of white womanhood. The white male's open rape of black women, coupled with his overweening concern for the chastity and protection of his wife and daughters, represents an extreme of sexist and racist hypocrisy. While on the one hand she was held up as the standard for purity and virtue, on the other the Southern white woman was never asked if she wanted to be on a pedestal, and in fact any deviance from the male-defined standards for white womanhood was treated severely. (It is a powerful commentary on American racism that the historical role of blacks as slaves, and thus possessions without power, has robbed black women of legal and economic protection through marriage. Thus black women in Southern society and in the ghettoes of the North have long been easy game for white rapists.) The fear that black men would rape white women was, and is, classic paranoia. Quoting from Ann Breen's unpublished study of racism and sexism in the South, "*The New South: White Man's Country,*" Frederick Douglass legitimately points out that, "had the black man wished to rape white women, he had ample opportunity to do so during the civil war when white women, the wives, sisters, daughters, and mothers of the rebels, were left in the care of blacks. But yet not a single act of rape was committed during this time. The Ku Klux Klan, who tarred and feathered black men and lynched them in the honor of the purity of white womanhood, also applied tar and feathers to a Southern white woman accused of bigamy, which leads one to suspect that Southern white men were not so much outraged at the violation of the woman as a person, in the few instances where rape was actually committed by black men, but at the violation of his property rights." In the situation where a black man was found to be having sexual relations with a white woman, the white woman could exercise skin-privilege, and claim that she had been raped, in which case the black man was lynched. But if she did not claim rape, she herself was subject to lynching.

In constructing the myth of white womanhood so as to justify the lynching and oppression of black men and women, the white male has created a convenient symbol of his own power which has resulted in black hostility toward the white "bitch," accompanied by an unreasonable fear on the part of many white women of the black rapist. Moreover, it is not surprising that after being told for two centuries that he wants to rape white women, occasionally a black man does actually commit that act. But it is crucial to note that the frequency of this practice is outrageously exaggerated in the white mythos. Ninety percent of reported rape is intra- not interracial. . . .

Indeed, the existence of rape in any form is beneficial to the ruling class of white males. For rape is a kind of terrorism which severely limits the freedom of women and makes women dependent on men. Moreover, in the act of rape, the rage that one man may harbor toward another higher in the male hierarchy can be deflected toward a female scapegoat. For every man there is always someone lower on the social scale on whom he can take out his aggressions. And that is any woman alive.

This oppressive attitude toward women finds its institutionalization in the traditional family. For it is assumed that a man "wears the pants" in his family—he exercises the option of rule whenever he so chooses. Not that he makes all the decisions— clearly women make most of the important day-to-day decisions in a family. But when a conflict of interest arises, it is the man's interest which will prevail. His word, in itself, is more powerful. He lords it over his wife in the same way his boss lords it over him, so that the very process of exercising his power becomes as important an act as obtaining whatever it is his power can get for him. This notion of power is key to the male ego in this culture, for the two acceptable measures of masculinity are a man's power over women and his power over other men. A man may boast to his friends that "I have 20 men working for me." It is also aggrandizement of his ego if he has the financial power to clothe his wife in furs and jewels. And, if a man lacks the wherewithal to acquire such power, he can always express his rage through equally masculine activities—rape and theft. Since

male society defines the female as a possession, it is not surprising that the felony most often committed together with rape is theft. . . .

★ ★ ★

Rape is an act of aggression in which the victim is denied her self-determination. It is an act of violence, which if not actually followed by beatings or murder, nevertheless always carries with it the threat of death. And finally, rape is a form of mass terrorism, for the victims of rape are chosen indiscriminately, but the propagandists for male supremacy broadcast that it is women who cause rape by being unchaste or in the wrong place at the wrong time—in essence, by behaving as though they were free.

The threat of rape is used to deny women employment. (In California, the Berkeley Public Library, until pushed by the Federal Employment Practices Commission, refused to hire female shelvers because of perverted men in the stacks.) The fear of rape keeps women off the streets at night. Keeps women at home. Keeps women passive and modest for fear that they be thought provocative.

It is part of human dignity to be able to defend oneself, and women are learning. Some women have learned karate; some to shoot guns. And yet we will not be free until the threat of rape and the atmosphere of violence are ended, and to end that the nature of male behavior must change.

But rape is not an isolated act that can be rooted out from patriarchy without ending patriarchy itself. The same men and power structure who victimize women are engaged in the act of raping Vietnam, raping black people and the very earth we live upon. Rape is a classic act of domination where, in the words of Kate Millett, "the emotions of hatred, contempt, and the desire to break or violate personality," take place. This breaking of the personality characterizes modern life itself. No simple reforms can eliminate rape. As the symbolic expression of the white male hierarchy, rape is the quintessential act of our civilization, one which, Valerie Solanis warns, is in danger of "humping itself to death."   [1971]

520 *CHAPTER VII: VIOLENCE AGAINST WOMEN*

Rape Law Reform

AMY SILVESTRO

Feminists have struggled to align rape law with the twenty-first century. However, the penal system continues to be confounded by the almost religious adherence to the belief that a woman's word is inherently unreliable. Such prejudice is manifested in the chameleonlike definition of consent in rape law. As a result, 30 years of rape law reform have not deterred the commission of rape nor increased its prosecution or conviction rates.[1]

For example, at first glance, recent changes to marital rape law seem progressive. In fact, in every state there is now protection for wives who are raped by their husbands. But, in several of those states, women must prove the use of physical force—that being the court's only proof that she really *meant* no.

Rape shield laws have been a failure.[2] Repeated challenges have rendered them all but ineffective, revealing the continued power of the myth that once a woman says yes, she is no longer entitled to say no. Most notable are cases where a woman has previously consented to sex with the defendant, or has allowed some degree of intimacy. A woman's prior, consensual sexual behavior should be irrelevant to the question of whether she consents to sexual intercourse with any individual man.

Reformers argue that nothing less than an explicit verbal yes (the affirmative permission requirement)[3] should ever count as consent. It is not enough to demand that the law assert that "no" means "no" as in some cases a woman may abstain from saying no in order to protect herself; silence is not consent. State laws are inadequate when they declare that nonconsent is only established when ". . . the victim clearly expressed that he or she did not consent to engage in such act, and a reasonable person in the [defendant's] situation would have understood such a person's words and acts as an expression of lack of consent to such act under all the circumstances" as New York did in 2001.[4] Here, "no" is taken at face value only if the *perpetrator* believes she really means no.

The next, and final wave of rape law reform must establish an affirmative permission requirement in which consent is given freely and not as a result of coercion or threat. Control of our sexual lives is our right, and must be protected.

---

[1]See Ilene Seidman and Susan Vickers, *The Second Wave: An Agenda for the Next Thirty Years of Rape Law Reform,* Suffolk University Law Review 38 (2005), p. 1.
[2]See generally Michelle J. Anderson, *From Chastity Requirement to Sexuality License: Sexual Consent and a New Rape Shield Law,* George Washington Law Review 70 (2002).
[3]See Seidman and Vickers, p. 485.
[4]N.Y. Penal Law 130.05 (2)(d) (McKinney, 2001).

141

Whose Body Is It, Anyway?

PAMELA FLETCHER

RAPE

I never heard the word while growing up. Or, if I had, I blocked it out because its meaning was too horrific for my young mind: a stranger, a weapon, a dark place, blood, pain, even death. But I do remember other people's responses to it, especially those of women. I specifically remember hearing about Rachel when I was in high school in the seventies. The story was that she "let" a group of boys "pull a train" on her in the football field one night. I remember the snickers and the looks of disgust of both the girls and the boys around campus. It was common knowledge that nobody with eyes would want to fuck Rachel; she had a face marred by acne and glasses. But, she had *some* body.

While I am writing this essay, I remember the stark sadness and confusion I felt then. This same sadness returns to me now, but I am no longer confused. Then I wondered how she could "do" so many guys and actually like it (!). Then I thought maybe she didn't like it after all, and maybe, just maybe, they made her do it. But the word rape never entered my mind. After all, she knew them, didn't she? There was no weapon, no blood. She survived, didn't she? And, just what was she doing there all by herself, anyway? Now, I know what "pulling a train" is. Now I know they committed a violent crime against her body and her soul. Now I know why she walked around campus with that wounded face, a face that none of us girls wanted to look into because we knew intuitively that we would see a reflection of our own wounded selves. So the other girls did not look into her eyes. They avoided her and talked about her like she was "a bitch in heat." Why else would such a thing have happened to her?

I tried to look into Rachel's eyes because I wanted to know something—what, I didn't know. But she looked down or looked away or laughed like a lunatic, you know, in that eerie, loud, nervous manner that irritated and frightened me because it didn't ring true. Now I wonder if she thought such laughter would mask her pain. It didn't.

PAINFUL SILENCE AND DEEP-SEATED RAGE

I remember another story I heard while I was in college. Larry told me that his close friend, Brenda, let Danny stay over one night in her summer apartment after they had smoked some dope, and he raped her. Larry actually said that word.

"Don't tell anyone," Brenda begged him. "I never should have let him spend the night. I thought he was my friend."

Larry told me not to ever repeat it to anyone else. And, trying to be a loyal girlfriend to him and a loyal friend to Brenda, I didn't say anything. When we saw Danny later at another friend's place, we neither confronted nor ignored him. *We acted as though everything was normal.* I felt agitated and angry. I wondered why Larry didn't say anything to Danny, you know, man-to-man, like: "That shit was not cool, man. Why you go and do somethin' like that to the sista?"

It never occurred to me to say anything to Brenda, because I wasn't supposed to know, or I was supposed to act as though I didn't know, stupid stuff like that. I sat there, disconnected from her, watching her interact with people, Danny among them, acting as though everything was normal.

DENIAL

Since I began writing this essay two months ago, I have had such difficulty thinking about my own related experiences. I hadn't experienced rape. Or, had I? For months, in the hard drive of my subconscious mind, I searched for files that would yield any incidence of sexual violence or sexual terrorism. When certain memories surfaced, I questioned whether those experiences were "real rapes."

I have some very early recollections that challenge me. Max, my first boyfriend, my childhood sweetheart, tried to pressure me into having sex with him when we were in junior high. Two of my friends, who were the girlfriends of his two closest friends, also tried to pressure me because they were already "doing it" for their "men."

"Don't be a baby," they teased. "Everybody's doing it."

But I wouldn't cave in, and I broke up with Max because he wasn't a decent boy.

A year later, when we reached high school, I went crawling back to Max because I "loved" him and couldn't stand his ignoring me. He stopped ignoring me long enough to pin me up against the locker to kiss me roughly and to suck on my neck long and hard until he produced sore, purple bruises, what we called hickies. I had to hide those hideous marks from my parents by wearing turtleneck sweaters. Those hickies marked me as his property and gave his friends the impression that he had "done" me, even though we hadn't gotten that far yet. We still had to work out the logistics.

I hated when he gave me hickies, and I didn't like his exploring my private places as he emotionally and verbally abused me, telling me I wasn't pretty like Susan: "Why can't you look like her?" And I remember saying something like, "Why don't you go be with her, if that's what you want?" He answered me with a piercing "don't-you-ever-talk-to-me-like-that-again" look, and I never asked again. He continued, however, to ask me the same question.

In my heart, I realized that the way he treated me was wrong because I felt violated; I felt separated from my body, as if it did not belong to me. But at 16 I didn't know how or what to feel, except that I felt confused and desperately wanted to make sense out of what it meant to be a girl trapped inside a woman's body. Yes, I felt trapped, because I understood that we girls had so much to lose now that we could get pregnant. Life sagged with seriousness. Now everybody kept an eye on us: our parents, the churches, the schools, and the boys. Confusion prevailed. While we were encouraged to have a slight interest in boys (lest we turn out "funny") so that ultimately we could be trained to become good wives, we were instructed directly and indirectly to keep a safe distance away from them.

We liked boys and we thought we wanted love, but what we really wanted as youth was to have some fun, some clean, innocent fun until we got married and gave our virtuous selves to our husbands just as our mothers had done. We female children had inherited this lovely vision from our mothers and from fairy tales. Yet now we know that those visions were not so much what our mothers had experienced, but what they wished they had experienced, and what they wanted for us.

We thought "going with a boy" in the early seventies would be romance-filled fun that involved holding hands, stealing kisses, exchanging class rings, and wearing big lettered sweaters. Maybe it was, for some of us. But I know that many of us suffered at the hands of love.

I soon learned in high school that it was normal to be mistreated by our boyfriends. Why else would none of us admit to each other the abuse we tolerated? These boys "loved" us, so we believed that they were entitled to treat us in any way they chose. We believed that somehow we belonged to them, body and soul. Isn't that what many of the songs on the radio said? And we just knew somehow that if we did give in to them, we deserved whatever happened, and if we didn't give in, we still deserved whatever happened. Such abuse was rampant because we became and remained isolated from each other by hoisting our romances above our friendships.

We didn't define what they did to us as rape, molestation, or sexual abuse. We called it love. We called it love if it happened with our boyfriends, and we called other girls whores and sluts if it happened with someone else's boyfriend or boyfriends, as in the case of Rachel and "the train."

We called it love because we had tasted that sweet taste of pain. Weren't they one and the same?

REALIZATION

One sharp slap from Max one day delivered the good sense I had somehow lost when I got to high school. After that point I refused to be his woman, his property. When I left home for college, I left with the keen awareness that I had better take good care of myself. In my involvement with Max, I had allowed a split to occur between my body and my soul, and I had to work on becoming whole again.

I knew that I was growing stronger (though in silent isolation from other young women and through intense struggle) when I was able to successfully resist being seduced (read: molested) by several college classmates and when I successfully fought off the violent advances and the verbal abuse (what I now recognize as an attempted rape) of someone with whom I had once been sexually intimate.

But how does a woman become strong and whole in a society in which women are not permitted (as if we need permission!) to possess ourselves, to own our very bodies? We females often think we are not entitled to ourselves, and many times we give ourselves away for less than a song. The sad truth of the matter is that this is how we have managed to survive in our male-dominated culture. Yet, in the wise words of the late Audre Lorde, "the Master's tools will never dismantle the Master's house." In other words, as long as we remain disconnected from ourselves and each other and dependent on abusive males, we will remain weak, powerless, and fragmented.

Just imagine how different our lives would be today if we were not injured by internalized misogyny and sexism. Imagine how different our lives would be if we would only open our mouths wide and collectively and loudly confront males and *really* hold them accountable for the violent crimes they perpetrate against females. Imagine how our lives would be if all mothers tell their daughters the truth about romantic love and teach them to love themselves as females, to value and claim their bodies, and to protect themselves against violent and disrespectful males.

What if we girls in junior high and high school believed we deserve respect rather than verbal and sexual abuse from our male classmates? What if we girls in my high school had confronted the gang of boys who raped Rachel that night in the football field 20 years ago, rather than perpetuated that cycle of abuse and shame she suffered? What if Larry and I had confronted Danny for raping Brenda that summer night in her apartment? What if Brenda had felt safe enough to tell Larry, me, and the police? What if we females believed ourselves and each other to

be as important and deserving of our selfhood as we believe males to be? Just imagine.

Envision a time when we women are connected to ourselves and each other, when we no longer feel the need and desire to conspire with men against each other in order to survive in a misogynist, violent culture. We must alter our destructive thinking about being female so that we can begin to accept, love, and cherish our femaleness. It is the essence of our lives.

Readjusting our lens so we can begin to see ourselves and each other as full, capable, and mighty human beings will take as much work as reconstructing our violent society. Neither job is easy, but the conditions and the tasks go hand in hand. Two ways to begin our own transformation are to become physically active in whatever manner we choose so we can take pleasure in fully connecting to ourselves and in growing physically stronger, and to respect, protect, support, and comfort each other. Once we stop denying that our very lives are endangered, we will soon discover that these steps are not only necessary but viable in empowering ourselves and claiming our right to exist as whole human beings in a peaceful, humane world.   [1993]

🌿 142

Rape and Gender Violence: From Impunity to Accountability in International Law

RHONDA COPELON

"I would like to once again prosecute the Japanese military. They damaged my body and I cannot be productive any more and I would like to have the Japanese government apologize and also pay reparations. I am an old woman and I don't know how long I will live but I will not give up until I win my victory."
—Yuan Zhu-lin of China testifying before the Women's International War Crimes Tribunal on Japan's Military Sexual Slavery

524   *CHAPTER VII: VIOLENCE AGAINST WOMEN*

Less than a decade ago, it was openly questioned whether rape was a war crime. Human rights and humanitarian organizations largely ignored sexual violence and the needs of its victims. The connection between sexual conquest of women and war was considered natural and inevitable, an essential engine of war, rewarding soldiers and readying them to fight again. The rape of women in prison was not considered torture but was usually noted as a lesser abuse and even excused in law as a mere personal indiscretion, while official toleration of privately inflicted gender violence was ignored as a human rights issue. Rape was the fault of unchaste women or brushed under the rug, and thus raped women were consigned to invisibility, isolation, and shame.

These cultural attitudes and practices were reinforced by the evolution of the classification of rape in the laws of war. In the 1907 Hague Convention, rape was delicately coded as a "violation of family honor and rights," simultaneously invoking male entitlement and female chastity. Rape was thus explicitly cast as a moral offense, not a crime of violence; the fault lay with the victims, not the perpetrators. The 1949 Geneva Conventions did not name rape, but subsumed it within other offenses. Rape was specifically mentioned, along with "enforced prostitution and indecent assault," as among the "outrages against personal dignity" in the 1977 Second Geneva Protocol relating to non-international armed conflict. With rare exceptions, impunity for rape was the rule of the day.

Courageous and concerted actions of women around the world forced a sea change in international law, culminating in the recognition of gender violence as a human rights concern and in its codification as among the gravest international crimes in the Rome Statute of the International Criminal Court (ICC). In the early 1990s, Korean former "comfort women" broke 50 years of silence to expose Japan's systemization of military sexual slavery during the Second World War. Soon thereafter, survivors, committed journalists, and feminist human rights advocates forced the story of the rape of women in the former Yugoslavia into the media and into international consciousness; and Haitian women, working underground, organized

to document the rape of women under the illegal Cedras regime. A growing women's human rights movement and reports by human rights groups demanded recognition of the crime of rape and discredited the notion that women wouldn't talk about it. In a series of United Nations conferences and other forums, survivors and activists from around the globe challenged the exclusion of gender violence and women's human rights from the human rights agenda.

The turning point was the 1993 World Conference on Human Rights in Vienna, which prioritized violence against women and gender mainstreaming throughout the human rights system. Responding to women's demands, the International Criminal Tribunal for the former Yugoslavia began to prosecute rape and sexual violence, including torture and enslavement as crimes against humanity, while the International Criminal Tribunal for Rwanda prosecuted rape as genocide.

These developments laid the foundation for the gender provisions of the Rome Statute of the ICC, which created the world's first permanent criminal court with jurisdiction over genocide, war crimes, and crimes against humanity and provides for future jurisdiction over the crime of aggression. As a result of the interventions and organizing of women's human rights activists and allies, largely through the vehicle of the Women's Caucus for Gender Justice, the Rome Statute is a landmark in the struggle for gender justice, codifying a broad range of sexual and gender crimes as well as structures and procedures necessary to make gender justice a reality.

The Rome Statute names a broad range of sexual and reproductive violent crimes—rape, sexual slavery including trafficking, forced pregnancy, enforced prostitution, enforced sterilization, and other serious sexual violence—as among the gravest crimes of war. These are also "crimes against humanity" when committed as part of a widespread or systematic attack on a civilian population, in times of peace as well as war, and by nonstate actors as well as officials. In addition, crimes against humanity include persecution based on gender. The Rome Statute's overarching principle against gender discrimination also prevents the ghettoization and trivialization of sexual and gender crimes and encourages their prosecution, where appropriate, as traditional crimes such as genocide, torture, enslavement, and inhuman treatment.

The adoption of gender crimes withstood virulent opposition from the Vatican, which has the privileges but not the responsibilities of a state in the U.N., and some Arab states. Opponents correctly perceived that crimes against humanity apply not only to rape in war but also to widespread or systemic sexual and gender crimes in everyday life. Thus, 11 Arab states sought explicitly to immunize rape, sexual slavery, and other sexual violence when committed in the family or as part of religion, tradition, or culture. In addition, the United States urged that slavery be confined to commercial exchange and sought more generally to immunize tolerance of these crimes from criminal responsibility.

Furthermore, after intense negotiations, "gender" was defined to include the social construction of male and female roles and identities, in opposition to efforts to define gender biologically and thereby exclude persecution against gender nonconformists, whether they be single women or transgendered people. Though some compromises were made, the fundamentalist positions were largely rejected, leaving the final word to the ICC judges in accordance with the principle against gender discrimination.

The Rome Statute also encompasses groundbreaking structures and processes to ensure that crimes will be prosecuted in a nondiscriminatory, respectful manner that minimizes the potential for retraumatization and overcomes women's reluctance to participate. Court personnel at every level must reflect a fair or equal representation of women and include experts on violence against women. As a result, 7 women were elected to the first ICC bench of 18 judges.

Investigations and trials contain safeguards that protect the safety and privacy of victims and enhance their role in the process. Evidentiary rules minimize some of the worst traditional features of rape trials, including distrust of women's testimony and humiliation through cross-examination about consent or their sexual histories. In addition, the statute anticipates the active participation of victims before the court and responds to the disconnect between punishment of perpetrators and the needs of victims by recognizing a role for the court in ensuring reparations.

Significantly, the ICC treaty should also affect domestic laws. It is not only the blueprint for the court; it reflects accepted minimal international norms for the operation of a justice system worldwide. The principle of complementarity encourages states to adopt its provisions as local law in order to retain the right to try national offenders. The ICC thereby powerfully supports women's domestic law reform efforts.

But will the ICC help to transform the legal and cultural acceptance of sexual violence? If the ICC survives the current assault by the Bush administration and implements its gender-inclusive mandate, it is possible that it will make a global difference. If its norms become accepted as military and domestic law, sexual violence will no longer be exempt from punishment and hopefully will become less tolerated legally as well as culturally. The survival of the court and of its norms is crucial to legitimating norms of gender justice and shifting both blame and shame from victim to perpetrator. Most importantly, perhaps, the court will contribute to the process of empowering women to say "no" to the shame that society has demanded and will increase the possibility of reparations and participation in peacebuilding. All this requires committed and knowledgeable judicial personnel as well as persistent monitoring and engagement by NGOs at every level.

Women's myriad campaigns around the world, including the continuing struggle for justice by the "comfort women," make clear that women's sexual autonomy and gender-inclusive justice are critical components of women's full citizenship. But formal justice alone will not eliminate these crimes, nor ensure women's empowerment, nor address the roots of militarism. Rape and sexual violence are products of long-standing male entitlement to control and abuse of the bodies and lives of women and perpetuate women's economic, political, cultural, sexual, and psychological subordination. Gender norms and accountability must, therefore, be part of a larger human rights mobilization for full equality,

526   *CHAPTER VII: VIOLENCE AGAINST WOMEN*

human rights, and empowerment of women as well as for peace, economic justice, and security. The Rome Statute is a watershed and the ICC a fragile, partial, yet crucial opportunity.   [2005]

143

Catcalls, Groping, and Stalking in Public Places: How to Deal with Street Harassment

HOLLY KEARL

"Being harassed just for being alone on the street happens so regularly, in so many different forms that I just expect it now . . . Whatever I wear, whatever I am doing, walking to work past a building site or out for a run, men [harass me]. If I react aggressively then I risk their anger at my ingratitude at being [treated as] an object . . . I'm sick of it. I just want to go about my day uninhibited in this so-called free country."
    —Contributor to the Stop Street Harassment Blog

Often starting during their early teenage years, as many as 80 percent of women around the world face at least occasional unwanted, harassing attention in public places from men they do not know.[1] The harassment ranges from legal leers, whistles, honks, kissing noises, nonsexually-explicit evaluative comments, vulgar gestures, and sexually charged comments, to illegal actions like flashing, stalking, public masturbation, sexual touching, assault, and rape. This type of unwanted, gender-based attention is termed street harassment.

Street harassment, often along with an underlying fear of it escalating into rape or murder, causes most women to feel unwelcome and unsafe in public at least sometimes, especially when they are alone. Street harassment is a form of sexual terrorism. Women never know when it might happen, by whom, or how far it may escalate. Because of street harassment, from a young age women learn that public spaces are male territory. They learn to limit the places they go, they try not to be in public alone (especially at night), and when they are alone, they stay on guard.

Outside of feminist circles, street harassment is rarely seen as a serious issue or as bullying. Instead it is treated as a compliment or "only" a minor annoyance and as a woman's fault due to her attractiveness, what she wore, or where she went. Consequently, victim blaming, including self-blame, is rampant.

If a woman hears that she is at fault for the harassment, she may think it is something she has to put up with and she may not speak about it or work to end it. She may tell other women it is complimentary or no big deal. She may believe it is her fault and change her appearance or habits or try to avoid being alone in places where she could be harassed, which also limits her access to public spaces and the resources there.[2]

Ultimately, to end street harassment, the onus should be on men to stop harassing women, but achieving that goal will take time. In the short term, it is important to empower both girls and women to lead less fearful and restricted public lives by teaching them that street harassment is not their fault and by equipping them with tactics for dealing with harassment.

One of the most important messages for girls and women, then, is that any street harassment they experience is not their fault, no matter what people may tell them. Women are not at fault because of what they wore, where they went, or what time of day or night they were in public, nor because they looked "too attractive" or "too vulnerable." Men who harass are at fault.

RESPONDING TO HARASSERS

Harassed girls and women are put in the difficult position of having to decide how to respond. Overwhelmingly, most women and girls ignore, walk away from, or humor their harassers. Their reasons may include fearing for their safety, being socialized to be polite and not make a scene, not knowing what else to say, not having the time or energy to do anything more, and not wanting to give the harasser the satisfaction of any response.[3]

These responses may be necessary, but they rarely deter a harasser from continuing their behavior and can leave women feeling disempowered and frustrated.[4]

Ignoring harassers can be harmful to women's self-esteem and health. At Rutgers University, psychology scholars Kimberly Fairchild and Laurie A. Rudman studied street harassment and women's self-objectification. Self-objectification means seeing oneself through the eyes of others. In the case of street harassment, it means seeing oneself through the eyes of the men who harass them. Studies show that girls and women who self-objectify are more prone to depression, low self-esteem, and eating disorders. A preoccupation with their looks can keep them from having as much energy and time for other pursuits.[5] In Fairchild and Rudman's study of 228 college women, the women who ignored or denied that the harassment was harassment reported higher rates of feeling self-objectified compared with women who responded to the harasser, reported him, or discussed the experience with friends.[6] Taking action against harassers, when possible, is better for women.

Also, despite a common belief that ignoring a harasser is the best way to stay safe, it is not always true. Crime reports show that women who have the highest success rate in escaping sexual assault are those who use a combination of early verbal and physical resistance, so if a fear of rape is keeping women silent against harassers, it is usually better for them to speak up.[7] The former executive director of the Washington, D.C., Rape Crisis Center, Martha Langelan, noted that there are men who use street harassment as a rape test, and they may attempt rape depending on how a woman responds to street harassment. If she is assertive and forceful, they are likely to leave her alone, but if she cowers or humors them, they may attempt rape.[8]

There is no magic formula or "best" way to respond to every harasser in every circumstance. Individual girls and women are the only ones who can determine the best way to respond in any given incident so they will feel both safe and empowered. The more informed they are about options for responding, the better they can be at making that decision.

Here are some suggestions for assertive responses.[9]
How to talk to a harasser:

- Always use strong body language: Look the harasser in the eyes; speak in a strong, clear voice. Using your voice, facial expressions, and body language together, without mixed signals, show assertiveness and strength.
- Project confidence and calm. Even if you do not feel that way, it is important to appear calm, serious, and confident.
- Do not apologize, make an excuse, or ask a question. You do not need to say sorry for how you feel or what you want. Be firm. Instead of saying, "Excuse me . . . ," "I'm sorry, but . . . ," or "Please . . . ," say directly, "Stop doing X."
- Do not get into a dialogue with the harasser, try to reason with them, or answer their questions. You do not need to respond to diversions, questions, threats, blaming, or guilt-tripping. Stay on your own agenda. Stick to your point. Repeat your statement or leave.
- Do not swear or lose your temper: This type of reaction is the most likely to give a harasser an excuse to escalate his actions into violence or verbal threats.
- Decide when you're done. Success is how you define it. If you said what you needed to say and you're ready to leave, do so.

Ideas for what you can say to a harasser:

- Name the behavior and state that it is wrong. For example say, "Do not whistle at me, that is harassment," or "Do not touch my butt, that is sexual harassment."
- Tell them exactly what you want. Say, for example, "Move away from me," "Stop touching me," or "Go stand over there."
- Use statements, not questions, if you tell them to leave you alone. For example, say, "Leave me alone," not "Would you please leave me alone?"
- Make an all-purpose antiharassment statement, such as: "Stop harassing women. I don't like it. No one likes it. Show some respect."

528   *CHAPTER VII: VIOLENCE AGAINST WOMEN*

- Use an A-B-C statement (and be very concrete about A and C).
  - A. Tell the harasser what the problem is;
  - B. State the effect; and
  - C. Say what you want. Here is an example: "When you make kissing noises at me, it makes me feel uncomfortable. I want you to say, 'Excuse me, . . .'" from now on if you want to address me."
- Identify the perpetrator: "Man in the yellow shirt, stop touching me." (This is especially useful if there are other people around.)
- Use the "Miss Manners Approach" and ask the harasser something like, "I beg your pardon!" or "I can't believe you said that," combined with strong facial expressions of shock, dismay, and disgust.
- Ask a Socratic question such as, "That's so interesting—can you explain why you think it's okay to call me, a stranger, your baby?"
- Turn what the harasser said into a joke.
- Ask them how they would feel if someone treated their sister, daughter, mother, aunt, girlfriend, or wife the way they are treating you.
- If the harasser is in a car, write down the license plate of the car. Even if you can't see it, pretending to write it down can scare the perpetrator into stopping.
- Tell the harasser that you are conducting a street harassment research project or survey. Take out a notebook and start asking them questions such as, "How often do you do this?" or "How do you choose which people to harass?" or "Are you more likely to do this when you are alone or when you're with other people," or "Do you discuss people you harass with your mother, sister, or female friends?"

If the harasser is threatening, touching, or following you, flashing or masturbating at you, you can try reporting him to the police. Find out what the harassment statutes are in your city that may cover other types of harassment, too. For example, in Independence, Missouri, there is a $500 fine or jail time when someone in a car harasses a pedestrian. Since you do not know the name of the harasser or where he lives, taking down a physical description or snapping a picture of him and a description of where it occurred will help your case if you report it. If there are other people nearby, make sure they realize the man's behavior is unwelcome and harassing, and see if they would be willing to be a witness to the police

Depending on where the harassment takes place, you can also report a harasser to a store manager or transit worker. And if the harasser works for an identifiable company and is harassing you while he is on company time, report him to the company. Stores and transit groups don't want to lose customers due to harassers, nor do companies want their employees harassing people on company time, so you often will see them take action. When you report the harasser in these cases, include a description of the person, the time of day, and the place, if possible.

For further information about responding to street harassers, visit www.stopstreetharassment.com, or read Martha Langelan's book *Back Off! How to Confront and Stop Sexual Harassment* (1993), Sue Wise and Liz Stanley's book *Georgie Porgie: Sexual Harassment in Everyday Life* (1987), my book *Stop Street Harassment: Making Public Places Safe and Welcoming for Women* (2010), and Girls for Gender Equity's book *Hey, Shorty! A Guide to Combating Sexual Harassment and Violence in Schools and on the Streets* (2011). Street harassment can be disempowering, but by using your creativity and smarts to think about how to respond to harassers in an empowering, safe way, you can take back your power and own your right to be in public.

NOTES

1. More than a dozen studies illustrating this statistic are found in chapter 1 of my book *Stop Street Harassment: Making Public Places Safe and Welcoming for Women* (NY: Praeger, 2010).
2. Martha Langelan, *Back Off! How to Confront and Stop Sexual Harassment and Harassers* (New York: Fireside Press, 1993): 99.
3. Brooks Gardner, Passing By: *Gender and Public Harassment*, University of California Press 1995. 148–57; see also Kimberly Fairchild and Laurie A. Rudman, "Everyday Stranger Harassment and Women's Self-Objectification," *Social Justice Research* 21, no. 3 (2008): 344; see also Sue Wise and Liz Stanley, *Georgie Porgie: Sexual Harassment in Everyday Life* (London: Pandora, 1987): 169.
4. Langelan, *Back Off!*, 102.

"Hey, Man, That's Not Cool": Men Stopping Street Harassment

Men who are not harassers are especially positioned to help stop street harassment, because men look to other men for approval and many men harass women only while with men to prove their masculinity through aggression and sexual comments or acts. A societal acceptance of most forms of harassment also contributes to its prevalence. There are many ways, then, that men can help stop street harassment, including by supporting healthy definitions of masculinity, promoting respect for women, and educating men about street harassment. Specific examples include:

- Not encouraging or condoning violence in any form, especially men's violence against women. That means not watching music videos, movies, or pornography or playing video games in which violence against women is glorified or sexualized. This also includes not supporting companies that use violent imagery to sell products.
- Not putting pressure on friends to "score," nor rewarding men for having multiple sexual partners (or penalizing women who do).
- Not describing women as body parts or referring to them only as sex objects instead of as complete human beings with personalities, interests, and talents.
- Not penalizing men or women who act outside their gender norms.
- Eliminating language like "pussy," "wuss," "fag," and "girl" as insults used to punish men who are not being "macho."
- Not penalizing, mocking, or dismissing men and women who speak out against violence, inequality, and disrespectful behaviors.
- Talking to other men about street harassment. Asking them to find out about street harassment from women they care about so they can better understand the issue.
- Brainstorming and role-playing ways to intervene in a harassment incident: either before it occurs, if your friends are the would-be perpetrators, or when you see it.
- Always standing up for other people, for human rights, for human dignity.

For more information and examples of bystander tactics that work, see chapter 7 of Holly Kearl's book *Stop Street Harassment: Making Public Places Safe and Welcoming for Women* (2010) or visit www.stopstreetharassment for a section specifically for male allies. If you care about the women in your life, do something to stop street harassment to make public places safer for them.

5. Caroline Heldman, "Out-of-Body Image," *Ms.*, Spring 2008, http://www.msmagazine.com/spring2008/outOfBodyImage.asp.
6. Fairchild and Rudman, "Everyday Stranger Harassment," 353.
7. Margaret T. Gordon and Stephanie Riger, *The Female Fear: The Social Cost of Rape* (Urbana: University of Illinois Press, 1991), 120.
8. Langelan, *Back Off!*, 45.
9. Along with my own suggestions, this list includes ideas that have been suggested other experts, including Martha Langelan, Lauren R. Taylor, and Dr. Bernice Sandler.

144

High-School Gauntlet

RACHEL

In my high school there is a patio area where everyone hangs out in between classes and during lunch. The school is small, so you can see everyone from the benches at the end of the patio. That is where the most popular boys in the school used to sit. Every day, as each girl passed, these boys stared at her and rated her different body parts from one to ten. The girls dreaded walking out of the lunchroom. This practice had been going on for years and I'm pretty sure that's why our school had one of the highest eating-disorder rates in the state.

I was friendly with these boys. I knew them all, and actually I was always glad about that because even though they still rated me, at least they never publicly humiliated me by yelling out the numbers. Until one day.

"Six."

"What? No way. That's Rachel. Eight."

"Ha! Seven for the bottom, five and a half for the top."

I felt so degraded and worthless I spent the rest of the lunch period hiding in the bathroom.

But something else happened that day, too. The girls at my school, girls who were usually so competitive with and cruel to one another, started talking. It began in the bathroom, when I rallied us together by suggesting we take action against these boys.

The next day at lunch a bunch of us girls got to the "boys' bench" before they did. We sat and waited until they approached, and when they did we called out *their* ratings as they walked by. We had it all planned out: When they came up to us to talk, we lifted their shirts and grabbed at them just the way they did to us every day. Then we handed each a letter I'd written and gotten 158 girls to sign. It said they needed to stop their behavior right away and that we were not going to stand for it any more.

It sounds amazing, but from then on it all stopped. Instead of taking their intimidating places on the bench, the boys mingled in the lunchroom. If any of the guys made any angry or sexual comments toward us about what we had done, they were immediately silenced by their friends.

It feels great knowing I did something good for girls, especially something that will help those who have yet to enter the frightening halls of high school.   [2002]

🌿 145

Naming and Studying Acquaintance Rape

PEGGY REEVES SANDAY

"When it comes to my masculinity I get very defensive. Because I know that men are admired for having many partners, I set quotas—so many girls in one month. The joy of sex for me is the feeling of acceptance and approval which always goes with having sex with a new person."
                                    —Male college student[1]

Martha McCluskey went to college during a time when feminist activism for rape reform was well under way, though not yet widely publicized outside scholarly and legal circles. In 1977 she was sexually abused by a group of fraternity brothers while a student at Colby College. At the time, however, Martha thought that being assaulted by "normal white college men . . . was not significant" and she didn't understand it as "real violence." It wasn't until after graduating from Yale Law School that she wrote about the assault in an article in the *Maine Law Review* on "privileged violence in college fraternities."

It happened at the beginning of vacation, when her dorm was nearly empty. As she described it:

I am standing in the hallway looking out the window for my ride home. I turn around and my suitcase is gone; Joe and Bill from down the hall are laughing as they carry it away. I follow them. I hear a door lock behind me. They let go of my suitcase and grab me.

I am lying on the bare linoleum floor of Joe's bedroom. In the room are a group of Lambda Chi and KDR pledges who live on my hall; several of them are football players. Some are sitting on the bed, laughing. Two others are pinning my arms and my legs to the floor. Joe is touching me while the others cheer.

I am a friendly fellow-classmate as I reasonably explain that I'm in a rush to catch a ride, that I'm not in the mood to joke around; that I'd really like them to please cut it out. It takes a few long upside-down seconds before things look different. As I start to scream and fight I feel like I am shattering a world that will not get put back together. They let me go.

Later I don't talk about this, not even to myself. I sit near Joe and Bill in sociology and English classes. I don't talk in class.[2]

Starting in the 1970s, research on acquaintance rape conducted by psychologists, sociologists, and medical researchers began, and by the 1990s a significant body of knowledge on all aspects of sexual assault and abuse had been established. At first the research focused on the annual incidence and lifetime prevalence of acquaintance rape in order to establish the scope of the problem, but soon it expanded to include causes, consequences, social and psychological costs, and prevention. The studies operated within the legal definition of rape as sexual intercourse, including oral or anal penetration, due to force, the threat of force, or by taking advantage of a person's incapacity to consent. Most studies focused on the heterosexual rape of females. However, in recent years attention has turned also to the heterosexual and same-sex rape of male victims. Least attention has been given to same-sex rape of women.[3]

THE EARLY STUDIES

Studies making a distinction between jump-from-the-bushes stranger rape and rape involving people who know one another go back at least to the 1950s. In 1952 the *Yale Law Journal* recognized that rape ranges from "brutal attacks familiar to tabloid readers to half-won arguments of couples in parked cars." Kalven and Zeisel's distinction between "aggravated" and "simple" rape in their national study of 1950s trials was the first to demonstrate that a significant proportion (40 percent) of rape cases going to trial involved acquaintances. Both of these acknowledged that when the parties know one another, a conviction is much more difficult. Kalven and Zeisel were able to attribute the difficulty to juror prejudice by showing that judges were much more likely than jurors to believe that the evidence warranted a conviction in cases of simple rape.[4]

The best-known of the early studies acknowledging the scope of acquaintance rape was authored by

sociologist Menachem Amir. Based on an examination of police files of rapes occurring in 1958 and 1960, Amir concluded that rapists are generally "normal" men. About half of all the rapes were committed by men who knew their victims. Only 42 percent of the rapists were complete strangers to their victims, and not all of the victims resisted to the utmost.[5] More than half of the victims were submissive during the rape; about one-fifth of the victims put up a strong physical fight; and another quarter actively resisted in some other way, like screaming. Twenty percent of the victims were between the ages of 10 and 14, and 25 percent were between 15 and 19. The younger the victim, the less likely she was to resist.[6]

The first widely read feminist studies mentioning acquaintance or date rape were authored by Susan Brownmiller and Diana Russell in the mid-1970s. In her landmark study, *Against Our Will*, Brownmiller is the first to use the term "date rape." The kind of interaction Brownmiller labeled date rape was typical of men and women caught in the double bind of the sexual revolution. Men pressed their advantage thinking that all women now "wanted it," but nice girls hadn't yet learned to make a no stick.

Brownmiller's historic contribution to the anti-rape movement is in her valuable analysis of the cultural forces shaping female passivity when confronted with male sexual aggression and her conceptualization of rape as violence. Brownmiller urged a generation of young women to learn to say no and overcome their historical training to be nice. She recognized that date rapes hardly ever get to court and don't look good on paper because the "intangibles of victim behavior . . . present a poor case."[7] These are the kinds of cases that Kalven and Zeisel found usually ended in acquittals. Before she began researching rape in the early 1970s, Diana Russell held the "crazed stranger" theory of rape, believing that rape was "an extremely sadistic and deviant act, which could be performed only by crazy or psychopathic people." The idea had never occurred to her that rape by a lover, friend, or colleague was possible. She learned differently in 1971 while she was attending the highly publicized rape

532   *CHAPTER VII: VIOLENCE AGAINST WOMEN*

trial of Jerry Plotkin in San Francisco. Plotkin was a jeweler accused of abducting a young woman at gunpoint to his swank apartment, where he and three other men raped her and forced her to commit various sexual acts.[8]

During the trial, which drew many feminist protestors, Russell began hearing stories from other women who had been raped but who had not reported the rape, fearing the treatment they would probably receive in the courtroom. The outcome of the Plotkin trial was a grim reminder of why so few were willing to report. The jury acquitted Plotkin because of the complainant's prior sex life, which was gone over in minute detail in the courtroom.[9] Convinced of the injustice of the verdict and aware of the need for further education, Russell embarked on a program of research that would produce two of the most important early studies of acquaintance rape. The first demonstrated that rape is just as likely to occur between acquaintances as between strangers, and the second provided a statistical profile of acquaintance- versus stranger-rape in a diverse population of all social classes and racial/ethnic groups.

Of the 930 women surveyed in the second study, 24 percent reported at least one completed rape, and 31 percent reported at least one attempted rape.[10] Russell used the term "acquaintance rape" as an umbrella term to distinguish rapes involving people who know one another from rapes involving strangers. Thirty-five percent of the women in her study experienced rape or attempted rape by an acquaintance (ranging in degrees of intimacy from casual acquaintances to lovers) as compared with 11 percent raped by strangers and 3 percent by relatives (other than husbands or ex-husbands).[11] Only 8 percent of all incidents of rape and attempted rape were reported to the police.[12] These incidents were much more likely to involve strangers than men known to the victim.[13]

Another important early survey, of nearly 4,000 college students at Kent State University, was conducted in 1978 by psychologist Mary Koss. When she first designed the Kent State study, Koss preferred the label "hidden rape" to "acquaintance rape" because of the growing recognition in law enforcement circles that rape was "the most underreported of major crimes." She chose to study "unacknowledged victims of rape," women who have experienced forced sexual intercourse but do not call it rape.

Koss's goal was to determine the prevalence of hidden rape. For the survey, she identified four degrees of sexual aggression, ranging from what she called "low sexual victimization" to "high sexual victimization," in order to separate gradations of sexual abuse.[14] The category labeled "high sexual victimization" was the category that Koss defined as rape. It included women who said they had experienced unwanted intercourse or penetration of the mouth or anus from a man or men who used or threatened to use physical force. Koss separated this category of rape victims into two types: women who acknowledged they had been raped and those who did not name what happened to them as rape. Koss found that 13 percent of the women interviewed answered yes to at least one of three questions asking them whether they had experienced forced penetration at any time since the age of 14. Only 6 percent of the women interviewed, however, answered yes to the question "Have you ever been raped?"[15]

Less than 5 percent of the men in the study admitted to using force. Those who admitted to using force were remarkably similar to the sexually aggressive men described in Kirkendall's 1961 study of college men. For example, like their 1950s counterparts, the Kent State males expressed attitudes illustrative of the double standard. They were more approving of sexual relationships with prostitutes and more disapproving of sexual freedom for women than the less aggressive men in the study. They preferred traditional women, who were dependent, attention-seeking, and suggestible. Their first experiences with sexual intercourse tended to be unsatisfactory, but they expressed more pride in these experiences than the less aggressive men. When asked if they had sex the first time because it was socially expected, nearly half of the men in the sexually aggressive groups answered yes, as compared with only a quarter of the nonsexually-aggressive men.

There were other differences between the types of men in Koss's study reminiscent of Kirkendall's findings. The highly sexually aggressive men were more likely to identify with a male peer culture. More were likely to be in fraternities than those reporting no or low sexual aggression. They were more insensitive to the woman's resistance and more likely to think that sexual aggression was normal sexual behavior, part of the game that had to be played with women. They believed that a woman would be only moderately offended if a man forced his way into her house after a date or forced his attentions in other ways.[16]

To see whether she could replicate her Kent State findings in a nationwide sample, Koss joined with *Ms.* magazine in a 1985 survey of 6,159 students on 32 college campuses. The results of this survey would play a significant role in stepping up antirape activism on college campuses, and in inspiring the campus section of the Violence Against Women Act, which would be introduced into Congress five years later.

The survey questions were similar to those Koss used in the Kent State study. This time, however, she included a question about unwanted sexual intercourse that occurred because of the effects of alcohol or drugs. Robin Warshaw's *I Never Called It Rape*, the first major book on acquaintance rape, was based on Koss's study. Warshaw reported that one in four women surveyed were victims of rape or attempted rape, 84 percent of those raped knew their attacker, and 57 percent of the rapes happened on dates.[17] The women thought that most of their offenders (73 percent) were drinking or using drugs at the time of the assault, and 55 percent admitted to using intoxicants themselves. Most of the women thought that they had made their nonconsent "quite" clear and that the offender used "quite a bit" of force. They resisted by using reasoning (84 percent) and physical struggle (70 percent).[18]

Only one-quarter (27 percent) of the rape victims acknowledged themselves as such. Five percent reported their rapes to the police. Although many women did not call it rape, Koss reported that "the great majority of rape victims conceptualized their experience in highly negative terms and felt victimized whether or not they realized that legal standards for rape had been met."[19]

The results for the men were similar to what Koss had found at Kent State. One-quarter of the men reported involvement in some form of sexual aggression, ranging from unwanted touching to rape. Three percent admitted to attempted rape, and 4.4 percent admitted to rape.[20] A high percentage of the males did not name their use of force as rape. Eighty-eight percent said it was definitely not rape. Forty-seven percent said they would do the same thing again.[21]

Koss's findings that men viewed the use of force as normal were corroborated by other surveys conducted on college campuses. For example, one study cited by Russell found that 35 percent of the males questioned about the likelihood that they would rape said they might if they could get away with it. When asked whether they would force a female to do something sexual she really did not want to do, 60 percent of the males indicated in a third college study that they might, "given the right circumstances."[22]

Since the early studies conducted by Koss and Russell, a number of additional scientifically designed research studies conducted on campuses in various states and in various communities reveal that an average of 13 to 25 percent of the participating females respond affirmatively to questions asking if they had ever been penetrated against their consent by a male who used force, threatened to use force, or took advantage of them when they were incapacitated with alcohol or other drugs.[23] A more recent national study, published in 1992 by the National Victim Center, defined rape more narrowly by leaving alcohol and drugs out of the picture. Thirteen percent of this national sample of a cross-section of women reported having been victims of at least one completed rape in their lifetimes. Most of these women had been raped by someone they knew.[24]

ACQUAINTANCE GANG RAPE

In the 1980s quite a few cases of acquaintance gang rape were reported around the country. In the *Ms.*

article announcing the results of Koss's Kent State study, Karen Barrett describes an incident that took place at Duke University in the Beta Phi Zeta fraternity. A woman had gotten very drunk and passed out. Men lined up outside the door, yelling "Train!" Although the woman did not press charges, saying that she had been a willing participant, Duke moved against the fraternity after it was discovered that senior members had assigned a pledge the task of "finding a drunk woman for a gang bang."[25]

In her national study Koss found that 16 percent of the male students who admitted rape, and 10 percent of those who admitted attempting a rape, took part in episodes involving more than one attacker.[26] In 1985 Julie Ehrhart and Bernice Sandler wrote a report for the Association of American Colleges describing such incidents. They found a common pattern. When a vulnerable young woman is high on drugs, drunk, or too weak to protest, she becomes a target for a train. In some cases her drinks might have been spiked with alcohol without her knowledge. When she is approached by several men in a locked room, she reacts with confusion and panic. As many as 2 to 11 or more men might have sex with her.[27]

In a survey of 24 documented cases of alleged college gang rape reported during the 1980s, psychologist Chris O'Sullivan found that 13 were perpetrated by fraternity men, 9 by groups of athletes, and 2 by men unaffiliated with any group. Nineteen of the cases were reported to the police. In 11 cases, the men pleaded guilty to lesser charges. In five of the six cases that went to trial, all of the men were acquitted. The only finding of "guilty" in the 24 cases she studied involved black defendants on football scholarships.[28]

In 1983, I began hearing stories describing gang rape on college campuses in several parts of the country. One such incident became the focus of my book *Fraternity Gang Rape*. The incident was brought to my attention by a student, whom I called Laurel in the book. Laurel alleged that she was raped at a fraternity party when she was drunk

and too high on LSD to know what was happening. The local district attorney for sex crimes, William Heinman, concluded that a gang rape had occurred because from his investigation of Laurel's state during the party, "there was no evidence that she was lucid" and able to give consent. When her behavior was described to Judge Lois Forer, she also concluded that Laurel was "incapable of giving consent."[29]

The brothers claimed that Laurel had lured them into what they called an "express." Reporting the party activities that night, they posted the following statement on their bulletin board a few days later:

> Things are looking up for the [name of fraternity] sisters program. A prospective leader for the group spent some time interviewing several [brothers] this past Thursday and Friday. Possible names for the little sisters include [the] "little wenches" and "the [name of fraternity] express."[30]

One of the boys involved in the act, who lost his virginity that night, said that he thought what happened was normal sexual behavior, even though the trauma experienced by Laurel sent her to a hospital for a long period of recovery and kept her out of school for two years. He explained his behavior by referring to the pornography he and his brothers watched together at the house. "Pulling train," as they called it, didn't seem odd to him because "it's something that you see and hear about all the time."[31]

Another brother talked at length with me about what he thought happened. Tom [pseudonym] was adamant that it was not rape because Laurel did not name it rape at first. It was only later that she called it rape after talking to campus feminists, he said. He suggested that the real problem was "her sexual identity confusion" and that both men and women who are sexually confused indulge in casual sex. According to Tom, a lot of guys "engage in promiscuous sex to establish their sexuality," because male sexual identity is based on sexual performance. The male ego is built on sexual conquests as a way of gaining respect from other men.

For men, he said, there was lots of peer pressure to be sexually successful.[32]

When I asked Tom about Laurel's bruises, he admitted that she had been bruised that night because she had taken acid and was dancing wildly. He added that sex always involves some degree of force, which also explained the bruises. He went on to say that "subconsciously women are mad that they are subordinate in sex and are the objects of force."[33]   [1996]

HAS ANYTHING CHANGED?

Since I published *Fraternity Gang Rape* in 1990, a great deal has changed. The change has mostly come in two forms. There has been more writing about the rape-prone sexual culture on college campuses, and there is much greater awareness.

In 1996, I published an article describing rape-free versus rape-prone campus sexual cultures.[34] In the revised edition of my 1990 book *Fraternity Gang Rape* (2007), I include an opening chapter describing cases reported early in the twenty-first century.[35] I also broaden the explanatory framework for understanding fraternity gang rape by putting the subject in its personal, social, and historical context. In the afterword to that edition I focus on what has changed and what has not on rape-prone college campuses.

Greater awareness is evidenced in the recent nationwide awareness initiative to end sexual violence on college campuses. The initiative was announced by Vice President Joe Biden in a speech given at the University of New Hampshire on April 4, 2011, and accompanied by a "Dear Colleague" letter from the U.S. Office of Civil Rights, addressed to colleges and K–12 schools throughout the country.

The letter outlined schools' responsibilities under Title IX, the federal civil rights law banning sexual discrimination, harassment, and violence. The letter began with a discussion of Title IX's requirements related to student-on-student sexual harassment, including sexual violence, explaining the responsibility of educational institutions to take immediate and effective steps to end both.

The letter both supplemented requirements and guidelines issued in 2001 and provided additional guidance with practical examples of proactive preventative efforts and remedies to end sexual harassment and violence and address its effects. Biden's speech came just days after the U.S. Office of Civil Rights announced it would investigate a complaint filed under Title IX by 16 Yale University students in March 2011, listing behaviors occurring at Yale in violation of Title IX.

Such efforts demonstrate that much has changed. Abusive male sexuality in the interest of the "guyland" behavior Michael Kimmel describes is no longer the shadow culture on college campuses.[36] Like Kimmel's book, my book *Fraternity Gang Rape* is widely used around the country in college classrooms. Consequently, college administrators and students are no longer in the dark about the rape-prone environment that may confront vulnerable young women who wander into the all-male fraternity parties held on almost every campus in the country. Even a few fraternities are taking note of the problem by assigning designated watchers to protect their guests from the most egregious behaviors.[37]

Another important change is the frequency with which national and local campus surveys are conducted measuring student experience with rape while at college. Although consciousness has been raised, the statistics are not much different from those reported by Mary Koss and her colleagues. The most recent large-sample study was conducted by Krebs et. al. (2007), funded by the U.S. Department of Justice, and was entitled "The Campus Sexual Assault (CSA) Study."[38] The research team surveyed random samples of undergraduate students at two large public universities, one located in the South and the other in the Midwest.

The CSA Survey was administered in the winter of 2006, with a total of 5,446 undergraduate women and 1,375 undergraduate men participating. According to the report, the statistics for males are not reported because this component of the study was exploratory. The study found that one

536   *CHAPTER VII: VIOLENCE AGAINST WOMEN*

out of five (1 in 5) undergraduate women experienced an attempted or completed sexual assault during their college years. The majority of the sexual assaults occurred when women were incapacitated due to their use of substances (primarily alcohol). It was also found that freshmen and sophomores were at greater risk than juniors and seniors. Finally, as in other studies, the large majority of women reporting assault experienced it from men they knew.

In answer to the question—Has anything changed?—the answer is both yes and no. The sexual culture fueled by alcohol and "hooking up" has grown, not diminished, with more women than before embracing its behaviors. In local campus surveys the 1-in-5 statistic holds for women (on some campuses it is higher). In these surveys, males respond by admitting to their unwanted advances.[39] A small percentage of men (6.6 percent in one campus survey) are also admitting to experiencing sexual abuse, including unwanted touching and rape. Younger women who are not yet able to handle themselves in the alcohol-fueled, male-dominated sexual environment suffer more than the more advanced women students, who increasingly opt out of the party culture. Based on my speaking tours on college campuses, I can say also that for a few older male students the wild sexual narcissism of rape-prone campus sexual cultures is considered shallow and not particularly gratifying.   [2011]

NOTES

1. Interview with anonymous college student, spring 1984.
2. McCluskey (1992:261–62).
3. For an excellent summary of studies of the heterosexual and homosexual assault of male victims, see Struckman-Johnson (1991:192–213). Also see Hickson et al. (1994), which describes a study of 930 homosexually active men living in England and Wales in which 27.6 percent said they had been sexually assaulted or had had sex against their will. Some of these men reported being abused by women assailants. Another source on male–male acquaintance rape is Mezey and King (1992). For a study of partner abuse in lesbian relationships, see Renzetti (1992).
4. Kalven and Zeisel (1966:254).
5. Amir (1971). See LeGrand (1973:922–23) on Amir and for other studies on the proportion of stranger-rape versus acquaintance-rape cases. Also see Prentky, Burgess, and Carter (1986:73–98); these authors state that

a sample of 16 studies showed that the incidence of stranger rape ranged from 26 percent to 91 percent.
6. Amir (1971:245); LeGrand (1973:922–24).
7. Brownmiller (1975:257).
8. Russell (1984a:11). First published in 1974.
9. Ibid., 12.
10. Ibid., 35.
11. Ibid., 59.
12. Ibid., 35–36.
13. Ibid., 96–97, 284.
14. The kind of behavior Brownmiller (1975:257) called date rape (see discussion in the text) corresponded to Koss's (1985:196) "low sexual victimization" category, which Koss does not label rape.
15. Two of the three questions used to determine the 13 percent asked whether actual or threatened physical force had been used in nonconsensual intercourse. The third question asked whether oral or anal intercourse or penetration with an object through the use of force or threat of force had been used in nonconsensual intercourse. Koss (1981: table 4, 51). See also Koss and Oros (1982:455–57).
16. Koss (1981:21–27).
17. Warshaw (1988:11). See also Koss (1988:15–16).
18. Koss (1988:15–16).
19. Koss (1992a:122–26).
20. One and a half percent of the men said they had forced a woman into intercourse, oral or anal penetration, or penetration with objects by using threats or physical force; 4 percent of the men said they had intercourse with an unwilling woman by giving her drugs or alcohol. See Koss (1988:8).
21. Ibid., 18–19.
22. Malamuth study summarized by Russell (1984b:159); Briere study in Russell (1984b:64). See also Malamuth (1981:138–57).
23. For a summary of these studies and others, see Koss and Cook (1993:110).
24. For a summary of many studies, see Koss (1993:1062–1069). For the 1992 national study on rape, see National Victim Center (1992). Koss found that 16 percent of the women in her national sample said they had experienced nonconsensual sex due to a man's force, threat of force, or use of alcohol. When Koss excluded the question about alcohol, this figure was reduced to 11 percent; see Koss and Cook (1993:106).
25. Barrett (1982:50–51).
26. Warshaw (1988:101).
27. See discussion in Sanday (1990:1–2). See also Ehrhart and Sandler (1985).
28. O'Sullivan (1991:144; 151).
29. Sanday (1990:74–75).
30. Ibid., 5–7.
31. Ibid., 34.
32. Ibid., 71–72.
33. Ibid., 72.
34. Sanday (1996:191–208).
35. Sanday (2007).
36. Kimmel (2008).
37. Sanday (1996).
38. Krebs et al., "The Campus Sexual Assault (CSA) Study," (2007).
39. Sanday (1996:191–208).

🌿 146

Stronger Than You Know

RACHEL MODELL

I will never forget the day. It was four days into my freshman year of college. August 27th, 2003. I was coming back from dinner with my roommate. We were all going to watch a movie with some people. On the way up to the guy's dorm my friends all disappeared and I was alone. We went in the room and he overtook me. Locked the door and had his friends standing outside of it. I could have unlocked it and left but I thought that I would fare better being alone with one guy than with a team. A team is what they were—members of the school's basketball team.

I tried to fight back. I repeated the word no over and over and over again. The word has since lost meaning for me and I do not use it. I tried to push him off me, keep my legs closed, but he had a good 80 pounds on me.

I remember the promises he made me. About how I was the first girl he had slept with thus far and how in three months we would still be together. He told me I would be apologizing for having doubted him. All lies, everything that came out of his mouth was a lie. Including the date he said he was born on. I remember it all; every detail of that night stands out in my mind.

That night left me broken in a way I never dreamed possible. When I came home to my parents, I was afraid to leave my house for weeks and then only if my dog was with me. I could not sleep with the light off or have anything on top of me. The weight of even a sheet on top of me made me anxious. I remember he asked me over and over where I lived; I lived in fear that he could come and find me. He told me after he raped me that he would be back to my dorm later that night so we could go again. If I was too tired then he said he would be back the next night and the night after.

I went to the hospital immediately after the rape. I did not shower or go to the bathroom. I did change into pajamas but I brought the clothes that I had worn during the rape to the hospital. I had a rape kit done and it felt like I was being raped all over again. I hated that the policemen had to take pictures of my body; capturing the marks left there. However, without the rape kit, I would not have stood a chance in court.

I did not plan to take this to trial but the rape kit started the ball rolling and I did not want to stop it. I went back to the police station the next night and I gave them my statement. He gave one too and so did a bunch of his friends. Those statements were the only honest things those men said. At grand jury, he changed his story to make it sound like I wanted and initiated sex with him. At trial he changed the story again. His friends denied having ever been at the dorms that night. Luckily they had given statements that night that said otherwise.

I have learned that the truth is extremely precious and in this case it prevailed. The trial itself was hard. I was on the stand for three hours and he did not take his eyes off me that whole time. It's funny, but before I went into the courtroom I saw him outside. He was with his mother and he looked so much smaller than I remembered. The power had been taken away from him; I had it instead. The jury took two full days to deliberate and they found him guilty of rape in the third degree, and of three counts of sodomy. He has been serving a minimum sentence of four years (the max was 12) and he is up for parole March 23, 2006.

I have come a long way since that night. Its events shook me to the core and I have not been the same person since. I do not think that it would be possible to come out of such an event unchanged, I wish that life was different. Not a day goes by when I don't think about him; about what he did to me and the fact that I put him in jail. The justice system has many flaws but it is all we have. He did have numerous chances to stop his actions. That night when he raped me, it was his choice. After grand jury, we offered him a plea bargain which he did not accept. His actions put him where he is now.

It is not in my nature to stay quiet and within a month of my being raped, I had joined a support group for girls 16–22. I was right in the middle, being 18. The group and individual counseling were the best things that I could have done. They helped me move on in ways that I did not think were possible. I have since become an educator about rape in college. I think it is important that people understand that rape does happen. One out of three college women has been raped. Chances are that every day you meet someone who has been raped and you will never know it.

They call rape a crime of passion but that could not be farther from the truth. It is a crime of power and greed. The rapist derives a pleasure from executing total power over his victim. Most of the time rapists do not even get pleasure from the act. They are doing it to fulfill some need inside themselves, a need that leaves pain and destruction in its wake. If you have been raped I advise you to seek counseling or confide in an adult/professor that you trust. There are fears that no one will believe you or that you are just overacting. People are out there to help and that old saying about strength in numbers is true. You should not have to go through this alone; you have already been through enough. The healing process is not easy. I do not think that you can ever come out of a rape and accept it. However, no one deserves to have their body vandalized. You are stronger than you know and in time you will come to see just how much. I did.   [2006]

🌿 147

Protecting Male Abusers and Punishing the Women Who Confront Them: The Current Status of Child-Sex Abuse in America

LANETTE FISHER-HERTZ

Ashley was 14 years old and in the eighth grade when her father, Carmine, began grooming her to be his sexual abuse victim.[1] Although he had often been violent with Ashley while she was growing up—once grabbing her shoulder hard enough to break her collarbone—he now became unexpectedly tender. Every night after dinner, he took Ashley into his study, a room she had previously been forbidden to enter, and showed her pornographic magazines, instructing her on the way grown women should dress and display their bodies. He had Ashley practice posing, urging her to put on make-up, purse her lips, and toss her hair around like a model. It made Ashley giggle, one of the few times she remembers laughing with her dad.

"He wanted to show me how to get dressed up to look sexy for guys so I could get a good husband someday," Ashley told investigators.

When police asked Ashley if she resisted what came later—months of daily rapes—she said no. She wanted to believe her father was trying to help her, and besides, what he did to her with his penis hurt a lot less than the punishments he used to give her with his hands or his belt. It was only when he began to get violent with her again that she went to a guidance counselor for help.

★★★

In my second month as executive director of the Child Abuse Prevention Center in Dutchess County, New York, a team of sexual-abuse investigators walked into my office, flush with triumph, to tell me Ashley's horrifying story. They had obtained a signed confession from the 38-year-old father, Carmine, who had repeatedly raped and sodomized his oldest child during the summer of 2000. The team was thrilled to have persuaded Carmine to "tell his side of the story" since confessions are usually the only means of obtaining a felony conviction for sexual abuse of a minor. (A child's testimony alone is almost always considered insufficient evidence for an indictment.) In this case, our burly male investigator had assured Carmine he understood perfectly how provocative young girls could be—which was, apparently, all the macho encouragement Carmine needed. As he and the investigator shared coffee at Carmine's kitchen table, Carmine earnestly explained that he had engaged in oral, anal, and vaginal sex with his daughter because "she was getting older," and he "didn't want her learning about this kind of stuff from a stranger." By the time Carmine was done explaining himself, the team had enough information to file a 23-count indictment. Ashley's mother, who had been 14 herself when Carmine impregnated her, was also indicted.

Because I was new to the field of child sexual abuse, I had naïve hopes that justice would be served in this case. I was already discouraged by the low prosecution rates I had encountered; most child sexual abuse goes unreported, and, of those cases that are reported, fewer than one-third are "substantiated"—and of *those,* "most substantiated and founded child abuse cases do not lead to prosecution," and only a quarter result in incarceration (Cross et al., 2003). Child sex abuse prosecutors report "as many as 50–75% of *valid* cases [are] rejected for prosecution" (Murphy, 2003, italics mine).

Ashley's case demonstrated how difficult it was to land a conviction in even the most appalling cases: Because Ashley was over 13 years of age and had "consented" to have sex with her father, statutory rape laws did not protect her.[2] Additionally, because Ashley was sexually assaulted by her own father, he was able to use the "incest loophole" that allows lighter punishment for men who molest their own family members. If the perpetrator hadn't confessed to his own criminal activity, we probably wouldn't have been able to send him to jail at all. This is true in most sexual abuse cases—since most molestation leaves no physical evidence, and most victims do not report the crimes against them for months or years, if at all, and are either reluctant to testify against family members, are shielded from having to testify, or are not considered good witnesses (Staller and Faller, 2010).

Under America's current justice system, when girls (or boys, who represent 11 percent of sexual assault victims; Finkelhor et al., 2004) are raped or molested by strangers, their perpetrators can be criminally prosecuted, jailed, and—thanks to the passage of recent legislation such as Megan's Law and the Children's Safety Act of 2005—compelled to register as sex offenders so that their whereabouts

and access to children can be monitored. However, because at least three-quarters of sexual assaults on minors are committed by friends or family members (Finkelhor, 2010), an aggressive criminal response occurs in only a minority of cases—and no matter the relationship between victim and perpetrator, child sexual abuse continues to be "among the most underreported and infrequently prosecuted major offenses (Staller and Faller, 2010).

If a child's assailant is a family member, her case may not be considered a criminal matter at all; instead, the rape may be labeled sexual "abuse" rather than sexual "assault," a distinction that allows the rapist to be referred for counseling rather than prosecution—and to avoid jail time and classification as a sex offender. As of this writing in 2010, the majority of states still have "incest loopholes" that allow prosecutors to treat intrafamilial sexual abuse as a private matter in family courts. (New York closed its incest loophole in 2006, and the loophole has also been eliminated in California, Illinois, Arkansas, and North Carolina; PROTECT, The National Association to Protect Children, is continuing a state-by-state battle to close this loophole nationwide.)

With both of Ashley's parents in jail and the rest of Ashley's family blaming Ashley for speaking out, Ashley was estranged from every source of support she'd had—and placed in a group home many miles from the small town where she had lived all her life. Despite this grim outcome, the case was considered a major victory for our Child Abuse Prevention Center, garnering two felony convictions and sentences of record length. I struggled to understand why even the light sentence Carmine received (he wound up serving just three years in prison) was considered an exceptionally good outcome, given the outrage I elicited when I spoke of these crimes in public.

"The girl was over 13, and she was no angel," one attorney explained.[3] "Plus no force was used, which means some of these crimes may not qualify as felonies. But the bottom line is: judges hate to give any jail time when it's a family matter. This is a good outcome, believe me."

I had trouble understanding this at first; why *wouldn't* judges want to imprison men who raped young girls? Politically, going after child rapists seems like a smart move. Yet the more familiar I became with the system, the less I could avoid acknowledging its function: The legal, social, and family institutions surrounding child sexual abuse discourage the reporting and prosecuting of intra-familial sexual assault. Sexual abuse by strangers is treated somewhat more seriously, but fathers or father figures, including uncles, grandfathers, step-fathers, and other male authority figures trusted by their victims, account for the majority of sexual abuse (Levesque, 1999). Even when the abuse is perpetrated by strangers, most men's sex crimes are unreported.

Child abuse cases are less likely to result in charges being filed than most other felonies referred for prosecution, and those that are prosecuted have lower incarceration rates than all other felonies (Cross et al., 2003). Even the few men who are convicted *spend no time in jail in a majority of cases*—with probation and counseling the most routine recommendations. Once a case proceeds to court, most men "plead out" to a lesser offense; more than 83 percent of men awaiting trial for child abuse crimes accept a plea bargain arrangement (Cross et al., 2003). The more affluent the offender, the less likely he is to serve time in jail, since a man's role as breadwinner is often cited as a reason to recommend probation. Additionally, because children who are forced to testify in open court have poorer long-term mental health outcomes than those not required to testify (Quas et al., 2005), many abuse-investigation teams are eager to accept plea bargains to spare children further trauma.

Although not as unusual as we would like to think, Ashley's story is shocking because our culture continues to pretend that extreme sexual dangers to children exist more prominently outside the home than within it, but all of us working in the field of child sexual abuse know the reverse is true. A majority of child sexual abuse is perpetrated by trusted authority figures who use bribery, coercion, emotional manipulation, threats, and other

nonviolent methods to induce their young victims to cooperate, which means that few child sexual abuse victims fit the category of those most likely to be believed and supported when they disclose (i.e., those suffering physical injuries). Additionally, children may suppress conscious recollection of the abuse for weeks, months, or years—or may be frightened by threats that they will destroy their families if they tell. Finally, parents who do discover that their children have been sexually abused may choose, even when they believe the child, to handle the matter without police involvement.

Approximately 70,000 children each year are sexually abused, according to the Department of Health and Human Services' National Child Abuse and Neglect Data System, which tracks only *confirmed* cases of abuse (*Child Maltreatment, 2009*). Despite the extensive, often sensationalist, media coverage incest has received since the early 1980s, extreme secrecy still surrounds nearly all individual cases. Men at every level of society are systematically protected from a public examination of their crimes—which enables them to retain their jobs, their status in the community, and their access to new victims. Most cases that are pursued by the authorities are still settled in sealed family court proceedings with no criminal charges filed. Even when cases are not sealed, reports about them rarely appear in local newspapers. Well-meaning editors claim they are protecting the identity of victims, but the result is a collective silence that makes child sexual abuse appear rare.

The few sensationalized cases that do receive media attention, as did Ashley's case, usually involve acts of penetration—often on young children. However, most child sexual abuse does not involve penetration. Rather, millions of men each year betray the trust of young girls by fondling them, flashing them, fingering them, rubbing their erections against them, licking them, spanking them when they are naked (or with whips, belts, or paddles), exposing them to pornography, or posing them and photographing them in sexual positions (Wurtele & Miller-Perrin, 1992). (If reading that list felt prurient to you, take a moment to reflect upon the extent to which male abuse of young women has been eroticized in our culture.) Even those women who are not sexually abused may endure childhoods in which they are the objects of continuous, sexualized attention, which can have the same long-term effects as sexual abuse.

Though a multitude of studies have shown that 95 to 97 percent of offenders are males who are, on average, 10 years older than their victims (Fodor, 2001), the gendered nature of child sexual abuse and its link to the male power structure is rarely, if ever, discussed in the child-abuse prevention community. A tiny percentage of women *have* been found to be sexually abusive, but most have been "accomplices" of men (Wurtele & Miller-Perrin, 1992)—like Carmine's abused wife, Sandy. Itzin (1994) confirms: "Most incest is perpetrated by men. It is always an abuse of power: both adult and male power."

Instead, law enforcement officers and child-abuse investigators I met, while usually well-intentioned, frequently expressed the larger society's victim-blaming and mother-blaming sentiments. Mothers are often threatened with loss of custody because their husbands or boyfriends molested their daughters—a threat that ironically mimics the threats these women hear from abusive men who warn they will take away the woman's kids (or cause them to be taken by the state) if the man's authority is challenged (Barker, 2001).

Even girls themselves are often angrier at their mothers for failing to protect them than they are at the fathers or father figures who abused them. According to multiple studies, girls often retain stronger feelings of anger at their mothers for failing to protect them than toward the men who molested them in childhood. Meiselman (1978) found that in adulthood, 60 percent of incest survivors had at least somewhat forgiven their fathers, but 60 percent still had strong negative feelings toward their mothers—even though 75 to 95 percent of mothers were unaware of the abuse and, when told, were supportive of their daughters. More recent studies reflect similar findings.

Daughters' attitudes reflect those of the larger society, in which mother-blame has long been part of our cultural response to incest (Russell &

Bolen, 2000). Theorists claimed men molested their daughters because of the failings of their wives, who were said to be disabled, alcoholic, frigid, rejecting, or otherwise not fulfilling their wifely duties. More recently, the "dysfunctional family" is treated collectively, with an emphasis on helping mothers realize how they have "enabled" their men's abusive behavior. Most states have now created statutes that penalize mothers as severely for "failure to protect" a child from sexual assault as they penalize men for actually committing aggravated rape or sexual battery on a child (Fugate, 2001). Because the criminal burden of proof is so high, mothers are *more often* penalized by social service agencies and family court systems for "failure to protect" than fathers are charged with the actual sexual abuse from which the mothers "failed" to protect them. A U.S. Department of Health and Human Services study in 2000 found that 27 percent of sex abuse charges were actually being leveled against mothers for their "failure to protect" their children from the male abusers in their lives, even though fewer than 5 percent of actual perpetrators of sexual abuse are female (Bolen, 2001).

Cultural, racial, and class divisions also lead to misperceptions about the scope and extent of the problem—and in some cases leave women torn between their desire to protect their communities and their desire to protect their daughters. Studies show that blacks are sexually victimized in childhood at the same rate as whites, but African-American women are less likely than white women to involve police in cases of child sexual abuse (Stone, 2004).

Women who are members of marginalized communities may have valid reasons to distrust law enforcement officials and to be reluctant to fuel perceptions that their men are deviant or criminal. Although the majority of mothers of color do believe and support their daughters' disclosures, launching a child sexual abuse investigation forces women to rely on social service workers they may previously have viewed as the enemy—and with good reason. Black women who involved state child-protection agencies reported feeling "disempowered and devalued" (Bernard, 1997). When impoverished women call upon the system for help, they run the greatest risk of having their daughters removed from them. Children whose parents have a family income of $15,000 or less are 22 times as likely to be removed from their mothers as children in households with incomes above $30,000 (Sedlak & Broadhurst, 1984).

The innate, human desire to believe that the world is fair and that bad things only happen to people who behave badly makes us *want* to attribute at least some blame to mothers—and even to the child victims of sexual abuse (Lerner, 1980). Undergraduate students are among those most likely to blame victims of hypothetical child sexual abuse cases. Given a scenario in which a little girl behaved as most incest victims do—which is to say, she lay there in a state of bewilderment or disassociation while the abuse took place—many students insisted the little girl "should have resisted"; a full third said the incest was the girl's fault (Waterman & Foss-Goodman, 1984). Studies find that the more traditional one's beliefs are about gender roles, the more likely one is to blame the victim (Ford, Schindler, & Medway, 2001).

"The idea that children are responsible for their own seduction has been at the center of almost all writing on sexual abuse since the topic was first broached," notes Finkelhor (1981). Blaming children, particularly girls, for their own victimization began with Freud and continues to this day. "In 1937, girls who had been molested were said to be "unusually attractive children who made seductive overtures to their psychiatrists" and in 1968 were said "to act in ways that actively encourage adults to approach them sexually . . . and [to] have discovered that they can obtain attention and affection from an adult by arousing his sexual impulses." (Bolen, 2001).

Such presumptions about the female ability to drive a man wild—even when that female is a child—reflect the sexualized environment in which modern girls and women currently struggle to establish autonomy. As Gilmartin (1994) reminds us: "While the societal expectation is that women are supposed to make themselves attractive to men and are rewarded for doing so, they simultaneously are blamed if these same men view them as sex objects and/or attempt to sexually assault them."

This double message works powerfully on girls' sense of self, making all women afraid not just that an act of sexual violence will be visited upon them—but that they will have done something to deserve it. Nearly 70 percent of rape victims say they're afraid to discuss the crime for fear they will be blamed (National Women's Study, 1998). The range of symptoms sexual-abuse survivors exhibit—including anxiety, depression, eating disorders, sleep disturbances, migraines, substance abuse, and self-mutilation—are nearly all linked to self-blame.

While victims blame themselves, abusers seldom believe they have done anything wrong—a belief system our institutions support with low arrest and conviction rates for male sexual abusers, systematic and institutionalized blaming of mothers and victims, and our collective, shamed silence regarding the individual cases in our families and communities.

Given the ubiquitous cultural messages promoting male sexual power (including websites urging viewers to "CUM SEE FATHER-DAUGHTER INCEST AT ITS HOTTEST!"), good-intentioned men may feel proud simply to have avoided taking part in any acts of sexual violence. Unfortunately, the ways in which we perpetuate sexual abuse are often subtler than that. If, for example, a girl sees her father consume pornography that celebrates the hypersexualization of young girls—or react salaciously to pornographic images of teenagers in pop culture—she receives a clear message that *her* value as a (child) sex object exists not only "out there" in the wide world, but also at home, where her earliest self-images are formed.

The first draft of this article was written more than a decade ago, and I am tremendously heartened to see great progress has occurred since then: child sexual abuse is down 61 percent over the past 14 years, and is continuing to decline each year (Finkelhor et al., 2009). This dramatic drop from the peak year of sexual abuse reporting in 1992 appears to be the result of a massive groundswell of organized political action around this issue. To effect real change, we had to learn to speak plainly to the men in our lives about the fear in ours—and to keep speaking until they were as horrified by the preponderance of male sexual violence as we were. The result is that the number of persons incarcerated for sex crimes against children increased 39 percent during the 1990s—while the number of both reported and substantiated sexual abuse cases declined 2 to 11 percent each year since (Finkelhor and Jones, 2006).

While I support the recent spate of tough-on-crime laws (Megan's Law being just one example) that purport to protect our children from sexual predators, I know that such laws punish a minority of sexual offenders. Each of us is in a better position than any law enforcement agency to stop the majority of sexual abuse, since most abuse continues unfettered because we are covering it up to "protect the family," often our own family.

If there's a child molester in our lives, we must stop protecting him with our silence—and encourage every woman who confides her own dark secrets to do the same. We need to name and publicly shame every perpetrator we know—from the corporate manager getting his R&R in Bangkok and making "jokes" about teen prostitutes, to the family friend making inappropriately salacious comments about teen-girl celebrities, to the elderly uncle who held us too hard on his lap and still makes girls squirm at family gatherings. Finally, we need to celebrate the courage of the children like Ashley who endured these sexual atrocities—by telling them we believe them and are proud of them for speaking out—and by letting them know that they were not responsible for their abuse, no matter how little they "resisted," no matter how eager they were for attention and affection. Children, including teenagers, should not be held responsible when adults take advantage of their innocence—nor their absolutely natural desire to be loved, cradled in someone's arms, and singled out for special treatment. We must stop blaming children for "letting themselves" be abused, just as we must stop blaming mothers for failing to save all their children from a national epidemic. We need to make girls (and boys) glad, not regretful, when they speak out.

Our vibrant, sexually alive bodies, and the beautiful, hopeful bodies of all our children, deserve nothing less.   [2011]

NOTES

1. Although I regret protecting the identity of a single rapist, I have changed names and minor identifying details to protect the identities of the abuse survivors. No girl should ever be ashamed to have survived sexual assault, but girls and women are often still treated as if they have done something shameful simply by naming the acts that have been perpetrated upon them.
2. Historically, daughters, like wives, were considered their father's property—and rape laws were enacted only to protect men's financial interests in them. One legacy of this legal doctrine is that most statutory rape laws apply only to men who have sex with girls who are *not* family members. In February 2001, New York updated its statutory rape laws so that anyone over 21 who has sex with anyone 16 or younger is now committing a felony—but the year before, Carmine's penetration of his daughter was not considered a felony because he had not used force.
3. Sex abuse victims are often labeled promiscuous by caseworkers and district attorneys, particularly if the girls have been victimized more than once.

WORKS CITED

Armstrong, Louise. *Rocking the Cradle of Sexual Politics: What Happened When Women Said Incest.* Reading, MA: Addison-Wesley, 1994.

Barker, Karlyn. "Policy Turns the Abused into Suspects: Mothers Find Seeking Help Can Backfire." *Washington Post*, December 26, 2001, B1–B4.

Bernard, Claudia. "Black Mothers' Emotional and Behavioral Responses to the Sexual Abuse of Their Children." In *Out of the Darkness: Contemporary Perspectives on Family Violence*, ed. Glenda Kaufman and Jana L. Jasinski. Thousand Oaks, CA: Sage, 1997.

Bolen, Rebecca M. *Child Sexual Abuse: Its Scope and Our Failure.* Boston: Kluwer Academic/Plenum, 2001.

Child Maltreatment 2009. A U.S. Department of Health and Human Services Report. http://www.acf.hhs.gov/programs/cb/pubs/cm09/index.htm.

Cross, Theodore P., Wendy A. Walsh, Monique Simone, and Lisa M. Jones. "Prosecution of Child Abuse: A Meta-Analysis of Rates of Criminal Justice Decisions." *Trauma, Violence & Abuse* 4, no. 4 (October 2003): 323–40.

Finkelhor, David. *Sexually Abused Children.* New York: Free Press, 1981.

Finkelhor, David. "The Prevention of Childhood Sexual Abuse." CYC-Online. The International Child and Youth Care Network. Issue 132, February, 2010. http://www.cyc-net.org/cyc-online/cyconline-feb2010-finkelhor.html.

Finkelhor, David, H. Hammer, and A. J. Sedlak. "Sexually Assaulted Children: National Estimates and Characteristics." *OJJDP: Juvenile Justice Bulletin* (2004). U.S. Department of Justice. http://www.ncjrs.gov/pdffiles1/ojjdp/214383.pdf.

Finkelhor, David, and Lisa Jones. "Why Have Child Maltreatment and Child Victimization Declined?" *Journal of Social Issues* 62, no. 4 (2006): 685–716.

Finkelhor, David, Lisa Jones, and Anne Shattuck. *Updated Trends in Child Maltreatment, 2009.* http://www.unh.edu/ccrc/pdf/Updated_Trends_in_Child_Maltreatment_2009.pdf.

Fodor, Margie Druss. 2001. Megan's Law: Protection or Privacy. Hillside, N.J.: Enslow.Itzen, Catherine. "Pornography and the Organization of Intra- and Extrafamilial Child Sexual Abuse." Out of the Darkness. Glenda Kaufman and Jana Jasinski, eds. pp. 58–79.

Ford, Harriett, Claudia B. Schindler, and Frederic J. Medway. "School Professionals' Attributions of Blame for Child Sexual Abuse." *Journal of School Psychology* 39, no. 1 (2001): 25–44.

Fugate, Jeanne A. "Who's Failing Whom? A Critical Look At Failure to Protect Laws." New York University Law Review Vol. 76: 272 April, 2001, pp. 272–308.

Gilmartin, Pat. *Rape, Incest, and Child Sexual Abuse: Consequences and Recovery.* New York: Garland, 1994.

Lerner, Melvin. *The Belief in a Just World: A Fundamental Delusion.* New York: Plenum, 1980.

Levesque, Roger J. R. *Sexual Abuse of Children: A Human Rights Perspective.* Bloomington: Indiana University Press, 1999.

Meiselman, Karen. *Incest: A Psychological Study of Causes and Effects, with Treatment Recommendations.* San Francisco: Jossey-Bass, 1978.

Murphy, Wendy. "The Overlapping Problems of Prosecution Sample Bias and Systematic Exclusion of Familial Child Sex Abuse Victims from the Criminal Justice System." *Journal of Child Sexual Abuse* 12, no. 2 (2003).

National Association to Protect Children: America's First Political Lobby for Child Protection. http://www.protect.org.

National Women's Study, 1998. http://www.ncjrs.gov/pdffiles/172837.pdf.

Quas, Jodi A., Gail S. Goodman, Simona Ghetti, Kristen W. Alexander, Robin Edelstein, Allison D. Redlich, Ingrid M. Cordon, and David P. H. Jones. *Childhood Sexual Assault Victims: Long-Term Outcomes After Testifying in Criminal Court.* Boston: Blackwell, 2005.

Russell, Diana. *The Secret Trauma: Incest in the Lives of Girls and Women.* New York: Basic Books, 1986.

Russell, Diana E. H., and Rebecca M. Bolen. *The Epidemic of Rape and Child Sexual Abuse in the United States.* Thousand Oaks, CA: Sage, 2000.

Sedlak, Andrea J., and Diane D. Broadhurst. *Sexual Exploitation.* Beverly Hills, CA: Sage, 1984.

Staller, Karen M., and Kathleen Coulborn Faller. *Seeking Justice in Child Sexual Abuse: Shifting Burdens and Sharing Responsibilities.* New York: Columbia University Press, 2010.

Stone, Robin D. *No Secrets, No Lies: How Black Families Can Heal from Sexual Abuse.* New York: Broadway Books, 2004.

Third National Incidence Study of Child Abuse and Neglect (NIS-3): Final Report. Washington, DC: U.S. Department of Health and Human Services, Government Printing Office, 1996.

Tower, Cynthia Crosson. *Secret Scars: A Guide for Survivors of Child Sexual Abuse.* New York: Penguin, 1988.

Walker, Lenore E. A., *Handbook on Sexual Abuse of Children.* New York: Springer, 1988.

Waterman, C. K., and D. Foss-Goodman. "Child Molesting: Variables Relating to Attribution of Fault to Victims, Offenders, and Non-participating Parents." *Journal of Sex Research* 20 (1984): 329–49.

Weeks, Grier. "The North Carolina Experience." National Association to Protect Children website. October 16, 2002. http://www.protect.org/articles/nc_law.shtml.

Wurtele, Sandy K., and Cindy L. Miller-Perrin. *Preventing Child Sexual Abuse: Sharing the Responsibility.* Lincoln: University of Nebraska Press, 1992.

🦎 148

Making Sense of the Experience of Incest Survivors

PERI L. RAINBOW

I grew into adulthood with lingering questions about my past. Mostly, I wondered why I couldn't remember anything that happened to me before my parents' divorce, when I was 12. I wasn't quite sure what I was supposed to remember, and I cautiously asked friends about their childhood memories. "Do you remember when you were seven years old, or eight, or six?" I'd listen to the details my friends remembered, not just special occasions like birthdays or holidays, but daily occurrences and what it felt like to be a child, and I'd wonder why I didn't know this about my life. I never let anyone know why I was asking and never revealed my own gaps. I didn't understand why, but I felt ashamed about not remembering. I did have what I call "Kodak memories." I would look at a childhood picture and repeat stories that were told to me about those times, vaguely sensing familiarity. But I felt no real connection with the child in the photograph. It was as if I was looking into the eyes of a stranger. Some unknown child stared back at me. Although I knew intellectually that the child was me, I felt deep inside that I was someone different. I didn't know then that the sexual abuse I had suffered was too painful to remember and that by blocking it out, I had also blocked out the memories of my childhood. I couldn't remember what being a child actually felt like. Feeling and knowing were to remain separate and distinct experiences for me for a long time to come.

I was a daring and promiscuous adolescent. At age 14, I had my first consensual sexual experience, and I also began to experiment with drugs. The fear and anticipation I felt when taking risks were uncannily familiar. So was sexual stimulation, and I found some comfort in this familiarity. Something about these experiences, though, while familiar and therefore comforting, also felt unsatisfying and vaguely frightening.

I spent my adolescence escaping life and my feelings about it, through chemicals, sex, and music. I was fortunate to connect with people (friends my own age and older) who were able to keep me relatively safe, despite my muted awareness. I was, however, raped by a "friend" at age 15 and molested by my mother's (male) partner at around the same time. I dismissed these incidents as insignificant and my fault. Actually, I didn't think about these incidents or define them as sexual assaults until my first college women's studies course. Instead of attending to the life my mother provided, I created my own "family" and spent a lot of time away from home. I was introduced to Jerry Garcia and the Grateful Dead at age 14, and their world—concert touring, LSD, marijuana, and sex—became my own. My friends and acquaintances became my family. They kept me distant from the pain buried inside, and perhaps in some ways they gave me the love that I needed to survive. I found solace in my head, using drugs to stay there, and found love through sex, using my body to feel wanted. I didn't understand then how significant this separation was and how I was doing exactly what I had learned to do as a child to survive the incest. I survived without feeling very much for many years. I was blessed with a fair amount of intelligence, and that, coupled with charm and an air of aloofness possible for one who rarely feels, enabled me to do well in high school.

I took these patterns (survival skills) with me to college and spent the first two years experimenting with drugs and men. I barely passed my classes, as

I was rarely if ever fully present at any point during that time. Toward the end of my sophomore year, an incident occurred that I was absolutely unprepared for. I was working at a vacation resort to support myself through college. One day, as I was working by the swimming pool giving out sporting equipment, I looked up and saw Bill, my father's best friend. He had been my music teacher, my caretaker, my "uncle"; he was family. A flood of physical and emotional feelings engulfed me when I recognized him. I was repulsed and terrified, and I was confused, as I could not explain any of this. My body reacted to these feelings as if it were a completely separate entity. I choked. I couldn't breathe and gasped for air, immediately hyperventilating. I felt excruciating pain in my stomach and in my vagina. I doubled over, vomited, and began to cry uncontrollably. It was as if something horrible was happening to my body, only right then and there, nothing was. As soon as I could, I locked myself in the equipment hut and rocked myself to safety. Although my mind had no memory of the sexual abuse, my body remembered.

That first flashback set in motion a process in which I have been involved, both consciously and subconsciously, ever since. In the many flashbacks that followed, remnants of the past would surface, sometimes like torn pieces of still photos stored in my brain, other times like a flood. With each flashback I was thrown into the past, and I felt the terror and the pain I must have known as a little girl. I was fortunate that these experiences lasted only seconds or moments, but from each one I emerged frightened and confused. Memories would also surface, not only of the abuse but also of happy times in my childhood, times I had not previously recalled. During flashbacks, I felt as if I were occupying the past. I was fully conscious of the present during the memories and simply took a mental note of their surfacing. I am still aware when new memories surface and always declare it out loud. At one point I wrote down everything I remembered, good and bad, as I feared that I would forget again. I now know that once the mind releases these things, they are back forever. Survivors remember when our minds are convinced that our bodies can tolerate the pain of knowing. Once we know, we know. It's interesting to me that the memories of the abuse, although confusing, did not surprise me. Somewhere inside I had always known. Knowing and believing, however, are two very different things.

What happened for me next further confused me and made it difficult for me to trust my judgment. I told my mother. I said, "I think Bill did something to me." She said, "Oh, don't be ridiculous—you just never liked him." It felt like my head was about to pop off my shoulders. I felt invisible, and for a moment I believed her. "I must be crazy" was what went through my mind, but then quickly, perhaps because of the vividness of my recent emotions, I thought, "No way." I did not, however, try to convince my mother of what I barely knew myself. It wasn't until four years later, when Bill's picture appeared in a local paper as he was being led away by police for molesting a little girl, that my mother believed me. Interestingly, that arrest cracked my mother's own wall of denial, and she remembered that Bill had been arrested at least once before, when I was about seven years old. He had exposed himself to a group of young campers near the place where our families spent our summers. It is the place where my most severe memories of abuse are from.

Once I began to believe that something actually did happen to me, the memories and flashbacks, as vague and disjointed as they were, became more disturbing. Now that my body was mine, it felt like it was betraying me. I felt crazy. I had difficulty being alone and difficulty being with others. Drugs helped to numb the pain but also interfered with my ability to function as a college student. I took a leave from school and left the state for several months, most of which was spent in a marijuana fog.

I returned to college believing more than ever that I had experienced something horrible involving Bill but ready to focus on something outside myself. My memories were still vague, and perhaps shifting my focus was a much needed distraction. I also believed that because of my own suffering, my college education, and my newly recognized class privilege that I could and ought to help others. I had always wanted to work in

human services. I felt comfortable with pain and suffering and, as I could not touch my own, felt passionate about the suffering of others. I had declared a sociology major early on in my college career. After my hiatus, I stumbled upon an elective that was cross-listed with the Women's Studies Program. The course, entitled "Violence Against Women in the U.S.," was taught by a soft-spoken, even-tempered, radical feminist named Alice Fix. In this class, I realized that it was not my fault that a "friend" forced me to have intercourse against my will, despite the fact that I had invited him to my room. Redefining and clarifying that experience from my adolescence helped me to better understand my connection to suffering. Although I still didn't really know what had happened to me as a child, I did know that at age 15, Greg's behavior was not unfamiliar. The more I learned about other women's experiences, with sexual violence in particular and life in general, the more I felt a bond with other women. Like the survivors I work with in group therapy, I began to experience women's power. I learned about resistance and survival and became aware of my own.

It would be wonderful to say that my healing began there and progressed upwardly thereafter; however, healing from trauma does not work that way. Survivors take "baby steps" and often pace themselves so as not to be overwhelmed. I slowed down the process of recognizing my childhood abuse by doing what I had always done so skillfully: I split myself in two. I separated my mind (knowledge) from my body (feelings) as a child. I reentered a familiar dissociated state of being. Intellectually, I became passionate about feminism and learning about women's lives. I became politically active, joining organizations, demonstrating, educating others about violence against women. I worked at a shelter for battered women and became the director of a women's crisis center. I was a leader, using my head to guide me. My body, however, stayed in what was familiar and unsafe.

I struggled for two years to maintain this dichotomy. Feminism tugged at my body. The personal, after all, is the political, and I had difficulty keeping my body, my heart, distant from the lives of other women. I had, throughout my life, often found my body at risk from others and even tried on several occasions to take my own life as well. Now, I was meeting other women who did so too, and as we learned more about and valued each other, it didn't seem to make much sense. It took nearly dying at the hands of my partner, however, and a radical intervention by a women's studies professor to move me to take action on my own behalf. I left the abusive relationship and began therapy. I also pursued my professional development in a more focused way.

Through my study of sexual abuse I learned about the dissociative process and became determined to share this knowledge with others. I wanted survivors and those who care about us to know that the residual effects, those "crazy" thoughts and behaviors, make perfect sense and that there is hope for recovery. It was knowledge and feelings together, perhaps in sync for me for the first time, that convinced me to continue on this path. The emotions I felt were connected not only to my own experience as a victim but to the courage of millions of survivors, who have struggled to understand and improve the quality of their lives. My feminist beliefs gave me faith in the possibility of change and appreciation for passion as a wonderfully powerful force.

As a budding feminist therapist, I recognized the misogyny inherent in men's abuse of women and children. I believe that the sexist socialization of men plays an important role in this. I also believe that as a feminist, it is my responsibility to take action. And so, I have proceeded to learn and to share, helping others to understand and heal.

As a budding feminist therapist, I recognized the misogyny inherent in men's abuse of women. I believe that the sexist socialization of men plays an important role in this. I have come to understand however, that women also perpetrate sexual abuse, often upon other women. My queer identity coupled with my identity as an educator, a psychotherapist, a mother and a feminist, have sustained the belief that it is my responsibility to take action toward social change. I continue to learn and share, helping others to understand and to heal.   [1999]

149

Bubba Esther, 1888*

RUTH WHITMAN

She was still upset,
she wanted to tell me,
she kept remembering
his terrible hands:

> how she came, a young girl
> of seventeen, a freckled
> fairskinned Jew from Kovno
> to Hamburg with her uncle
> and stayed in an old house
> and waited while he bought
> the steamship tickets
> so they could sail to America
>
> and how he came into her room
> sat down on the bed, touched
> her waist, took her by the
> breast, said for a kiss
> she could have her ticket,
> her skirts were rumpled, her
> petticoat torn, his teeth were
> broken, his breath full of
> onions, she was ashamed

still ashamed, lying
eighty years later
in the hospital bed,
trying to tell me,
trembling, weeping with anger   [1980]

---

*Grandma